THE SOCIAL THOUGHT OF W.E.B. DuBOIS

Joseph P. DeMarco
Cleveland State University

UNIVERSITY
PRESS OF
AMERICA

Shambaugh Library

LANHAM • NEW YORK • LONDON

Copyright © 1983 by

University Press of America,™ Inc.

4720 Boston Way
Lanham, MD 20706

3 Henrietta Street
London WC2E 8LU England

Library of Congress Cataloging in Publication Data

DeMarco, Joseph P., 1943—
  The social thought of W.E.B. Du Bois.

  Includes bibliographical references.
  1. Du Bois, W.E.B. (William Edward Burghardt),
1868-1963. 2. United States—Race relations.
3. Pan-Africanism. 4. Peace. 5. Socialism. I. Title.
HM22.U6D684 1983   303.4'84'0924   83-6547
ISBN 0-8191-3235-7
ISBN 0-8191-3236-5 (pbk.)

To Bonnie

ACKNOWLEDGEMENTS

I wish to thank Tuskegee Institute and Cleveland State University for the research assistance each provided. Cindy Bellinger's typing and proof-reading are very much appreciated. The support of my family, and especially my wife, Bonnie, gave me the incentive to continue.

Grateful acknowledgement is made to the following for permission to quote from Du Bois' writings:

Professor David Du Bois, Dusk of Dawn;

Mr. Chester Higgins, The Crisis Magazine;

Mr. Julius Lester for use of his collection, The Seventh Son;

Atlanta University Press for quotations from the Atlanta University Publications;

International Publishers, John Brown and The Autobiography;

Russell & Russell, Black Reconstruction in America;

Parts of this book include revised material originally appearing in: "The Rationale and Foundation of Du Bois' Theory of Economic Cooperation," Phylon, (c) 1974, Atlanta University, Atlanta, Georgia, 30314, and "The Concept of Race in the Social Thought of W.E.B. Du Bois," The Philosophical Forum, Winter, 1971-72. I am grateful to the editors for permission to use these articles.

TABLE OF CONTENTS

INTRODUCTION

W.E.B. Du Bois was an unusually productive
scholar and social critic. Some of his works stand as
landmarks of scholarship, such as his pioneering
sociological study, The Philadelphia Negro (1899)
and the Suppression of the African Slave-Trade to the
United States of America, 1838-1870 (1896). Other
works are classic pieces of protest: The Souls of
Black Folk (1903), Darkwater (1920), and The World and
Africa (1947). And some are respected for their
theoretical innovation: "The Conservation of Races"
(1897), Black Reconstruction in America (1935) and
Dusk of Dawn (1940). Added to these he, almost single-
handed, pursued the first large-scale, significant
social research on black America. He edited (and
wrote most of) the 20 volume Atlanta University Publications (1896-1917) which covered various aspects of
Afro-American life.[1]

Du Bois apparently felt most comfortable in his
role as a historian, sociologist and social critic.
However, it seems that he felt compelled, at an early
age, to take an active part in social leadership. In
this position he followed Booker T. Washington in the
line of the four main black American social leaders,
beginning with Frederick Douglass and ending with
Martin Luther King, Jr. Standing opposed to
Washington's apparent compromise on social rights,
Du Bois took an initiating role in the Niagara Movement
of 1905. From the Niagara Movement he moved into a
central role in the more influential N.A.A.C.P.,
founded in 1910. While at the N.A.A.C.P. (1910-1934)
he founded, edited and wrote much of The Crisis
magazine, its main information outlet.

Du Bois also periodically worked at bringing
together peoples of African descent to form a common
approach to the common problems of racism. He organized several Pan-African Congresses and became inter-
nationally well-known as a founder of Pan-Africanism.

During his last two decades, he was occupied by a
crusade for peace and toward socialism. During the
fifties and sixties these activities were viewed by
many with disdain, but today they can be somewhat more
objectively evaluated. These activities showed unusual
personal qualities of courage and honesty.

Even though most of his activities centered on social and political advancement, he did significant work in aiding artistic activities among blacks by encouraging literary activity, producing plays, publishing poetry and fictional works of his own and of others; all of these give him a prominant place in what Alain Locke calls the "Negro Renaissance."[2]

This brief account is intended to provide with background support for two claims: (1) His life was unusually diversified, long, and productive. (2) The public activities part of his life derives its structure and emphasis from his basic intellectual outlook. The latter is noted because much comment on Du Bois has concentrated on his public activities usually without giving adequate attention to the intellectual underpinnings of activities. When we turn to the intellectual side, the problems of decades of diversity and a high level of productivity alone make difficult a comprehensive and in-depth analysis. Furthermore, the structure of much of his basic thought is complex, and not completely accessible from his works alone. For example, Du Bois received an early education at Harvard which, he claimed, changed his views from scholasticism to pragmatism. Philosophically the pragmatic movement, represented by people like William James, Charles Peirce and John Dewey, is complex and often misrepresented. Furthermore, the pragmatic influence on Du Bois is best seen in relation to the thought of Josiah Royce, an important figure in the history of philosophy who is nearly unknown outside specialists in the philosophical community. Du Bois was also highly influenced by some of the better known doctrines of Marxism, such as Marx's economic determinism and his notion of class struggle. But these tend to be complicated and their use by Du Bois significantly varied over the years. So this work attempts to describe and analyze his major writings, his basic positions on social, political, historical and sociological issues, and the changes in these and to locate the various influences on the philosophical basis of his social thought. Although set in various traditions, Du Bois' intellectual accomplishments are as unique as they are valuable. In this work he is considered mainly for his social/political philosophy, in which he centered on the crucial issues of identity, communal advance, and the pragmatic approach to collective policy.

II

Du Bois' intellectual development may be divided
into four periods.[3] The first period ranges from the
years of his adolescence to the end of his formal
education (1880-1894). These years were marked by a
major shift in attitude: during his boyhood he showed
a faith in laissez-faire capitalism and in an individualistic social Darwinism, which gradually gave way to
the belief that social groups have a greater historical significance than individuals and tend to specify
the abilities and achievements of its members. Thus,
he rejected his early individualism in favor of a
search for a genuinely communal basis for social
action. He also changed from a static conception of
reality in which the observer's notions play a passive
role, to a dynamic, pragmatic notion of meaning in
which people's actions and beliefs play a constitutive
role. These early years are linked together because
they were almost entirely years of development, without
the production of a well-formulated overall social
position. Nevertheless, two interlocking features
remained constant--his belief in the efficacy of
knowledge and, concomitantly, his faith in the talented.

The second period, from 1894-1905, was dominated
by his first full statement on the nature and significance of racial differences. This, his "early notion
of race," is distinguishable from the concept of race
developed in his third period. The early concept of
race relies on three beliefs present at the end of the
first period: (1) the primacy of the community, (2)
the pragmatic notion of meaning, and (3) faith in the
talented. Du Bois' concept of race delineates racial
groups as units (communities) of social action; these
groups have special features functionally contributing
to a definition of their goals, and at the same time
pushing toward realization of these goals. The goals
(and consequently the past action) that are most important are highly refined cultural expressions, such as
constitutional law, philosophy and art. The main
achievements of a race are along these lines and in
the final instance are produced only by the talented.
Yet this does not eliminate a communal basis: these
works express racial characteristics of the group and
are thereby supported by the defining traits of the
whole group.

Du Bois' faith in talent leads to his well-known

doctrine, present only in his early works, of the
"Talented Tenth." Advance comes through knowledge
and education, fostered by the talented. Truth and
understanding thus became important notions: knowledge
was the main weapon against rampant prejudice caused by
ignorance of the defining characteristics of racial
groups. Consequently, he proposed to overcome racism
through sociological knowledge.

The third period (1906-1940) is partly distinguished by Du Bois' turn from the social sciences
toward a social activism, that is, toward a more
public life. The dominant influence on this move was
his diminishing faith in the efficacy of knowledge.
His studies showed no abatement of racism: in fact,
those were years of apparently increasing racism. In
short, reasoned argument proved a futile weapon against
the lynch mob. This practical belief was supported by
theoretical change (though which comes first and to
what degree is conjecture): (1) The central reality
of society was no longer thought to be the product of
the culturally talented; instead he turned toward a
Marxian economic determinism holding that cultural
traits of the sort he admired were part of a superstructure molded by the production and distribution of
economic goods. (2) Racism was thus interpreted as
something different from ignorance of differing ideals;
instead he began to view it as initially set by the
economic realities of slavery. (3) Racism, although
beginning in slavery, maintains its staying power from
deep-seated psychological factors. Du Bois blended
his Marxian economic determinism with a Freudian
notion of subconscious motivation in one of the
earliest attempts to integrate these two significant
deterministic doctrines.

At the beginning of the third period Du Bois left
the academic life and began working with the N.A.A.C.P.
as editor of the Crisis. One of his most notable
intellectual achievements was his attempt to fight
racism by using racial unity to build a relatively
independent economic sub-system in the black community
through the techniques of economic cooperation. The
second main intellectual achievement of the period was
his incorporation of racial differences into a Marxian
analysis of historical change. His work, Black Reconstruction, is based on a revamped version of a Marxian
dialectic. In spite of the intellectual quality of
these attempts, at the end of the third period he began

to lose ground as a social leader. His plan for black
economic cooperation was largely ignored, his separatist
leanings drew sharp criticism, and his position as
editor of The Crisis came to an end. Du Bois returned,
in 1934, to academic life with a position at Atlanta
University.

His fourth period (1941-1963) started without a
significant leadership position. The beginning of
World War II and the end of the depression found him
without an overall plan for social advance. This
brought about a period in which his views were mainly
critical. His interest centered increasingly on Africa.
His efforts began to turn from American racial problems
to a focus on the issue of war as the proximate cause
of society's problems; and the cause of war was linked
to imperialistic ventures, especially in Africa. He
did, during this time, adopt a genuine socialism and
eventually espoused communism, but he saw both as historically relative to empirical conditions inevitably
to be worked out in different ways by different societies. He offered socialism, then, as the ideal to
which all societies were moving in a de facto way, but
he did not speculate on how this would come. Instead
he saved the major part of his attention for what he
took to be the barriers to socialism, such as war.

This period also includes a change in the importance of the race idea in his thought. The economic
unity fostering racial identity, in his view, began
to break down. Economic classes rather than racial
identity became the main analytic tool with which to
understand behavior. Race was increasingly displaced
by class; this tends to explain his move towards
communism and away from the brand of a racially and
psychologically modified Marxism characterizing his
third period.

III

In this work the examination of Du Bois' social
thought and its development and change will mainly be
based on his non-fictional writings. This, then, is
an intellectual portrait, with no detailed attention
given either to his personal life or to many of the
public events in his life as a social leader. Whether
some events involve illumination of theoretical and
intellectual issues is sometimes a matter of judgment.
For example, some of Du Bois' dealings with Booker T.

Washington did not involve a theoretical dispute, but rather focused on practical issues and events. In such cases the events are not included. But sometimes these aspects of Du Bois' life are difficult to separate; where social actions exemplify theoretical issues they are included. Often Du Bois' dispute over educational matters did so involve such key theoretical notions as the "Talented Tenth" and the role of higher and industrial education in social advance.

Several book-length secondary sources do deal with his private and public life. His second wife, Shirley Graham Du Bois, has written a personal memoir of her relationship to him, mainly covering his fourth period, entitled His Day is Marching On.[4] Two other works, not nearly as sympathetic, were written in the late fifties, and thus omit much of his later period; they both deal extensively with his public career, the changes he went through, his accomplishments and his rivalries. These are: Francis L. Broderick, W.E.B. Du Bois: Negro Leader in a Time of Crisis[5] and Elliot M. Rudwick, W.E.B. Du Bois: Propagandist of the Negro Protest.[6] Both works give good coverage, yet are marred by an occasional pejorative attitude toward his racial ideas. One of the best brief accounts of Du Bois' life and writings as well as fine edited collection of his writings is Julius Lester's The Seventh Son: The Thought and Writings of W.E.B. Du Bois, (two volumes).[7] A somewhat briefer collection, W.E.B. Du Bois Speaks (two volumes), edited by Philip S. Foner,[8] provides an excellent in-depth coverage of the major statements by Du Bois on many of the issues covered in this volume.

Foner also deals with Du Bois' relationship to socialism in a fascinating and thorough study, American Socialism and Black Americans: From the Age of Jackson to World War II.[9] Arnold Rampersad briefly covers many aspects of Du Bois' social thought in The Art and Imagination of W.E.B. Du Bois.[10] Rampersad provides in-depth coverage of Du Bois' literary works while the present volume almost entirely ignores Du Bois' fiction. He also offers an interesting account of the influence of religion on Du Bois which, although provocative, seems to me to be too speculative.

Added to these is Du Bois' own efforts at auto-biography. Throughout his career he recounted his life in relation to the major events of the times. These works include The Souls of Black Folk, Darkwater, Dusk

of _Dawn_, and his _Autobiography_. All of his biographi-
cal works provide interesting accounts of his public
life and recount elements in his basic intellectual
changes.

Another source of insight into his character is
his published correspondence edited by Herbert
Aptheker.[11] These volumes include letters to Du Bois
as well as characteristic responses by him. This collection, while generally helpful, is particularly use-
ful for the insights it provides into the sorts of
interpersonal problems Du Bois had, such as the tension
between him and several others at the N.A.A.C.P., and
his difficulties with the U.S. Department of Justice
late in his life.

Du Bois' social thought will be thoroughly analyzed
in the coming chapters. Many of his full-length works
are described in detail, all of his significant positions are placed into the context of his intellectual
development, and the major philosophical influences on
his thought are presented. He is treated throughout as
a social theorist; and by and large an objective presentation is attempted. Du Bois is allowed to speak for
himself with frequency, through quotations and close
paraphrase, so as to provide a check on the organization and interpetation of his writings.

NOTES

1. Julius Lester (ed.), _The Seventh Son: The Thought
    and Writings of W.E.B. Du Bois_ (2 Vols.: New York:
    Random House, 1971), II, pp. 740-767, contains a
    relatively thorough bibliography of his writings.

2. Alain Locke (ed.), _The New Negro_ (New York:
    Atheneum, 1970), pp. xvi-xvii.

3. My classificatory scheme is based almost entirely
    on Du Bois' intellectual development and change.
    Others have divided his life into periods without
    such a perspective. Of course, any division is
    meant to aid in understanding his life and involves
    some relatively arbitrary designations. See, for
    example, Julius Lester's work and Francis L.
    Broderick, _W.E.B. Du Bois: Negro Leader in a Time of_

Crisis (Stanford: Stanford University Press, 1959).

4. Shirley Graham Du Bois, His Day Is Marching On: A Memoir of W.E.B. Du Bois (New York: J.B. Lippincott Co., 1971).

5. Francis L. Broderick, W.E.B. Du Bois: Negro Leader in a Time of Crisis (Stanford: Stanford University Press, 1959).

6. Elliott M. Rudwick, W.E.B. Du Bois: Propagandist of the Negro Protest (New York: Atheneum, 1969).

7. Lester, The Seventh Son.

8. Philip S. Foner (ed.), W.E.B. Du Bois Speaks (two volumes) New York: Pathfinder Press, 1970).

9. Philip S. Foner, American Socialism and Black Americans: From the Age of Jackson to World War II, (Westport, Conn.: Greenwood Press, 1977).

10. Arnold Rampersad, The Art and Imagination of W.E.B. Du Bois, (Cambridge, Mass.: Harvard University Press, 1976).

11. Herbert Aptheker (ed.), The Correspondence of W.E.B. Du Bois (three volumes), (Amherst, Mass.: University of Massachusetts Press, 1978).

CHAPTER I

EARLY YEARS: 1868-1894

W.E.B. Du Bois' upbringing in Great Barrington, a town in Western Massachusetts with a population of about five thousand, molded his early social and political views; to a significant degree his early commitments, mainly political tendencies in his adolescent life and the positions he espoused in college and graduate school, can be traced back to what can be characterized as his "dual life": he was, to a significant extent, an accepted part of his small town, but he was also a member of the town's relatively segregated black minority. His position presented the makings of a dilemma for the young Du Bois because the virtues he saw in America were vitiated by the town's sometimes latent, sometimes overt racism. The individualistic emphasis implied in its laissez-faire attitudes was countered by the reality of socially defined group traits (in his case race) tracking action so that individual attempts at advance seemed pre-cast to at least partial failure. Early in life he took seriously both dominant cultural and political attitudes and the flaw of racism. The result was a movement away from the individualism he first accepted toward a commitment to the black community, a commitment intertwined with some of his early values. The real dilemma was not whether to give up individualism; after a time that appeared to him to be unrealistic as a social doctrine. The main problem he had to deal with over the years was whether the American society contained racism as an anomaly in an otherwise beneficial and healthy society or as an integral part of the system. He first tended to view racism as such an anomaly, while later in his life he believed that racism was an integral part of social life.

I

The black community in Great Barrington was small, probably less than fifty people, yet the members of Du Bois' family mainly associated in this closed circle.[1] The color line was clear, but not especially deep or vicious,[2] so he could also claim that as a boy he noticed almost no discrimination.[3] Of course he recognized differences in appearance and that economic and social inequalities tended to distinguish his small group from wealthier whites: the blacks he knew were not affluent and did not own businesses.[4]

Even though he experienced no strong sense of discrimination, he was sensitive to the occasional slights, especially when strangers visited.[5] In high school the racial distinctions were more frequent, but again not especially harsh; prejudice against Irish immigrants was more apparent to him than anti-black attitudes. In fact, Du Bois recollected the town's prejudice as mainly stemming from economic inequality and ancestral ties.[6] So, due to his family's long-standing ties in Great Barrington, he could, despite his economic status, view himself as part of the larger community, and his capacities underscored this outlook because as a youth he excelled in important activities, especially scholarship. His high school principal, in uncharacteristic style for those days, put him into the college preparatory program; he claimed this brought him into association with the upper social classes.[7]

In contrast with his experiences, he later judged the age as one in which strong, deepseated, and abiding racial attitudes had firmly developed.[8] Looking back at his youth, he recognized the forces of racism that affected him regardless of his initial awareness. This helps to explain a significant and apparently quickly formulated change, after high school, to a deep commitment to racial (as opposed to individual) progress: the change to a racial commitment is best understood not in terms of racial harmony in Great Barrington, but in terms of his attitude toward limitations caused by racial discrimination. For example, he often heard relatives talk of their problems in getting jobs, and implied in this was a recognition of color bars to which he was not yet subject.[9]

The most apparent influence of his experiences in Great Barrington had little to do with race or racism but rather concerned the formation of laissez-faire liberal attitudes. He was, of course, mainly a product of his time, with the essential difference of race; his attitudes typically followed a New England cast and tended to be supported by the character of his town and his position in it. Great Barrington had pronounced differences in wealth, but it seemed to him as a youth that, with inherited wealth at a minimum, all people worked for their income, even though their income "was not proportioned to the effort. . . ."[10]

2

Du Bois noted two significant minority groups;
one was the small group of blacks and the other was
composed mainly of Irish immigrants. The older Irish
families made up part of the "respectable poor," but
the newly arrived families lived in slums and were
feared by Du Bois, who was occasionally the recipient
of their racial slurs. Growing up, he assumed that
this group made and preferred the slums. Interjecting
his later view, he remarked, "Certainly in school
and church and on the street, I got no idea that the
town was responsible for the slums."[11] These slums
were not especially bad even though they repelled the
young Du Bois.[12] He did not identify with the poor;
in fact he considered, probably for reasons of
longevity in the town, the rich or at least the well-off
as the group to which he properly belonged![13] His
attitude toward wealth was in line with the dominant
sentiment of his age: "all who were willing to work
could easily earn a living; that those who had property
had earned it and deserved it and could use it as they
wished; that poverty was the shadow of crime and con-
noted lack of thrift and shiftlessness."[14] Du Bois'
earliest social views were aligned with the growing
popularity of social Darwinism and with laissez-faire
economics.

Looking back on his early life Du Bois pointed out
several other traits that were, to varying degrees,
significant in their affect on his later social views.
He recognized sexual inequality.[15] Women in the town
were by and large housekeepers.[16] Perhaps more significantly in terms of his later social outlook, he noted
an unconscious socialist tendency; that is, the town
owned its water supply, took care of the streets and
sewers, and provided for the few paupers. The benevolence of the town was not unmixed; he "early came to
understand that to be 'on the town,' the recipient of
public charity, was the depth not only of misfortune
but of a certain guilt."[17] And his elitist propensities
may have been dampened by work he did as a timekeeper
on a construction site; for the first time he witnessed
what it meant to do hard physical labor. His job included giving notices of discharge--an education about
the life of a laborer without the social protection of
labor unions and unemployment insurance.[18]

It is safe to say that the boyhood life Du Bois
experienced was not especially out of the ordinary;
the dominant opinions of the town became by and large

his opinions. Nevertheless the essential difference of race remained beneath his experiences. He was at once sensitive about it, and saw the distinction as a point of pride. The presence of a racial distinction carried with it the threat of prejudice and economic disadvantage, and also, for him, the realization of personal excellence. This dual experience of racial pride and racial suffering is apparent in many of the policies he adopted throughout his life.

Later, in looking back on his boyhood, he articulated some of the contradictory forces to which he was subject. Wealth and apparent advance were on one side: "It was a day of Progress with a capital P. Population . . . was increasing . . . ; cities everywhere were growing and expanding. . . . Wealth was God. Everywhere men sought wealth and especially in America there was extravagant living; everywhere the poor planned to be rich and the rich planned to be richer; everywhere wider, bigger, higher, better things were set down as inevitable."[19] But he could not overlook racism: "Apparently one consideration alone saved me from complete conformity with the thoughts and confusions of the then current social trends; and that was the problems of racial and cultural contacts."[20] He did not question the capitalistic system he saw as supporting the advance of the world, he simply questioned the relation of blacks to this movement.[21] He eventually sought ways for blacks to become a full part of this world movement. In effect the problem was that blacks were separated from, or alienated from the mainstream of social life, but this alienation, like all alienation experiences, was significant because the separation was from the social life that otherwise tended to constitute his social experience.

It seems that early in his life he did experience what he later called a "double consciousness." ". . . the Negro is a sort of seventh son, born with a veil, and gifted with second-sight in this American world.--a world which yields him no true self-consciousness, but only lets him see himself through the revelation of the outer world. It is a peculiar sensation, this double consciousness, this sense of always looking at one's self through the eyes of others, of measuring one's soul by the tape of a world that looks on in amused contempt and pity. One ever feels his twoness,-- an American, a Negro; two souls, two thoughts, two un-reconciled strivings; two warring ideals in one dark

4

body, whose dogged strength alone keeps it from being torn asunder."[22] Here the expression is one of a deep alienation, of a despair which is clearly lacking in his youth. Yet the germ of this alienation and the search it evokes was present early on.

The earliest answer to the situation, which comes before his rejection of individualism, was that the color problem in general could be solved in the way he attempted to solve it for himself. Prejudice was over-shadowed by his personal, mainly intellectual, success: "The secret of life and the loosing of the color bar, then, lay in excellence, in accomplishment; if others of my family, of my colored kin, had stayed in school, instead of quitting early for small jobs, they could have risen to equal whites. . . . There was no real discrimination on account of color--it was all a matter of ability and hard work."[23] Two features were essential to Du Bois' early outlook: (1) prejudice was not a fundamentally serious matter and (2) self-help, involving hard work and intellectual excellence, was the only efficacious solution to the racial problem. This outlook influenced his life and writings to various degrees until around 1905. The second point formed part of the foundation of the doctrine of the "Talented Tenth" and the rationale behind his early social studies. This view was adopted during his boyhood and in ways was strengthened by his later education, yet his progress in intellectual life involved an understanding of those kinds of things which eventually destroyed it.

II

At the age of 15 Du Bois began writing articles for the New York Globe (later the New York Freeman). Besides simple reports on social activities, he often offered paternalistic advice to the black community. In 1883 he warned that not enough blacks were attending town meetings: "it seems that they do not take as much interest in politics as is necessary for the protection of their rights."[24] Blacks, he insisted, held the balance of voting power in Great Barrington, thus, "If they will only act in concert they may become a power not to be despised. It would be a good plan if they should meet and decide which way would be most advantageous for them to cast their votes."[25] He also advised that a most beneficial action for the community would be the establishment of a literary society[26] and that he should be consulted before personal libraries were

5

revised.[27]

This early concern for group development was briefly expressed and fell within an individualistic discourse. So in general his boyhood years, living on the outskirts of Great Barrington, gave him a kind of quintessence of 19th century Americanism, except for often unnoticed racial differentiating. The American side of the double consciousness was well formed. And accordingly, he hoped to go on after high school graduation in 1884, as the natural course of events, to Harvard for his college education. But there were difficulties--the preparatory quality of the Great Barrington school and his lack of funds.[28] Some people in Great Barrington apparently believed that he would be better off enrolling in a black college and money was raised to send him to Fisk University in Nashville, Tennessee. Du Bois was not troubled by this since he believed he would attend Harvard eventually and because he wanted to be at Fisk among people physically like himself. He realized that "as I grew older, the close social intermingling with my white fellows would grow more restricted."[29] And, characteristically, he saw himself as being sent to the black South to continue the New England crusade against slavery into a post-war period of promise. Even at seventeen he conceived of himself as the leader of a people he felt himself to be a part, but in reality knew little about.

At Fisk it is safe to say that Du Bois consciously adopted the previously weakly experienced black side of the double consciousness. The beginning was physical: "I was thrilled to be for the first time among so many people of my own color or rather of such various and such extraordinary colors, which I had only glimpsed before, but who it seemed were bound to me by new and exciting and eternal ties."[30] But the physical tie quickly developed into a sense of commitment growing out of common and harsh problems. At Fisk he encountered a world trenchantly divided by racial barriers, "where the darker half was held back by race prejudice and legal bonds, as well as by deep ignorance and dire poverty."[31] He witnessed at close hand the reality of lynching: from 1885 through 1894 seventeen hundred blacks were lynched. "Each death was a scar upon my soul . . . ,"[32] He experienced the beginning of wide-spread Jim Crow accommodations, racially divided cities and towns, public insult, and violence. "My knowledge of the race problem became more definite. I

6

saw discrimination in ways of which I had never
dreamed. . . ."[33] During two summer terms he taught
in a backward rural black school. "I saw the hard,
ugly drudgery of country life and the writhing of
landless, ignorant peasants. I saw the race problem at
nearly its lowest terms."[34] Such experiences, of
course, had a profound effect on the young Du Bois.
Here he could see the power of racism as a cause of
human degradation. The effect of this, one may speculate, was to contribute to his eventual doctrine of the
"Talented Tenth." Slavery and its aftermath contributed to a situation of relative helplessness occupied
by the average black. As a result Du Bois began to
believe that salvation of the race would come from the
top down. He seems not to have had a sense of despair--
which only began to appear in the early 1900's--but
rather a sense of commitment and a desire to study the
black problem while advocating a strong community led
by the "Talented Tenth." Yet these sorts of experiences
began to suggest the depth of the errors of the assumptions of laissez-faire social policy.

He claimed that at Fisk his consciousness became
social so as to replace his previously egocentric world
by the concerns and needs of the black world. His
studies and plans began to take definite direction as
a course of action for the eventual amelioration of the
black problem.[35] These new experiences and goals turned
him away from his "Americanism," or perhaps it is better
to say his "laissez-faire" attitudes to his race: "A
new loyalty and allegiance replace my Americanism:
henceforward I was a Negro."[36] The new loyalty he expressed was to a community previously known in a limited
way, and it was fostered by the problem faced by blacks
in the South, including the students at Fisk. This
change in a young man at Fisk is presented by Du Bois
as a kind of grand leap from an environment of little
realized discrimination and from nearly complete agreement with the dominant culture. But this is not entirely true; he did recognize the discrimination present in
Great Barrington. Further, his reporting activity suggests some group awareness. All of this indicates that
the changes were already initiated in Great Barrington.
The change at Fisk was partly a matter of emphasis.
Nevertheless, his experiences at Fisk were quantitative-
ly and qualitatively different and established in a
concerted way themes which would influence and permeate
his social thought throughout his years: his "double
consciousness," and his search for the bounds and

7

strengths of a cohesive community. Both stem from the
divisions and persecution plaguing a minority in a
country dominated by the white majority.

The double consciousness Du Bois spoke of is a
form of alienation which can cause a search for roots--
for a community with strength and cohesiveness so as to
offset that feeling of alienation. Du Bois' social
thought involved an attempt to define and create such
a community, an attempt which proved frustrating and
often futile. The beginnings of his first fully articulated notion of a community were tentatively formulated at Fisk. Unsurprisingly, his views at Fisk were
consistent with the influence of his days in Great
Barrington. He relied on the potential power of knowledge as a way to group advance; he concentrated on cultural class distinctions in order to mold an effective
community structure. He divided the black group into
two main sections: first of all the talented, those
with knowledge and skill, and, secondly, the overwhelming majority lacking these traits. The masses of oppressed blacks form the body of the community as an
amorphous class needing direction and strength. The
direction was to come from the educated few, the
"Talented Tenth," who could use their knowledge and
education to lead the group out of its problems.[37]
The knowledgeable elite was to provide the binding
leadership to direct a powerful and effective community,
already receptive to leadership by being subject to a
common problem.

The college program at Fisk brought together
students from an educational elite who followed a
traditional liberal arts program. Thus, the Fisk program provided a model for his class consciousness.
The students, though distinct by the special background, were part of the cultural life of black Americans and faced a similar pattern of discrimination.
Cultural continuity and similar problems could supply
the needed impetus behind a socially committed Talented
Tenth. The beginnings of Du Bois' first full efforts
at establishing a community relied on these key points
and also on a faith that progress could be achieved by
the sorts of efforts that the talented could undertake.
So there was little reason to look beyond an educated
leadership for a solution. "Nor did I pause to enquire
in just what ways and with what technique we would
work--first, broad, exhaustive knowledge of the world;
all other wisdom, all method and application would be

added unto us."[38]

As editor of the student newspaper, the <u>Fisk
Herald</u>, Du Bois began his career as an earnest social
critic with a statement entitled, "An Open Letter to
the Southern People;" he attacked arbitrary class
differentiations between whites and blacks and the
hypocrisy of refusing education to blacks while justi-
fying discrimination on account of ignorance. His
faith in educated elites also seemed to apply to
whites; he appealed to the Southern aristocracy to join
hands with black men of talent to lead both races.[39]

Perhaps the early extent of his social commitment
is best illustrated by his selection of Bismarck as the
topic of his graduating oration in 1888. Bismarck was
his hero because "He had made a nation out of a mass of
bickering people."[40] This was what, in effect, he saw
as his own goal. Reflecting back he realized the inad-
equacies of his early position: he accepted dominant
notions and social structures without asking fundamental questions about the foundations of wealth and
success and about the basis of "Progress": ". . . I
did not understand at all, nor had my history courses
led me to understand, anything of current European
intrigue, of the expansion of European power into
Africa, of the Industrial Revolution built on slave
trade. . . . I was blithely European and imperialist
in outlook; democratic as democracy was conceived in
America."[41] His admission here should be read as
meaning that in his early days he did not understand
the complicated significance of social and political
life. To understand what is needed for solutions to
large scale social and political problems requires,
first of all, a thorough appreciation of the factors
that cause the problem. He eventually came to believe
that the American social system, including its links
with Europe and its treatment of colonial lands, caused
racism. So, a solution seeking entry by appealing to
and using talent and knowledge, missed the fundamental
realities. His education at Fisk had avoided the realities of economic questions which he eventually saw as
crucial to race relationships and development. His
schooling, especially pertaining to social and political
questions was just beginning; after Fisk it was continued at Harvard (as a college junior) through a scholarship partly designed to diversify Harvard's student
body.[42]

III

When Du Bois arrived in Harvard in 1888 he continued, in the predominantly white environment, the loyalty
he developed at Fisk. The few blacks at Harvard were
mostly integrationists, seeing integration as the only
possible solution to the problems blacks faced. Du
Bois held to the separate development of the black side
of the dual consciousness; he adopted the policy of "a
Negro self-sufficient culture even in America,"[43] He
tolerated the segregation he found at Harvard and used
his second college, in distinction to Fisk, almost
entirely as an educational experience and minimized it
as part of his social life. He believed that it was
essential to work within the black group, to heighten
a sense of culture as a way of combating problems of
discrimination. Race marked a group separated from the
dominant structure, but he had not yet clearly defined
a concept of race--after leaving Harvard his outlook on
race as defining a community became more adequately
formulated. In the practical sense, though, his commitment was already well formed: ". . . I went to
Harvard as a Negro, not simply by birth, but recognizing myself as a member of a segregated caste whose
situation I accepted but was determined to work from
within that caste to find my way out."[44] Note the
significance of the expression. He was not dedicated
to segregation; his effort was directed to eventually
destroying it. Group loyalty is not equivalent to
segregation.

Knowledge, as we have seen, was for Du Bois the
force by which discrimination could be overcome; he
took this seriously enough so that he intended at
Harvard to study among other things knowledge itself.
". . . above all I wanted to study philosophy! I
wanted to get hold of the basis of knowledge, and explore foundations and beginnings."[45] He obviously
found unsatisfactory the standard concensus of what
knowledge meant and could do. He seemed to intuit that
knowledge had been conceived in a way that made it too
abstract, with too little impact on day to day life, to
be the sort of force he required. Instead he began to
conceive knowledge as essentially empirical, or based
on observed data, rather than on rationalistic speculation: ". . . I was [at Harvard] in possession of the
average educated man's concept of this world and its
meaning. But now I wanted to go further: to know what
man could know and how to collect and interpret facts

face to face. And what 'facts' were."[46]

He was attracted to the unusually great philoso-
phers at Harvard, among them William James, Josiah
Royce and George Santayana. He studied Immanuel Kant's
Critique of Pure Reason in a private tutorial with
Santayana, ethics with James, and carried on his most
active social life on campus with these men; this may
have strengthened his belief that education could overcome prejudice because he apparently found no prejudice
in this extraordinary group.

His initial idea of philosophy was traditional--he
called it scholastic without elaboration. Scholastic
philosophy was speculative, theological and static. It
was theological because it put the role of God in a
central position; it sought certain, that is un-
shakeable and indubitable, knowledge about God and His
creation. The world was seen as fixed in its basic
structures, independent of mankind, and only dependent
on God's sustaining force. This philosophy was non-
empirical: the test of belief was its position in the
philosophical system which assigned everything its
place. Philosophical speculation in the middle ages
was, in the main, most concerned with that aspect of
reality which did not change--the essence (or the nature) of a thing. Philosophical understanding of human
beings, for example, centered on the commonly shared,
universal ingredients of all humans who ever lived and
ever would live in the future. Needless to say, these
shared features were quite abstract and rarefied, and
thereby not observable in themselves: humans were
defined and speculated on simply as "rational animals."
To know right from wrong, for instance, meant to speculate on what sorts of actions would be rational, that
is, in conformity with the nature of human beings. For
Du Bois' attempt to use knowledge to solve social problems, such a philosophy appeared too detached.

During his stay at Harvard, William James was
developing his pragmatic philosophy; this new point of
view attracted Du Bois as the sort of empiricism he was
looking for. He claimed, "William James guided me out
of the sterilities of scholastic philosophy to realist
pragmatism. . . ."[47] Pragmatism became, as we shall
see, one of the prime methodological influences on
Du Bois' early concept of race and on his first clearly
articulated formulation of an adequate black community.
For now, we briefly characterize the main points of the

11

pragmatic movement. Pragmatism, America's first original contribution to philosophy, is not to be characterized by a body of doctrines or substantive beliefs; rather it is best thought of as a method of inquiry which structures all attempts at gaining knowledge after a model of scientific inquiry. Experimentation, and thereby action molds the pragmatic viewpoint: and the pragmatist's empiricism insists that certainty is never assured since beliefs must be subject to change in light of new evidence. Concepts are tools to be used to solve problems; the test of thought is its effectiveness in solving problems.

The main pragmatists were Charles S. Peirce, William James, Josiah Royce,[48] and John Dewey. Du Bois' experiences were mainly with Royce and James. James held that a belief is considered true for an individual if it works, if it aids that person, i.e., if it helps to organize experience, makes life more tolerable, makes the person happier, etc. James' influence on Du Bois can best be seen in Du Bois' acceptance of the notion that the test of a belief is its ability to accomplish prescribed goals; he also accepted the view that beliefs or theories are subject to revision.

Du Bois' communal commitments can find support in Josiah Royce's philosophy. Royce placed a basic emphasis on commitment to a community. The following chapter explores Du Bois' early concept of race and shows its relationship to pragmatism in general and to Royce's commitment to community.

Du Bois, of course, was never a professional philosopher and while it is safe to say that he always remained pragmatic, his tended to be a loose sort of pragmatism in which he accepted broad ideals and struggled with the means through which they are attained; this means changing ground as a plan becomes unworkable or superceded by an alternate plan of action. The right course of action, including the ideal in view, was not thought of by Du Bois as something intuitive, speculative or assumed; rather, social ethics was a question of factual analysis. The observation of facts pointed to problems and problems called for solutions. This was a basic feature of Du Bois' earliest studies, and this is what he meant when, in a term paper at Harvard, he interpreted James and Royce as attempting "to base ethics upon fact--to make it a science."[49]

12

However, James added in the margin that he believed
that this was impossible. Perhaps Du Bois' emphasis
on science led him to turn away from philosophy to a
pursuit of the social sciences, even though he claimed
he turned from philosophy because of James' advice that
"It is hard to earn a living with philosophy."[50]

Du Bois' philosophical and social views easily led
to an ethical analysis of historical and social facts.
That is, history became a moral primer, and sociology
pointed the way to understanding and progress. He began a study of United States history under Albert
Bushell Hart and "conceived the idea of applying philosophy to an historical interpretation of race relations." He went on, "In other words, I was trying to
take my first steps toward sociology as the science of
human actions. . . . But I began with some research in
Negro History and finally at the suggestion of Hart, I
chose the suppression of the African slave trade to
America as my doctor's thesis."[51] The first draft of
the thesis was finished in 1891.

Harvard did not recognize sociology but was, in
his view, grasping towards a scientific approach to
human action. Du Bois' turn toward history and sociology was, to a small degree, coupled with economics,
which he would see later in his life as central in
basic relationships; he claimed, "It was not until I
was long out of college and had finished the first phase
of my teaching career that I began to see clearly the
connection of economics and politics; the fundamental
influence of man's efforts to earn a living upon all
his other efforts."[52]

At Harvard there was little awareness of the overriding importance of economics. Marx was hardly mentioned, free trade was supported, and there was little
sympathy for labor. "We reverenced Ricardo and wasted
long hours on the 'Wages-fund.' I remember Frank
Taussig's course supporting dying Ricardean economics.
Wages came from what employers had left for labor after
they had subtracted their own reward. Suppose that this
profit was too small to attract the employer, what would
the poor worker do but starve?"[53] Harvard tended to
view strikes as lawless; trusts and monopolies were
seen as inevitable. Socialism was feared. He concluded
that Harvard was rich and reactionary: "This defender
of wealth and capital, already half ashamed of Sumner
and Phillips, was willing finally to replace an Elliott

with a Lowell. The social community that mobbed
Garrison, easily hanged Sacco and Vanzetti."[54]

While Du Bois accepted many of the political views
at Harvard he was critical of the white world and knew
well the problems of the black world. So his outlook
was still essentially to gain full social benefits for
blacks, and this was to be achieved eventually from
the strength of a segregated closed cultural circle.
This goal was mainly limited to the United States.
There was some passing mention of an expanding racial
consciousness to include all darker people in the world
in the struggle for self-determination.[55] However, he
claimed that he knew little about colonialism, its
methods and the condition of the people living under
its rule. "The Congo Free State was established and
the Berlin Conference of 1885 was reported to be an
act of civilization against the slave trade and liquor.
French, English and Germans pushed on in Africa, but
I did not question the interpretation which pictured
this as an advance of civilization and the benevolent
tutelage of barbarians."[56]

At Harvard he maintained his earlier view that it
was possible to solve problems of discrimination quiet-
ly through applied knowledge. He also began to note
the importance of economics. In an unpublished manu-
script, "Harvard and the South" (June, 1891) he claimed
that ignorance of economic realities caused many problems in the South.[57] The South's problems were caused
by over-rapid industrialization, accelerated by an
unhealthy political environment and a poor economic
foundation. These problems were excusable and could
be solved by an educated elite and a real university
system.

Du Bois' Harvard years led him to a belief in
pragmatic empiricism and strengthened his commitment
to the black group. But in these years he perceived
social dynamics only vaguely--a recognition of entrenched economic forces was coupled with a faith in knowledge as capable of solving all problems. A desire for
a separate culture was coupled with a high regard for
and desire to emulate the achievements of predominantly
white Western civilization. Regard for problems of
black Americans was not linked to the problems of
colonial blacks. Politics and economics, in the main,
were viewed separately, world events and conditions
were seen in isolation, and the key to success was

14

education, hard work, and moral righteousness.

IV

Change in these views involved a long, slow process beginning with the continuation of his graduate training from 1892 to 1894 at the University of Berlin, through a special fellowship from the Slater Fund.

In Germany, Du Bois claimed to have expanded both his intellectual capacities and his "humanity." He did not encounter the level of racial discrimination he met in the United States and thus he claimed to have emerged from the "extremes," of his "racial provincialism."[58] And he "began to understand the real meaning of scientific research and the dim outline of methods of employing its techniques and its results in the new social sciences for the settlement of the Negro problems in America."[59] Presumably Du Bois meant that he began to understand the sorts of empirical techniques of collecting, displaying and interpreting data that he used in The Philadelphia Negro and the Atlanta University Publications.

At Berlin he worked mainly in economics, history and sociology. He became acquainted with such famous figures as Schmoller, Heinrich von Treitschke, and Max Weber. His closest association was with the economist, Gustav Schmoller, who directed his doctoral disseration (in German) entitled, "The large-and small-scale management of agriculture in the Southern United States, 1840-1890;" it was not accepted for the degree due to residency requirements. Schmoller claimed the thesis was otherwise acceptable.[60] Schmoller tended toward a blend of empiricism and normative evaluation operating within the parameters of a particular historical period.[61] This seems to be the same sort of emphasis Du Bois began to develop at Harvard, and, as we shall see, is apparent in his Harvard doctoral dissertation. Without detailing influences, Du Bois recounted in retrospect, that under the instructors at Berlin he "began to see the race problem in America, the problem of the peoples of Africa and Asia, and the political development of Europe as one. I began to unite my economics and politics; but I still assumed that in these groups of activities and forces, the political realm was dominant."[62] He did not fully realize the interrelationship of world economic and political events: ". . . how gold and diamonds of South Africa

15

and later the copper, ivory, cocoa, tin and vegetable oils of other parts of Africa and especially black labor force were determining and conditioning the political action of Europe."[63]

In those days Du Bois considered political events to be predominant--politics refers, in this case, to the conscious policies adopted by a person or group of people, and the authoritative actions taken by these people with the intention of securing policy goals. By claiming these events are autonomous, he was, in effect, contending that a political order is capable of selecting policy goals from among a wide assortment of alternatives. These alternatives can be freely selected within broad parameters, and not closely constrained by economic realities. Two further beliefs are easily inferred from the autonomy of politics: (1) That moral culpability rests with those who make (morally) bad decisions, and (2) political decisions can dominate and thereby change social reality. Du Bois held both views; his conclusion was that the main constraint on proper political decisions was knowledge--his task, until 1905, was to get the facts straight so that those who want to make the right decisions in relation to the race problem could. Those who did not want to make the right decisions were to be condemned as immoral.

In Germany Du Bois was also introduced in a serious way, to socialism and Marxism. Writing in his diary, he spoke of the natural attractiveness of socialism but regretted that the development of Marxism was, in his words, "too complicated for a student like myself. . . . I was overwhelmed with rebuttals of Marxism before I understood the original doctrine."[64] His main intellectual attention was not to Marxism but to social studies; however, he did attend meetings of the Social Democratic Party.[65]

Returning to the United States in 1894 brought him back to the realities of prejudice and discrimination. He had a clearer idea of how to investigate social issues and what they meant. He also felt clear about the course of action he would follow; he would try to use the knowledge gained from the study of history and sociology as a weapon for equality. These views were still those of a relatively young man and his aims would change; his grasp of social forces would become clearer. Yet his foundation was extraordinary. Few people in the United States received as good an education as Du Bois. This, of course, placed him in an elite group. Du Bois' commitment to the use of sociology and history as a weapon for racial advance was aristocratic in the sense that it required an educated elite to guide and lead the mass into a coherent and powerful group. He would eventually question the power of truth and the leadership role of an educated elite, and he finally accepted in late life a thorough Marxian position. During the next period of his life he would rely on knowledge and elitism in his development of a concept of race loyalty, of a notion of a "Talented Tenth," and he would copiously apply his scholarly capabilities to historical and sociological studies.

V

A main accomplishment of Du Bois' education was his Harvard doctoral dissertation on the efforts, mainly by governmental action, to abolish the slave trade. At Harvard, as we have seen, he claimed to have "conceived the idea of applying philosophy to an historical interpretation of race relations."[66] His commitment was to the power of knowledge as the solution to racial problems and this approach involved "sociology as the science of human action."[67] His dissertation, The Suppression of the African Slave Trade in the United States of America: 1638-1870,[68] published in 1896, as the first volume of the Harvard Historical Series, perhaps best shows how he hoped to use an historical study as a way of understanding human motivations and as a guide to normative prescription.

The Suppression is a most significant work; it stands as an historical landmark. As John Hope Franklin comments: "The year 1896 marks a significant turning point in the study of American history. Harvard University began, in that year, to issue its Historical Studies, the first series of scholarly historical works to be published by an American university."[69] Du Bois' book, as the first volume, attests to its pioneering inquiry into the slavery period. Du Bois gathered much of the material single-handed, and a final version clearly displays the careful and meticulous quality of his work; even today it is held in high regard.[70]

The point of studying the attempts to limit the importation of slaves to the United States was not simply to gather data on little known laws and protests, but to find out why people acted as they did. That is,

17

why certain groups, states, and finally the federal
government attempted to suppress slavery by suppressing
the slave trade and, on the other hand, why others
resisted the suppression of slavery? For Du Bois
slavery was, and remained, the focal point as both
the molding force behind interracial relations and
behind the problems of the black community. His first
published book was an attempt at a "philosophical"
sociology, an attempt thereby to solve racial problems.
The Suppression was intended to locate causes for human
actions and to evaluate those same actions. For Du
Bois, in his early years, history and sociology were
designed to be prescriptive as well as descriptive.
Also, his early studies involved an attempt to provide
knowledge about his own racial identity and about the
structure and condition of the black community. Although this became clearer in later works, it was an
essential ingredient in his earliest study of interracial relations.

A main thesis of the work is that there is a
functional combination of clearly identifiable varia-
bles behind the formulation of attitudes towards slavery. The main factors are moral, economic and what
we might call the "fear" factor. These motivations
operated differently in different sections of the country and at different times and with varying force.
Throughout the inquiry Du Bois placed judgment on the
extent to which moral beliefs guided action. In fact,
he adopted a particularly strong moralizing tone,
placing judgment on the moral fortitude of the various
sections of the country and on the founding fathers.
But this work also indicates that from an early period
Du Bois placed economic factors as an important moti-
vating force behind social activities. In distinction
to the work's moralizing tone he showed that even the
fear of slave insurrections and the fear of a dispro-
portion between slaves and free citizens occupied a
stronger role than moral motivation.

Even though this is the case, the ultimate recourse Du Bois used was moral--that is, the solution
to social problems depended more on strong moral fibre
than on a change in economic or political structures.
This presents an interesting paradox because economic
conditions were presented as overriding morality as an
influence on social action, but morality was viewed as
capable of affecting change even in the face of conflicting economic pressures. But the paradox is

apparently solved on the level of knowledge: Once the influence on social activities is exposed, and the consequences of these activities are clearly seen, he apparently believed that it then became possible to be freed from even the adverse influence of economics; he consequently offered his admonitions in a directly moral framework.

After beginning the work with a brief description of early attempts mainly in England to channel and tax the African slave trade, and with statistics on the numbers of slaves imported,[71] he asserted, "That the slave-trade was the very life of the colonies had, by 1700, become an almost unquestioned axiom in British practical economics. The colonists themselves declared slaves 'the strength and sinews of this western world,' and the lack of them 'the grand obstruction' here, as the settlements 'cannot subsist without supplies of them.' "[72] The encouragement of the slave trade seemed, to England, to be the natural course. Bare economic necessity established slavery, but it was a brutal institution, especially in its earliest years.[73] As a consequence, insurrections and acts of violence by the slaves were frequent. Many colonists lived under fear which was "the prime motive back of all earlier efforts to check the further importation of slaves."[74] Thus, the fear factor appears. However, the severity of conditions and the number of slaves were not evenly proportioned among the colonies; so he turned to an examination of each region separately.

Du Bois considered the attitudes of the "planting colonies" to be the most significant. These southern settlements had soil and climate suitable to slavery, whereas in the other colonies "the institution was by these same factors doomed from the beginning."[75] Thus the crucial factor in the survival of slavery in North America was the attitude of the Southern colonies. The point Du Bois made is this: powerful economic motives militate for an institution which many saw as immoral. Only very strong moral motives could combat the rise of slavery. Slavery set up a kind of moral test of the colonies; he assumed it was possible to have the moral awareness and political courage to overcome the predisposition of economic factors. A strong moral and political position can realistically accept or reject an economic institution. This emphasis on morality in his early writings begins to disappear in his later works as he gradually accepted a Marxian economic determinism.

19

The Marxian emphasis on class struggle, so pertinent
in Du Bois' Black Reconstruction of 1935 is also absent
in the Suppression. Instead he wrote as if the colonists formed a homogeneous mass without class differentiation, but for the existence of slaves.

As he began his analysis of a particular region,
his moralizing tone is apparent. "In Georgia we have
an example of a community whose philanthropic founders
sought to impose upon it a code of morals higher than
the colonists wished."[76] Oglethorpe believed slavery
to be against the teachings of the gospels and against
the laws of England. So the trade was prohibited in
1735 and the colonists were told that slaves would be
a source of weakness to the colony, and that white
labor could be imported to do the work of the slaves.
Here is a case where Du Bois offered evidence that
indicates a gap between politics and economics. In
Georgia a moral view, arrived at free of the influence
of economics, was adopted on the highest political
level in the state. However, the colonists were opposed
to the law, frequently violated it and in 1749 forced
its repeal. The fact that the law was repealed can be
viewed in two ways: (1) that the apparent autonomy of
politics was merely a temporary anomaly. (This would
be consistent with his later views.) Or, (2) one can
claim moral strength on the part of political leaders
which was overruled by moral weakness and immoral political activity on the part of the constituency. This
route saves the autonomy of politics, and is the course
Du Bois took in Suppression. In his view, immorality
won out over morality and in doing so further weakened
an already poor "moral fibre" by frequent violation of
law. The lawlessness inaugurated by slavery and slave
trade forms a motif in Du Bois' work--the consequence
of slavery is the general weakening of the nation.

A similar sort of analysis was applied to the other
colonies. After close analysis of the various colonies,
Du Bois concluded that up to and including the revolutionary period, they displayed similar general patterns
that towered over their diversity. From 1638 to 1664,
there was "a tendency to take a high moral stand
against the traffic."[77] The period from 1664 to 1760,
was "marked by statutes laying duties varying in design
from encouragement to absolute prohibition, . . . and
by the slow but steady growth of a spirit unfavorable
to the long continuance of the trade."[78] And finally,
from 1760 to 1797, there was a "pronounced effort to

regulate, limit, or totally prohibit the traffic."[79]

The revolutionary period witnessed a unity of opinion: the system of slavery would wither away. "It seemed certainly a legitimate deduction from the history of the preceding century to conclude that, as the system had risen, flourished, and fallen in Massachusetts, New York, and Pennsylvania, and as South Carolina, Virginia, and Maryland were apparently following in the same legislative path, the next generation would in all probability witness the last throes of the system on our soil."[80] This showed a widespread desire to prohibit the trade, but concurrently there was a potentially dangerous shift in the South away from a moral condemnation of slavery to the view that it was a "perhaps unfortunate necessity."[81] He also noted that the colonies were on the verge of great industrial expansion and that slavery would play a significant role in that expansion.[82] His intention in looking ahead to industrial expansion was probably to focus on the revolutionary times as a key opportunity to rid the country of slavery--an opportunity which would tend to be cut off in the future by new economic conditions. Slavery was presumed to have failed economically in all but the South, which, it was believed, would soon follow suit. The revolutionary philosophy of freedom and universal rights provided a sufficient background for abolition. The war itself gave further incentive: fear of slave uprisings added to the turmoil of war. And the slave trade was an important part of the colonial traffic with England which the revolutionaries saw as exploitative. Added to these factors was the oversupply of slaves making continuance of the trade seem temporarily unappealing.[83]

Though the time was right to end the traffic in slaves, "As the war slowly dragged itself to a close, it became increasingly evident that a firm moral stand against slavery and the slave trade was not a probability."[84] Those who suffered economically at the war's hands sought to regain their old strength: ". . . all the selfish motives that impelled a bankrupt nation to seek to gain its daily bread did not long hesitate to demand a reopening of the profitable African slave trade."[85] Consequently, the trade resumed at its prewar level.

Du Bois also offered a moral evaluation of the Federal Convention of 1787. All those at the convention

21

agreed that slavery was a temporary institution and that without a flourishing trade it could not survive. There was a discernible "underlying agreement in the dislike of slavery."[86] Yet the convention missed "the opportunity for a really great compromise," and descended "to a scheme that savored unpleasantly of 'log-rolling.'"[87] It agreed not to prohibit the trade before 1808. Du Bois believed that this policy resulted from, on the one hand, a strong and unified position on the slavery side and, on the other, the "forces of freedom were . . . divided by important conflicts of interests, and animated by no very strong and decided anti-slavery spirit with settled aims."[88] United and determined effort overcame halfhearted and disunified effort. A morally committed opposition could have triumphed. "The student of the situation will always have a good cause to believe that a more sturdy and definite anti-slavery stand at this point might have changed history for the better."[89]

The problem of dealing with slavery became more serious as the new technology of the industrial revolution required huge amounts of cotton. England's consumption of cotton in 1781 was 13,000 bales, but in 1860 it had increased to 3,366,000 bales! The South then put its energy into cotton as its staple product. The consequences of compromise became more serious: "Here it was that the fatal mistake of compromising with slavery in the beginning, and of the policy of laissez-faire pursued thereafter, became painfully manifest; for, instead now of a healthy, normal, economic development along proper industrial lines, we have the abnormal and fatal rise of a slave-labor large-farming system, which, before it was realized, had so intertwined itself with and braced itself upon the economic forces of an industrial age, that a vast and terrible civil war was necessary to displace it."[90]

Cotton production by 1838 was in the hands of powerful, large plantation owners who were about to "corner" the market; by 1850 "it had not only gained a solid economic foundation, but it had built a closed oligarchy with a political policy."[91] The compromise with slavery had thus allowed the development of an entrenched political power defeatable only by a very strong moral consciousness or a great fear of rebellion.

In a tone which is almost Marxian, except for the moral note, Du Bois condemned the owners of the large plantations. The South had succeeded in reducing labor to its minimum status: ". . . there is but one limit below which his labor's price cannot be reduced. The limit is not his physical well-being, for it may be, and in the Gulf States it was, cheaper to work him rapidly to death; the limit is simply the cost of procuring him and keeping him alive a profitable length of time. Only the moral sense of a community can keep helpless labor from sinking to this level; and when a community has once been debauched by slavery, its moral sense offers little resistance to economic demand."[92] Again the emphasis was on the results of compromise and the possibility, affirmed at some point, of morality overcoming economic reality.

The final result of the attempt at compromise was a split in the country between a free-labor system and a slave-system leading to the horrors of the Civil War.

The moral lesson was driven home by Du Bois: "Every experiment of such a kind . . . where the moral standard of a people is lowered for the sake of a material advantage, is dangerous in just such a proportion as that advantage is great. In this case it was great."[93] He saw moral apathy at work in the attempts to limit the trade, leading to an "indisposition to attack the evil with the sharp weapons which its nature demanded. Consequently, there developed steadily, irresistibly, a vast social problem, which required two centuries and a half for a nation of trained European stock and boasted moral fibre to solve."[94] But even the final collapse of slavery, he briefly asserted, was due more to economic collapse of the large-farming slave system than to moral appeal.[95]

After viewing the evidence, Du Bois offered the hope that the United States would not have to face such a moral problem again, because he claimed that as a people Americans seem to lack a strong moral sense. "One cannot, to be sure, demand of whole nations exceptional moral foresight and heroism; but a certain hard common sense in facing the complicated phenomena of political life must be expected in every progressive people."[96]

Du Bois' study did the sorts of things he hoped to do with history. It pointed to causes for social actions. In the case of the slave trade the causes were economic, social (fear factor) and moral. He

23

used the knowledge gained to postulate a moral principle. When he asked the question "How far in a State
can a recognized moral wrong safely be compromised?"[97]
his answer was: ". . . it behooves nations as well as
men to do things at the very moment when they ought to
be done."[98] This was the lesson of the history of the
suppression of the African slave trade. And it was a
lesson for the nation because his position throughout
was that "nations" act as a people and that through the
people, the course of actions could have been changed.
What was required was moral courage.

The idea of the compromise with evil and the moral
strength needed to combat moral problems recurs in
Du Bois' forthcoming writings. But this is perhaps less
interesting than the fact that his tone changes when
similar matters are examined later in his life, most
notably in Black Reconstruction, in which power relationships override the moralizing tone. This represents
a weakness in the Suppression--but the general level of
insight into the period and the quality of the empirical
study overshadow that weakness. Indeed the recognition
of the complexity of factors, and his sensitivity for
each, gives the book much of its strength.

VI

During Du Bois' long life he witnessed a series of
dramatic changes. The tremendous economic growth of
America, two world wars, the adoption of communism in
Russia and China, dramatic changes in the government of
Africa and other colonial lands, and civil rights
agitation. Du Bois did show a willingness to accommo-
date his thinking to change. This Du Bois learned
early when he gave up his faith in the individualism of
laissez-faire economics and in social Darwinism. His
first basic change was his partial rejection of individualism. His group dedication would eventually grow
stronger. The examination that follows shows his perspective on social problems went through a thorough
self-evaluation, a series of frustrations, and sometimes dramatic changes.

His early period contained most of the basic
positions he later (until around 1905) refined. Although he committed himself at Fisk to the development
of a racial community led by the Talented Tenth, the
explicit rationale for that commitment did not come
until the 1897 publication of "The Conservation of

Races." His faith in knowledge and the tractability of social problems, given moral resolve, remained relatively constant until 1905. Up to around 1905 he mainly continued the work of studying black history through sociological and historical studies, especially in The Philadelphia Negro and in the systematic annual survey done at Atlanta University.

NOTES

1. W. E. B. Du Bois, Dusk of Dawn: An Essay Toward an Autobiography of a Race Concept (New York: Schocken Books, 1968), p. 5.

2. Ibid., p. 10.

3. W. E. B. Du Bois, The Autobiography of W. E. B. Du Bois: A Soliloquy on Viewing My Life from the Last Decade of Its First Century (New York: International Publishers, 1968), p. 74.

4. W. E. B. Du Bois, "My Evolving Program for Negro Freedom," What the Negro Wants, ed. Rayford W. Logan (Chapel Hill, N.C.: University of North Carolina Press, 1944), p. 32.

5. Du Bois, Darkwater (New York: Schocken Books, 1969), p. 12.

6. Du Bois, Dusk of Dawn, p. 14.

7. Ibid., p. 16.   8. Ibid., p. 5.

9. Du Bois, "My Evolving Program," p. 33.

10. Du Bois, Autobiography, p. 78.

11. Ibid., pp. 82-83.

12. Du Bois, Dusk of Dawn, p. 16.

13. Du Bois, Darkwater, p. 10.

14. Du Bois, Dusk of Dawn, p. 18.

15. Du Bois examines the status of women in society in "The Damnation of Women," Darkwater, pp. 163-186.

16. Du Bois, _Autobiography_, p. 78.

17. Ibid., p. 95.   18. Ibid., pp. 106-107.

19. Du Bois, _Dusk of Dawn_, pp. 26-27.

20. Ibid., pp. 25-26.   21. Ibid., p. 27.

22. W.E. Burghardt Du Bois, _The Souls of Black Folk_ (Greenwich, Conn.: Fawcett Publications, 1961), pp. 16-17.

23. Du Bois, "My Evolving Program," p. 33.

24. Julius Lester, ed., _The Seventh Son: The Thought and Writings of W.E.B. Du Bois_ (2 vols; New York: Random House, 1971), I, p. 154.

25. Ibid., pp. 156-157.   26. Ibid., p. 155.

27. Ibid., p. 161.

28. Du Bois, _Dusk of Dawn_, pp. 20-21.

29. Du Bois, "My Evolving Program," p. 35.

30. Du Bois, _Dusk of Dawn_, p. 24.

31. Du Bois, "My Evolving Program," p. 36.

32. Du Bois, _Dusk of Dawn_, pp. 29-30.

33. Ibid., p. 30.   34. Ibid., p. 31.

35. Du Bois, "My Evolving Program," p. 37.

36. Du Bois, _Autobiography_, p. 108.

37. Du Bois, "My Evolving Program," p. 38.

38. Ibid.

39. Elliot M. Rudwick, W.E.B. Du Bois: _Propagandist of the Negro Protest_ (New York: Atheneum, 1969), p. 21.

40. Du Bois, _Dusk of Dawn_, p. 32.

41. Ibid.

42. Du Bois, Autobiography, p. 125.

43. Du Bois, "My Evolving Program," p. 40.

44. Du Bois, Autobiography, p. 132.

45. Ibid., p. 133.

46. Du Bois, "My Evolving Program," p. 39.

47. Du Bois, Autobiography, p. 133.

48. Royce is considered, with much justification, to
    be a Hegelian idealist and not a pragmatist, but
    in his reliance on Peirce for the development of
    his concept of community and in much of his ethi-
    cal thought, which for the purposes of this book
    is most important, Royce exhibits a real continu-
    ity with the pragmatic movement.

49. Quoted in Francis L. Broderick, W.E.B. Du Bois:
    Propagandist of the Negro Protest (New York:
    Atheneum, 1969, p. 31.

50. Du Bois, Dusk of Dawn, p. 39.

51. Du Bois, Autobiography, p. 148.

52. Du Bois, Dusk of Dawn, p. 41.

53. Du Bois, Autobiography, p. 141.

54. Du Bois, Dusk of Dawn, p. 40.

55. Du Bois, Autobiography, p. 125.

56. Ibid., p. 143.

57. Quoted in Broderick, W.E.B. Du Bois, p. 18.

58. Du Bois, "My Evolving Program," p. 42.

59. Ibid.

60. Herbert Aptheker, ed., The Correspondence of
    W.E.B. Du Bois, Vol. I: 1877-1934 (Amherst, Mass.:
    University of Massachusetts Press, 1972), p. 28.

61. See Hans Gehrig, "Gustav von Schmoller," in Edwin

R.A. Seligman, ed., Encyclopedia of the Social Sciences (New York: Macmillan Company, 1934), Vol. XIII, p. 576.

62. Du Bois, Dusk of Dawn, p. 47.

63. Ibid., p. 49.

64. Quoted in Du Bois, Autobiography, p. 168.

65. Ibid.

66. Du Bois, Autobiography, p. 148.

67. Ibid.

68. W.E. Burghardt Du Bois, The Suppression of the African Slave-Trade to the United States: 1638-1870 (Baton Rouge, La.: Louisiana State University Press, 1969).

69. John Hope Franklin, "Forward" in The Suppression, p. v.

70. Julius Lester, The Seventh Son, Vol. I, p. 170.

71. For example, between 1713 and 1733, "fifteen thousand slaves were annually imported into America by the English. . . ." Du Bois, Suppression, p. 3. "It is probable that about 25,000 slaves were brought to America each year between 1698 and 1707," Ibid., p. 5. About 20,000 slaves were imported per year between 1733 and 1766. And "Before the Revolution, the total exportation to America is variously estimated as between 40,000 and 100,000 each year. . . . The Census of 1790 showed 697,897 slaves in the United States," Ibid.

72. Du Bois, Suppression, p. 4.

73. Ibid., p. 6.   74. Ibid.

75. Ibid., p. 7.   76. Ibid.

77. Ibid., p. 39.   78. Ibid.

79. Ibid.   80, Ibid., p. 40.

81.	Ibid.	82.	Ibid.
83.	Ibid., p. 41-42.	84.	Ibid., p. 49.
85.	Ibid.	86.	Ibid., p. 68.
87.	Ibid., p. 58.	88.	Ibid., p. 57.
89.	Ibid., p. 58.	90.	Ibid., p. 152.
91.	Ibid., p. 153.	92.	Ibid., p. 168.
93.	Ibid., p. 194.	94.	Ibid., p. 195.
95.	Ibid., p. 197.	96.	Ibid., p. 198.
97.	Ibid., p. 199.	98.	Ibid.

CHAPTER II

RACIAL SOLIDARITY AND THE TALENTED TENTH

Du Bois' commitment to a racial community led by
the talented was firmly established during his stay at
Fisk. Such a commitment, however, was not without
theoretical and practical problems, partly made apparent
by the intellectual trends of the times. First of all,
advance through racial loyalty conflicted with the views
of social Darwinism. Secondly, blacks viewed race as
an illicit category, used mainly for proscription.
Finally, exclusive behavior tends to be antagonistic to
ethical requirements: The moral life seems to demand
that human beings be equally treated at least in relevant social respects, and that actions accepted as
morally right for some, are right for all others in
similar circumstances. Exclusive reference to a particular group must be justified--argued for by giving the
sorts of reasons that permit such an exclusive loyalty.
In short, an exclusive racial commitment must be defended against the charge of racism, albeit a racism in
reverse.[1]

Two further aspects of Du Bois' early commitment
indicate need for a fuller articulation. (1) The
background support of a racial commitment is unclear.
What group does this commit oneself to? Can racial
groups be precisely defined? What traits of a group
make such a commitment philosophically significant? Is
the group international in scope or is it restricted to
some locality such as the United States? To the analytical eye of the developing sociologist, these issues
had to be taken seriously. (2) Lack of clarity in his
commitment was not restricted to definitional questions.
He also had to consider, in greater depth and in relation to ethical questions, the full purpose of a racial
community. What sorts of projects would be involved
and why would these projects be selected? These are
the sorts of questions and issues to which we now turn.

I

One of Du Bois' earliest works, the 1897 pamphlet
"The Conservation of Races,"[2] contains his most complete
statement on the nature of racial distinctions and includes a plea to the black community to maintain a
separate racial identity. He began by assuming that
the world's people are divided into racial units and

that in the United States the "two most extreme types of the world's races have met. . . ."3 The interaction between these races became, for Du Bois, a great world-historical event. He claimed, for reasons which will become clearer, that "the history of the world is the history, not of individuals, but of groups, not of nations, but of races, and he who ignores or seeks to override the race idea in human history ignores and overrides the central thought of all history."4

While racial distinctions maintained a central function in history, it was difficult to reach any conclusion as to the sorts of differences that define a race. Du Bois argued that the normal criteria proposed relied on physical differences such as skin color, hair texture and cranial measurements, and individuals did seem to form a continuum of coloration, hair texture and bone structure. But these distinctions proved to be elusive: "All these physical characteristics are patent enough, and if they agreed with each other it would be very easy to classify mankind. Unfortunately for scientists, however, these criteria of race are most exasperatingly intermingled. Color does not agree with texture of hair, for many of the dark races have straight hair; nor does color agree with the breadth of the head. . . ." Du Bois concluded that no scientific definition of race was possible. He supported this claim later on in his short study, The Negro (1915):

> We find, therefore, in Africa to-day,
> every degree of development in Negroid
> stocks and every degree of intermingling
> of these developments, both among
> African peoples and between Africans,
> Europeans, and Asiatics. The mistake is
> continually made of considering these
> types as transitions between absolute
> Caucasians and absolute Negroes. No
> such absolute type ever existed on
> either side. Both were slowly differ-
> entiated from a common ancestry and
> continually remingled their blood
> while the differentiation was pro-
> gressing. From prehistoric times down
> to to-day Africa is, in this sense,
> primarily the land of the mulatto. So,
> too, was earlier Europe and Asia; only
> in these countries the mulatto was

32

bleached by the climate, while in
Africa he darkened.[6]

Du Bois' sense of the intermingled nature of
physical racial distinctions was heightened by his own
white French background.[7] As a mulatto Du Bois clearly
identified with the black group, an identification not
entirely accounted for by physical differences. And
even in a purely physical sense these differences were
not important and were overshadowed by physical similarities: ". . . great as is the physical unlikeness
of the various races of men their likenesses are greater, and upon this rests the whole scientific doctrine
of Human Brotherhood."[8]

While the concept of race was beyond a clear,
physical scientific definition, Du Bois believed it
could be clearly defined by historians and sociologists.
From such a perspective he defined the concept of race
in a dynamic sense involving two main aspects besides
physical differentiations, viz., a common history and
common ideals: "It [a race] is a vast family of human
beings, generally of common blood and language, always
of common history, traditions and impulses, who are both
voluntarily and involuntarily striving together for the
accomplishment of certain more or less vividly conceived
ideals of life."[9] The significant differences, then,
are not physical but rather what he called spiritual
and psychical differences based on, but greatly transcending, the physical. Using his twofold criterion of
a physical base and shared ideals he identified eight
groups as historical races: Slavs, Teutons, English,
Romance nations, Negroes, Semitic people, the Hindoos
and the Mongolians. Other minor racial units were recognized, and he understood that variations and sub-
divisions existed within each group.[10]

Races developed by a process with two major accomplishments. First, historical growth differentiated
people according to spiritual and mental attributes
covering increasingly larger units, and, second, it
tended to integrate physical differences. When units
were first distinguished as separate nomadic tribes,
each small group maintained the great physical similarity of family resemblance. But as various small
families came together to form stationary households in
towns and cities, they began to lose close physical
identity through inter-breeding, and thus they began to
form a larger racial group. As cities developed in size

33

their inhabitants tended to take on a cultural unity while at the same time they became intermixed physically, causing each to lose its close family resemblance. The spiritual unity of the larger group depended, in part, on their different ideals.[11] The process of racial development went on to include cities under a nation, furthering the breakdown of clear physical differentiation and increasing historical ties and spiritual similarity. "The larger and broader differences of color, hair and physical proportions were not by any means ignored, but myriads of minor differences disappeared, and the sociological and historical races of men began to approximate the present division of races. . . ."[12] Du Bois thereby presented races as developing through a historical process generating broad cultural unity from the intermingling of physical differentiation.

Through this development each group took on particular defining cultural traits: "The English nation stood for constitutional liberty and commercial freedom; the German nation for science and philosophy; the Romance nations stood for literature and art. . . ."[13] He believed that each race strives to perfect itself for its own particular cultural ideal. Apparently, he held that racial units contain particular and unique capacities or potentialities; these separately contribute to the cultural development of the world. And humanity, evolves culturally by each group contributing its peculiar attainment to a thereby enriched world community. Human life is perfected by the contributions, which members of any group may share in, of diverse groups. All racial "groups are striving, each in its own way, to develop for civilization its particular message, its particular ideal, which shall help to guide the world nearer and nearer that perfection of human life, for which we all long, that

'one far off Divine event.' "[14]

This provided the foundation for his brand of nationalistic separatism: Races must maintain their cultural identity to be able to make their special contribution, and so historical progress depended on clearly established cultural differentiation among races. Development required not an individual growth but the growth of racially distinct groups: "For the development of Japanese genius, Japanese literature and art, Japanese spirit, only Japanese, bound and welded together, Japanese inspired by one vast ideal, can work

out its fullness the wonderful message which Japan has
for the nations of the earth. For the development of
Negro genius, of Negro literature and art, of Negro
spirit, only Negroes bound and welded together, Negroes
inspired by one vast ideal, can work out in its fullness
the great message we have for humanity."[15] Blacks must
strive for racial solidarity and organization not out of
a sense of chauvinism, but to realize that "broader
humanity which freely recognizes differences in men,
but sternly deprecates inequality in their opportunities
of development."[16]

     Du Bois proposed the establishment of black organ-
izations including colleges, businesses and newspapers
to aid black accomplishments in intellectual and artistic matters. Furthermore, his concept of race led him
to aid in the establishment of a Pan-African movement
at the Pan-African conference of 1900 in London. As
Clarence Contee pointed out, "The origins of Pan-Africanism were grounded in black cultural nationalism."[17]
And that Du Bois' attitude in "The Conservation of
Races" fostered a negritude "about the ethos of Negro
life and heritage,"[18] which initially permeated his
attitudes toward Pan-Africanism. In reviewing the Pan-
African idea, Du Bois asserted that the movement centered on the commonality of culture and experience as its
basis: "The idea of one Africa uniting the thought and
ideals of all native peoples of the Dark Continent be-
longs to the twentieth century and stems naturally from
the West Indies and the United States. Here various
groups of Africans, quite separate in origin, became so
united in experience and so exposed to the impact of a
new culture that they began to think of Africa as one
idea and one land."[19] Du Bois here situates the rationale for the Pan-African movement in his notion of
race, with the unity of culture and experience dominating. But note the extent to which the idea of a common
African culture is attributed to the Americas. Du Bois'
real cultural contact with Africa was, indeed, limited.
Du Bois eventually drew back from the notion of cultural unity and focused instead on unity of economic interest. Perhaps this is why Du Bois' emphasis on Pan-
Africanism was quite weak in 1900; in fact the movement
itself amounted to little: "This meeting [1900] had no
deep roots in Africa itself, and the movement and the
idea died for a generation."[20]

     In his early concept, race was, in sum, the unit
of cultural advance in world-historical development.

Common history and ideals created a racial community
with special cultural traits allowing it to make unique
cultural contributions. The types of contributions
Du Bois stressed were mainly with artistic and intellectual development, such as literature, philosophy and
science; all of these require special capacities normally found only in the elite of a particular racial group.
This is important; the concept of race was intended to
establish a foundation for the racial community supporting the unique capabilities of a few. The entire racial
heritage bestowed singular capacities on the elite. The
concept of race, then, included a normative appeal to
retain racial identity and to establish the sorts of
institutions capable of developing special talents. He
admonished the American Negro Academy, for which he
wrote "The Conservation of Races," to seek "to comprise
something of the best thought, the most unselfish striving and the highest ideals. There are scattered in
forgotton nooks and corners throughout the land, Negroes
of some considerable training, of high minds, and high
motives, who are unknown to their fellows, who exert far
too little influence. These the Negro Academy should
strive to bring into touch with each other and to give
them a common mouthpiece."[21] Also, Du Bois insisted
black Americans formed the "advance guard" of all
African peoples and therefore needed to establish cultural leadership through the maintenance of their racial
identity.[22]

The notion of race he adopted clearly centered on
cultural traits and rejected an emphasis on physical
contours. This was consistent with his rejection of
scholastic philosophy, in which meaning centered on
static concept, and is instead a dynamic, result-ori-
ented, pragmatic approach. For the pragmatist the
meaning of an object is discovered in its actions, in
what it does and how it interacts. Further, the importance of an object, and thereby the main ingredients of
its definition, depended on its purpose. In Du Bois'
notion of race the meaning of a racial unit was to be
found in its cultural life, its language, laws, religion, art, etc.; these features were highlighted because the ultimate purpose of a racial unit was to make
a unique contribution toward a world cultural development.

II

Du Bois' definition of race was pragmatic,

but this alone could not solve the ethical problems of commitment limited by the adoption of a racial per- spective. Du Bois seemed to be aware of this problem, and although he did not attack it systematically, two features of "The Conservation of Races," do suggest an ethical rationale. (1) The first was a factual claim amounting to a rejection of individualism and an affirmation of a social group as the unit of significant historical action: he wrote, as we have seen, that "the history of the world is the history, not of indi- viduals, but of groups, not of nations, but of races. . . ."[23] In this sense, the group became the significant bearer of actions and thereby the most significant ethical unit. Adoption of an emphasis on a racial unit thus stood for ethical realism, to be ignored at the cost of an illusory individualism. (2) The racial unit was affirmed not as an ultimate datum to be valued only for itself but rather as an agent with an overriding universal purpose. He affirmed, throughout the article, the reality of "Human Brother- hood." He also approved Darwin's belief that people resembled one another more than they differed.[24] Du Bois claimed that the ultimate goal of race development was the "perfection of human life."[25] For him racial development was analogous to individual development undertaken for the purposes of aiding humanity; an ultimate goal few would consider ethically objectiona- ble.

Du Bois' position on group commitment as ethically proper was not systematically defended, but it is, at key points, highly analogous to the ethical theory de- veloped by his mentor at Harvard, Josiah Royce. The notion of racial commitment dominated most of Du Bois' life, so a full understanding of its rationale is important. The following comparison of Du Bois with Royce, with its possible historical connection, is in- tended to provide a more complete rationale as a possi- ble foundation for his view. In this sense, it becomes a defense against the charge of ethical exclusiveness.

The intention here is not to engage in the risky enterprise of claiming a precise historical influence, made even more troublesome by the fact that Royce's main philosophical works, the Philosophy of Loyalty[26] and The Problem of Christianity[27] were published re- spectively in 1908 and 1914, a decade or so after Du Bois' "The Conservation of Races." However, the anal- ogies between these works are pronounced, and it seems

37

plausible that Royce and Du Bois discussed their ideas during the Harvard years. Also, Royce was interested in the race idea, as is evidenced by his work, Race Questions, Provincialism and Other American Problems.[28]

It is quite possible and defensible by publication dates that Du Bois' views proved an influencing factor on Royce. The real question here is not the problem of influence, but that of developing a full rationale, as an amplification for analytic reasons, of Du Bois' only partially expressed theoretical views. Significant parts of Royce's philosophy of loyalty provide such a possible and plausible theoretical background.

Royce's philosophy, with its ethical implications, focused, as did Du Bois', on loyalty to a community. Royce believed that people are social beings; communities make up the culture and civilization of human beings. People come to self-consciousness through what he called "spiritual warfare,"[29] including rivalry, criticism, and mutual observation. But the social tensions that breed the self are assuaged by the legal codes and customary rules established by the social demands of the individual's community. Paradoxically, in complex civilizations, individualism outstrips the collectivism of the primitive societies, and yet collective interdependence is maximized. Even food production tends to become relegated to a small percentage of the society. Each individual sees himself or herself as an isolated unit yet is collectively dependent. This creates a tension between the individual and the society that can be overcome only by devotion to or love of a community. That is, when the individual freely identifies himself or herself with a community, the tension of modern life tends to be dissolved. Therefore, Royce's community centers on an individual commitment to a social group.

Royce viewed each individual as unique.[30] Even though people are individuals, they are not immediately aware of their own selves, but instead the individual interprets himself or herself as spread out in time because of an identification with both past and future events. In less technical language, this means, for example, that people view their pasts as part of themselves. Therefore, when individuals, although distinct, look back to some common event or look forward to a common purpose, then, insofar as they interpret the common event as part of themselves, they form a commu-

38

nity involving a shared identity. The members of the
community, who have all consciously interpreted their
individual lives so as to include a common past and a
common expected future, must be aware, to dissolve
tension, that their individual deeds are needed for
the community's success. The individual interprets
his or her own past and future as contributing to the
life of the community.

In "The Conservation of Races" Du Bois clearly
referred to race as primarily involving a common past
and hoped for future. He also consciously tried to
persuade people to adopt the past and ideals of the
black community and to adopt them cognitively.[31]

Du Bois' insistence on racial loyalty is similar
to Royce's ethic of loyalty. Royce's The Philosophy of
Loyalty builds an ethical system around the concept of
loyalty. He defined loyalty as "the thoroughgoing and
loving devotion of an individual to a community."[32]
Loyalty is needed in the "community of interpretation"
(the name Royce gave to his concept of community due to
the central role of interpretation of the past and
future within it) as a sustaining force. And he claimed
that loyalty fulfills the entire moral law; a moral
person is one who wants to have a thoroughgoing devotion
to a cause. Loyalty requires that an individual appro-
priates for himself or herself some model presented by
society. This creates a unity between the individual
and the society. The cause then brings fulfillment,
life, and opportunity to the person. Royce claimed
that loyalty as a moral principle is social, that is,
a person should not be loyal to his or her private
desires; an individual's desires are varied and conflicting, creating disharmony within the individual.
Loyalty brings consistency and harmony within the individual by adopting a single, dominant, society-oriented
goal.

Royce explicitly dealt with ethical problems of
exclusiveness. He made loyalty to a cause the supreme
good, but causes can be in conflict and even instill
hatred between groups. He observed, "If loyalty is a
supreme good, the mutually destructive conflict of
loyalties is in general a supreme evil."[33] To eliminate
this problem he proposed that the following maxim be
followed: ". . . by reason of your choice and of your
service, there shall be more loyalty in the world rather
than less."[34] Therefore, any cause is to be judged in

terms of its value to mankind as a furtherance of loyalty. Royce called his highest maxim "loyalty to loyalty;" he insisted that loyalty to loyalty tends to increase human ties through an overriding cause which is the 'unity with the unity of all human life."[35] The unity of persons loyal to a cause forms a personal unity transcending the individual person. By identifying oneself on the side of loyalty in general, supra-personal loyalty in principle may include everyone. Just as the object of loyalty is interpersonal community, the final object of the community goes beyond a specific common history and idealized future to include, for Royce, all humanity.

Two concepts which are basic in Royce's concept of community bear special relationship to Du Bois' notion of race. The first is that each community must go beyond itself to embrace all humanity so as to avoid conflicts and hostility. And, secondly, the community is engaged in a pragmatic task, which for Royce is the interpretation of the world.[36]

In "The Conservation of Races" Du Bois made it plain that the work of Africans and Afro-Americans was to contribute to humanity. A previously quoted passage in "The Conservation of Races" is similar to the Roycean message. Du Bois stated that each race is striving "in its own way, to develop for civilization its particular message, its particular ideal, which shall help to guide the world nearer and nearer that perfection of human life for which we all long, that

'one far off Divine event!'"[37]

Du Bois envisioned the possibility of a pluralistic society, one with many loyalties, supporting separate strivings in political, economic and religious harmony. There is no reason why "two or three great national ideals might not thrive and develop, that men of different races might not strive together for their race ideals as well, perhaps even better, than in isolation."[38] The pragmatic task of a racial community in Du Bois' early work was a cultural contribution to human civilization. All contributions were seen as necessary for the perfection of mankind, and implied in his message was that all conflicts can be harmonized in an advanced civilization.

Royce's ethical position is capable of weakening

the charge that a group loyalty, in Du Bois' case a racial loyalty, is inconsistent with the ethical requirements of universality. It does so with the explicit proviso that loyalty to group must contribute to a universal advance, a proviso Du Bois clearly incorporated into his position. Royce's position obviously differs considerably from Du Bois' in terms of substantive commitment of the ultimate object of the Universal community. Royce was greatly influenced by the highly abstract theories of the 19th century German philosophy, Georg Hegel; the notion of the universal community as a kind of universal "mind" is nowhere in Du Bois, yet he came close to this. He was interested in a particular type of achievement, one that does not concentrate on "practical" matters, such as economic development. Rather the community he envisioned would be dedicated to cultural achievement, to art, literature, philosophy, law, enterprises which are not the usual achievements of the ordinary person. So just as Royce's community in its ultimate mission seems best geared to the philosophical enterprise of interpreting the universe, Du Bois' racial community was to be dedicated to supporting the work of the culturally talented.

Royce's position opens up a further insight into Du Bois' position: loyalty to the racial group can be viewed as constituting the identity of the individuals within it in such a way as to bring harmony to basic social conflict. So together, in the unity of a racial community, a consistent self-image can be formed in a way that attacks the problem of the double consciousness. For Royce, modern society leaves the individual with conflicting desires and tendencies because of the real dependence on varying social groups; as an individual one is doomed to conflict. But with the strength of a group, harmony can result. For Royce, a person is communal, and must recognize this for psychic health; the same was true for Du Bois. He understood that without consciously adopting a racial loyalty, an individual would constantly encounter the realities of social identification without its unity and thereby its strength.

III

So far we have examined some of the philosophical background and a possible theoretical support for Du Bois' concept of race. "The Conservation of Races"

41

goes beyond, in various ways, the kind of philosophical basis already explored. It is also an objection to a purely physical notion of race and it is a rejection of an individualistic social Darwinism. In both of these Du Bois was reacting to debates well known during his time but now usually forgotten. Some of these controversies are examined in this section, beginning the development of racial thinking and, with it, racism.

Race and racism, as influential categories, are a relatively recent development. Du Bois noted that "The world has always been familiar with black men, who represent one of the most ancient of human stocks. . . ." But he added, "The medieval European world . . . knew the black man chiefly as a legend or occasional curiosity, but still as a fellow man--an Othello or a Prestor John or an Antar." He contrasted this attitude with the attitude of the modern times in which he found "a widespread assumption throughout the dominant world that color is a mark of inferiority."[39] Thomas D. Gossett similarly remarked that even though racism existed in ancient times, "before the eighteenth century physical differences among people were so rarely referred to as a matter of great importance that something of a case can be made for the proposition that race consciousness is larely a modern phenomenon."[40]

The fact that Du Bois became aware of this change in emphasis toward a racial consciousness presents a clue to his eventual rejection of his early concept of race. In his earlier years he did not consider the causes of this change. Instead we simply find Du Bois writing on race and race commitment at the end of the nineteenth century, a period during which race theories were enormously influential in the writings of social scientists.[41] The concept of race could not be easily ignored. Herbert Spencer, Lester Ward, Charles Cooley, Ludwig Gumplovitz, and Charles Sumner, all prominent social scientists of their day, made race a significant element in their theories. Even Ralph Waldo Emerson thought that race fostered national character.[42] Du Bois' history teacher and mentor at Harvard, Albert Bushnell Hart accepted, as a fundamental principle of American History, the racially motivated theory that American institutions are Teutonic in origin.[43]

That Du Bois used racial theorizing to support his own commitments fits in well with leading inclinations during the time. Of course, he did reject the racist

overtone, those efforts to inflict harm and pejorative
characteristics on people because of the race, dominating the writings of many. For example, when Robert
Knox said, in 1850, that "Race is everything," his
message was about what he took to be the innate inferiority of most of the people of the world.[44]

It is not surprising, from the point of view of
Du Bois' personal development and from the dominant
ideas of the social science of the day, that he adopted
a race idea as a central trend in history; it is somewhat more difficult to account for his rejection of
scientific validity of physical traits as the defining
characteristics of race. Biologists and anthropologists today are questioning the scientific utility of
race classifications; however, many seem to believe that
this is a recent development.[45] Ashley Montagu adds to
this puzzlement by characterizing himself, in 1941, as
one of the "earliest to state clearly and unequivocally
what was wrong with the traditional conception of race
held by most physical anthropologists. . . ."[46] He
did, however, give a list of critics of the race concept, going back two centuries, including two re-
searchers named in "The Conservation of Races,"
Johann Blumenbach and Henry Huxley.[47] The idea that
physical racial differences are not scientifically
definable in a precise way has a fairly long tradition;
Du Bois never claimed that this was his discovery.

Racism was present, to some degree, even in
ancient time; the division of the world into racial
groups, on the other hand, is a 17th century notion.
In 1684 Francois Bernier, a French physician, was
probably the first to divide the world into racial
categories. He proposed four groups: Europeans, Far
Easterners, "blacks" and Lapps.[48] As race thinking
caught on there were a series of attempts to delineate
the number of racial groups (the numbers offered varied
from 3 to 400), to specify the physical traits that
defined racial units, and to explain why racial diversity existed (climate, evolution, divine creation,
etc.). These attempts were often linked to racist
motivation. All sorts of definitional traits were
used in order to specify the nature of racial differences, including, cranial measurements, hair texture
and brain size. All of these attempts failed, essentially for the reason Du Bois presented. Blumenbach,
(whom Du Bois mentioned) for example, claimed, "The
more my daily experience, and, as it were, my familiar-

ity with my collection of skulls of different nations increases, so much the more impossible do I find it to reduce these racial varieties . . . to the measurement of any single scale."[49]

The second major problem was to explain the origins of racial differences. The main causes appealed to in the 19th century were environment and genetic "sporting" or chance variation. However, many felt that devices used to explain racial diversity developing from racial homogeneity failed; these theorists held instead that the original world population was divided into different races (the polygenetic theory). To many taking a religious orientation this view conflicted with the Bible and was thus rejected. However, polygenetic theory was widely supported and again with racist overtones. Some argued that if races formed different species, then one specie may well be superior to another. Darwin rejected such a view because he believed similarities between racial units were too close to have been independently acquired.[50] Du Bois may have had this in mind when he cited Darwin as supporting the scientific principle of Human Brotherhood.[51]

The monogenetic thesis (asserting that all races derive from common original ancestors) was also used as a racist weapon through ad hoc claims that some races are lower than others on the evolutionary scale. While racists could be found on both sides of the argument, neither position necessarily supported a racist view, and it may have been that Du Bois sided with the polygenetic theory. Du Bois stated his theory of racial development as follows:

> The age of nomadic tribes of closely related individuals represents the maximum of physical differences. They were practically vast families, and there were as many groups as families. As the families came together to form cities the physical differences lessened, purity of blood was replaced by the requirement of domicile, and all who lived within the city bounds became gradually to be regarded as members of the group; i.e., there was a slight

and slow breaking down of physical
barriers. This, however, was
accomplished by an increase of the
spiritual and social differences
between cities . . . The ideals of
life for which the different cities
struggled were different. When at
last cities began to coalesce into
nations there was another breaking
down of barriers which separated
groups of men . . . At the same
time the spiritual and physical
differences of race groups which
constituted the nations became
deep and decisive.[52]

He characterized the growth of racial units as one
which proceeds from physical heterogeneity to an increasing physical homogeneity: "The whole process
which has brought about these race differentiations
has been a growth, and the great characteristic of this
growth has been the differentiation of spiritual and
mental differences between the great races of mankind
and the integration of physical differences."[53] The
process Du Bois described does not broach the question
of the origin of the maximal physical differences
present during the age of nomadic tribes. This does
not easily fit in with a Darwinian monogenetic account
in which heterogeneity proceeds from physical homogeneity. Rather it seems to fit better with polygenetic
thesis. Du Bois did not attempt to explain the origins
of maximal physical differences--but it seems to play
the role of an unaccountable beginning, or an original
datum.

Du Bois' notion of racial origins is only briefly
presented and not at all satisfactorily defended. It
appears as more of a hunch than as a piece of science.
Others writing at the end of the 19th century did
present more extensive theories, some showing marked
similarities with Du Bois. For example, Ludwig
Gumplovitz' produced a widely noticed treaty on racial
and national development in Race and State (1875), and
tend years later in his better known The Outlines of
Sociology.[54]

Gumplovitz not only argued for the polygeneticist
view, but claimed this position to be more consistent
with Darwinism than Darwin's monogeneticism. He

pointed out that Darwinism evidence showed only that
some organic origination is evolutionary, but
Gumplovitz saw this as consistent with and supportive
of genetic difference.[55] Accordingly he argued that
the premise of sociology is the polygenetic origin of
physically differentiated groups. "Sociology begins
with the countless different social groups of which,
as can be irrefutably proven, mankind is constituted."[56]
These heterogenous groups eventually come into contact
with each other and an amalgam begins. Gumplovitz
describes the process in terms partly similar to Du
Bois': "Analysis shows that the positive binding
force is association and simple consanguinity with the
resulting community of language, religious ideas,
customs and mode of life, while the contrast with the
stranger lies in his lack of participation in them."
Further: "Social development presupposes the junction
of heterogeneous or the differentiation of homogeneous
elements. In the former case the combining elements
are united by common interests and fall into social
opposition for lack of them."[57] Common interests are
brought about by a cultural conditioning. "Birth and
training are social factors. The latter, especially,
imparts the language, morals, ideas, religion and
usages of the group and causes the individual to appear
to himself and to others to belong to it. All together
bind the members to each other by a common interest,
which is patriotism in its earliest form."[58]

    The emphasis on the group as the primary focus of
social advance, common to both Du Bois and Gumplovitz,
was not unusual during the 19th century, especially in
Germany. Gumplovitz, again like Du Bois, combined a
group loyalty with an internal class structure[59] and
with the notion that conflict is a necessary condition
of group development.[60] Gumplovitz believed classes
were based on social power relations, but did not support the sort of class structure based on cultural
achievement that Du Bois espoused. Du Bois also accepted, in a less than enthusiastic way, the notion of
progress through conflict. While Du Bois explicitly
rejected the conflict between individuals as a vehicle
for social advance, he did not reject all conflict as
a means to advance. In effect he only rejected social
Darwinian individualism. In an early essay entitled
"The Talented Tenth," he hinted at the means through
which the talented are created, a form of social
Darwinism. He claimed that slavery usually nullified
the leadership role of the talented because slavery was

"the legalized survival of the unfit. . . ."[61] In
The Souls of Black Folk, Du Bois made his Darwinian
adherence clearer: "It is, then, the strife of all
honorable men of the twentieth century to see that in
the future competition of races the survival of the
fittest, shall mean the triumph of the good, the
beautiful, and the true. . . ."[62] Further, in "The
Conservation of Races" Du Bois defined race prejudice
in a way that suggested that racial groups have a
tendency toward conflict: "If we carefully consider
what race prejudice really is, we find it, historically,
to be nothing but the friction between different groups
of people; it is the difference in aim, in feeling, in
ideals, of two different races; if, now, this difference exists touching territory, laws, language, or even
religion, it is manifest that these people cannot live
together in the same territory without fatal
conflict. . . ."[63] He added that racial groups in the
United States, however, have enough in common so that
conflict may be avoided and that cooperation may be
mutually beneficial.

    The note of conflict between groups was not strong
in Du Bois. It is only found in a few early passages
and sometimes in ambiguous form, suggesting a play on
words, as when survival of the fittest is called upon
to be restricted to the good and the beautiful. He
eventually emphasized cooperation over conflict and
talk about socially beneficial conflict dropped from
his writings. Also, the account of racism, making it
a function of a natural conflict gave way to the more
comfortable view for Du Bois, namely that racism is
mainly the product of ignorance (the sort of ignorance
that the Talented Tenth can displace).

    Du Bois' early concept of race, while not
especially original in its basic features did provide
a rationale for group loyalty, and a point of departure concerning required activities and the need for
cultural leadership. And in it was what appears to be
a genuine concern for overall human development. Any
exclusive reference to a racial unit runs the risk of
racism; Du Bois' obvious outward looking concerns
mitigate that charge.

IV

    With the exception of the mention of race con-
flict, the major themes of "The Conservation of Races"

47

maintained a central role in Du Bois' writing until around 1905. The form of commitment supported by his early doctrine of race solidarity was present from his early years. From his youth, he valued intellectual achievement. Early in his life he regarded talent, maximizing one's own ability, as a solution to problems of poverty. With the defense of a race doctrine in "The Conservation of Races," the support of talent, articulated as the "Talented Tenth," became systematized and was made to function on the group level. The group as a whole, through its evolution, supported the milieu in which the talented got their capacity to make racially unique cultural contributions. When Du Bois spoke of a Japanese literature or a Negro literature, he was referring to a literary mode of expression based on the life of the whole community, taking its character from the whole; by its nature it is a refined art form expressible only by the talented. That is, the contributions made by a race are made through the talented as its representatives. There is a symbiotic relation here. The talented are supported by the group; that support, and the possibility of developing talent to higher levels, depends on the level of sophistication of the whole group. The level of the group is raised by the work of the talented and so forth. So the responsibility of the talented is twofold: (1) To make those race contributions to the cultural development of a heterogeneous world that only the talented are capable of making and (2) to raise the general level of the group, both socially and economically, so that cultural achievements are best supported.

This notion, however, has implications that are difficult to accept. The talented in Du Bois' earlier writings functioned as a merit class--a class which deserves more social power and recognition than others; this implies a sharp distinction between social classes. The Philadelphia Negro, the great pioneering social study of life of blacks in Philadelphia's seventh ward, published in 1899, was written at the height of his reliance on the talented. In that work, he drew sharp distinctions between grades of blacks: (1) Those living well, (2) those living in comfort, (3) the poor, and (4) the "submerged tenth," the "criminals, prostitutes and loafers. . . ."[64] This classification indicates a moral disapproval of the submerged tenth and a moral commendation of the talented. He coupled his classification with a condescending provision of social responsibility: ". . . better classes have their chief

48

excuse for being in the work they may do toward lifting
the rabble."[65] His early views, in opposition to his
later thoughts, were explicitly, even if mildly, anti-
democratic: "If the Negroes were by themselves either
a strong aristocratic system or a dictatorship would
for the present prevail. With, however, democracy thus
prematurely thrust upon them, the first impulse of the
best, the wisest and the richest is to segregate themselves from the mass. This action, however, causes
more of dislike and jealousy on the part of the masses
than usual because those masses look to the whites for
ideals and largely for leadership."[66] Du Bois envisioned the ideal political system, for blacks in the
1900's, as including "aristocractic" power resting
with the talented to use in ways benefitting the masses.
Knowledge and skill would then be used to solve urgent
social problems.

The Philadelphia Negro, widely considered a classic and pioneering study in American sociology, reflects
Du Bois' intense desire to make a thorough empirical
investigation of the sociological situation of blacks
in America. This means complete knowledge of the historical background, economical and employment conditions, social and political interaction, and class
relationships among blacks. His concern in the study
was not mainly with the amelioration of the talented
group--as the doctrine of the "Talented Tenth" might
suggest. The extent of the doctrine is to lay on the
talented the responsibility for the growth and enrich-
ment of the masses. His ultimate concern was with
the entire race through the knowledge and skill of the
talented. Thus, in setting out the problem for investigation in The Philadelphia Negro, Du Bois focused
on the "problems of poverty, ignorance, crime and
labor."[67] Yet it is also true that he showed special
concern for the problems of the "social elite": "many
are well-to-do, some are wealthy, all are fairly educated, and some liberally trained. Here too are social
problems--differing from those of the other classes,
and differing too from those of the whites of a corresponding grade, because of the peculiar social environment in which the whole race finds itself, which the
whole race feels, but which touches this highest class
at most points and tells upon them most decisely."[68]
The social uplift generated by the talented would also
redound to their own benefit.

Du Bois' study, after surveying the remote history

of black migration into the city and the general demo-
graphic facts about the black community in general,
provides a detailed, block by block, description of the
inhabitants of the seventh ward, as broken down into
various groups or grades: Grade 1-Middle classes and
above, Grade 2-Working people, Grade 3-the poor,
Grade 4-Vicious and criminal classes. He also noted
the residences of whites, stores and public buildings.
He presented detailed data on marital, sexual and
family relationships, education and literacy, occupa-
tional and income property status, health information,
church membership, crime and case studies dealing with
racial prejudice.

       He ended the study with an evaluative chapter, "A
Final Word," spelling out what blacks and whites must
do to solve social problems. The concrete proposals
were meager. Blacks were called upon to maintain a
spirit of calm, to kindle a desire for education; to
spend money wisely. He added, without programmatic
specification, "Above all, the better classes of the
Negroes should recognize their duty toward the masses.
They should not forget that the spirit of the twentieth
century is to be the turning of the high toward the
lowly, the bending of Humanity to all that is human;
the recognition that in the slums of modern society lie
the answers to most of our puzzling problems of organization and life, and that only as we solve these problems is our culture assured and our progress certain."[69]
Du Bois here is clearly on the side of the masses, but
the solution for the masses rests mainly with the elite.

       Du Bois' main advice to whites was to set adequate,
non-prejudiced standards for black employment, to live
by standards, and to "recognize the existence of the
better class of Negroes and . . . gain their active aid
and co-operation by generous and polite conduct. Social
sympathy must exist between what is best in both
races. . . ."[70]

       All in all, his advice to blacks and whites has
more the flavor of a gentle admonition than a programmatic solution. The Philadelphia Negro, then, stands
mainly as a careful, pioneering sociological study, as
a way to gain knowledge rather than as a work in social
criticism in the style of The Souls of Black Folk or
Dusk of Dawn.

       In The Philadelphia Negro there is support for

50

class contact and interaction; however, a few years
later Du Bois' attitudes on class distinctions and
social interaction between classes seem to have become
more rigid. In The Black North in 1901 he concluded:
"Social distinctions should be observed. A rising race
must be aristocratic; the good cannot consort with the
bad--not even the best with the less good."[71] Once
again the aristocratic moralizing tone was strong. In
the same work he identified and quantified the class
differences (with moral overtones) among Northern
blacks. The "submerged tenth," comprise 6 percent of
the population, the poor 30 percent, those working hard
with "rapidly improving morals" 52 percent and finally
12 percent "form an aristocracy of wealth and education."[72]

It is difficult to accept his statement of class
separation as consistent with the general mutual aid
doctrine of the "Conservation of Races," because it
would tend to limit contact among people of a racial
unit and thereby would truncate the experiences that
inform cultural expression. By and large these sorts
of statements seem to be exceptions to the more compas-
sionate hope that the talented would consciously aid
the whole group. The rationale of his position on race
advance underscored the theme of commonality even if
this comes within the context of a class structure head
by the talented. The statements of moral disapproval
tend to establish gaps in the unity he otherwise
supported.

The full doctrine of the Talented Tenth was most
explicitly and fully formulated in his essay "The
Talented Tenth" (1903). In it Du Bois argued that
priority should be given to the training of talented
blacks as the only solution to the problems blacks
faced. He took the view that cultural advance could
solve problems; this was consistent with his formulation
of racial mission in "The Conservation of Races." And
here he made explicit the theme of elevating the masses:
"Was there ever a nation on God's fair earth civilized
from the bottom upward? Never; it is, ever was and
ever will be from the top downward that culture filters.
The Talented Tenth rises and pulls all that are worth
saving up to their vantage ground. This is the history
of human progress. . . ."[73]

The Talented Tenth was not simply to remain active
within the group, but also to work against the forces

of racism. As already seen, he defined race prejudice
in "The Conservation of Races," as group conflict and
made racism into an expected concommitant of the sorts
of differences he supported. Racism viewed as almost
natural is counterproductive for a group suffering from
its bad effects. So it is not surprising that this view
of racism played virtually no role in most of his early
writings. A different concept, tenuously related to
the earlier view of the causes of racism, was implicit
in much of his early work and was made explicit in
Du Bois' reflections from later years: "The world was
thinking wrong about race, because it did not know.
The ultimate evil was stupidity. The cure for it was
based on scientific investigation."[74] Racism was thus,
in the main, caused by ignorance, so its cure was
knowledge.

Du Bois saw it as his mission to set racial
thinking straight through sociological studies of
black America. After completing his study of blacks
in Philadelphia, he proposed in November, 1897, to the
American Academy of Political and Social Sciences that
a black college be established to do systematic social
studies of blacks in the United States with the close
co-operation of Harvard, Columbia, Johns Hopkins, and
the University of Pennsylvania. In a period when
American Universities were blatantly racist such cooperation was not likely. (Du Bois, for example, even
with his exceptional educational background and publications, had no hope of getting a teaching position at
such schools, and while at the University of Pennsylvania during his sociological investigations, he was
not permitted to teach.)[75]

Even though the sort of combined effort he hoped
for was out of reach, he secured a position at
Atlanta University in 1897, as the director of a series
of studies on various aspects of the social life of
black Americans:

> We studied during the first decade
> Negro mortality, urbanization, the
> effort of Negroes for their own
> social betterment, Negroes in
> business, college-bred Negroes,
> the Negro common school, the Negro
> artisan, the Negro Church, and
> Negro crime. We ended the decade
> by a general review of the methods

and results of this ten year study
and a bibliography of the Negro.
Taking new breath in 1906 I planned
a more logical division of subjects
but was not able to carry it out
quite as I wished, because of lack
of funds. We took up health and
physique of American Negroes,
economic co-operation and the Negro
American family. We made a second
study of the efforts that social
betterment, the college-bred Negro,
the Negro common school, the Negro
artisan, and added a study of morals
and manners among Negroes instead of
further study of the church. In all
we published a total of 2,172 pages
which formed a current encyclopedia
on the American Negro problems.[76]

In 1935 Du Bois attempted to reinstitute the
Atlanta University studies, and, in doing so, he
talked explicitly about what he hoped would be accomplished by such a series. His remarks seem to be
applicable to his earlier efforts as well: "No social
study can in itself effect changes and reforms. It can
find the facts, present the findings and suggest ways
for improving certain conditions. This study will
propose remedial and constructive programs to be carried
out in certain fields. . . . The study will ascertain
the specific maladjustments, relate those to the group
believed best adopted to handle the problems, and
propose certain programs and policies for
action. . . ."[77]

The Atlanta University studies, much in the style
of The Philadelphia Negro, had, as their main purpose,
the development of thorough, scientific, sociological
knowledge about the general conditions, and the
strengths and weaknesses of the black community. Detailed analysis of the problems facing the masses was
intended as a vehicle through which racism, fostered by
ignorance, could be overcome. Much of the material in
these works is about the average condition of the
masses; apparently with this knowledge, the elite could
better perform their social responsibility. Consequently, the Atlanta University Publications presents a
further development of the notion of the Talented
Tenth's responsibility for social uplift. For example,

53

the 1898 study, Some Efforts of American Negroes for
Their Own Social Betterment, contained the observation
that beneficial societies, such as the Masons, Knights
of Pythias, Odd Fellows, and the Jollifee Union, should
allow for the development of the sorts of class traits
that aid in economic advance.[78] In the 1907 study,
Economic Co-operation Among Negro Americans he again
advocated an aristocracy of talent:

> . . . a race in the state of devel-
> opment in which the Negro American
> is today must of necessity depend
> tremendously upon the individual
> leader. He is in the period of
> special individual development,
> and while group development is
> going on rapidly, yet it is the
> individual as yet who stands
> forth. Consequently, very often
> we must touch upon individual
> effort and touch upon things
> which strictly speaking are not
> co-operative. . . because the
> leader has been called forth by
> a group movement and not simply
> for his own aggrandizement. In
> other words, the kind of co-
> operation which we are going to
> find among the Negro American is
> not always democratic co-opera-
> tion; very often the group organ-
> ization is aristocratic and even
> monarchic, and yet it is co-oper-
> ation, and even the monarch does
> the same, as in the case of the
> small Baptist church.[79]

This was written shortly before the role of the
Talented Tenth was dropped, by and large, from his
writing. While it explains the relationship between
the individual and the group in non-democratic terms,
the emphasis on talent seems more pragmatic than in his
earlier statements. Early on the manifestations of
talent (in refined cultural achievements) were part of
the goal of racial development. In 1907 Du Bois spoke
in an almost apologetic way about the necessity, at a
particular stage of development, for the individual to
stand out from the group. Of course, there was never
an articulated position claiming that only a small

portion of the people could be among the talented;
nevertheless, the sorts of traits he admired most have
been restricted to the few. Yet, in this paragraph
he was not referring to refined cultural achievements,
but to business. The rationale for a Talented Tenth
begins to weaken once the emphasis is taken off such
enterprises as philosophy, literature, and constitutional law. Perhaps the real significance of the
paragraph is that it reflects a shift in his attention
increasingly away from cultural matters and toward
economic achievements.

In Chapters III and V this shift is discussed in
greater detail, but for now these later developments
can be anticipated and related to the well-known debate
with Booker T. Washington. The shift that eventually
occurred in Du Bois' thought toward economic determinism
tended to mitigate some of his criticisms of Washington:
In a speech, "Education and Work" delivered in the
Commencement Address at Howard University on June 6,
1930 he tried to bring the debate up to date with a
view toward reforming then present economic and industrial conditions. These took the place of the most
important aspect of either an industrial or academic
education: He argued, "Whatever human civilization
has been or may become, today it is industry."[80] With
the focus on industry and on economic conditions in
general, the role of knowledge in cultural advance
became secondary. He thus began to criticize black
colleges and trade schools in relation to economic
realities. The main fault he found with trade schools,
such as Tuskegee Institute (before its reorganization
as a comprehensive institution of higher learning) was
that they poorly prepared students to become part of
modern industry: "The industrial school assumed that
the technique of industry in 1895, even if not abso-
lutely fixed and permanent, was at least permanent
enough for training children into its pursuit and for
use as a basis of broader education. Therefore, school
work for farming, carpentry, bricklaying, plastering
and painting, metalwork and blacksmithing, shoemaking,
sewing and cooking was introduced and taught. But,
meantime, what has happened to these vocations and
trades? Machines and new industrial organizations have
remade the economic world and ousted these trades either
from their old technique or their economic significance."[81]

In 1930 the vantage point from which he viewed

the controversy with Washington was the reform and the
use of the industrial system; no mention was made of
the Talented Tenth. His balanced critique accepted the
goals of industrial education, but found it deficient
in its conception of how those goals could be realized.
Looking back in 1940 Du Bois pursued a different line
of criticism: he recounted his early belief in a
Talented Tenth and his early faith in higher education
and he noted the poor quality of achievement of
Washington's industrial training.[82] He added a further
claim that the real controversy between him and
Washington was over power.[83] He charged that from
Tuskegee, with the financial support of northern industry, Washington had developed around him what Du Bois
called the "Tuskegee Machine," which attempted to
hammer all black opinion into conformity.[84] He claimed
that the "Tuskegee Machine," with its government and
industrial connections, could veto the distribution of
funds to other institutions and even veto government
appointments.[85] And so the black community, Du Bois
felt, was essentially controlled by Washington. Arnold
Rampersad, in The Art and Imagination of W.E.B. Du Bois,
forcefully argues that Du Bois saw Washington's control
as serving his own selfish interests in alliance with
"white politicians and big businesses at the expense of
blacks in general."[86] Rampersad concludes that Du
Bois' "charges, including his belief that the Tuskegee
Machine" would move "against universities such as
Atlanta for refusing to silence intellectuals in public
disagreement with Washington, or against the nonpartisan
Atlanta Publications in its search for financial
support. . . ," were well founded based on the
Washington papers which show an ethos "somewhat more
suited to a corrupt political ward than to an institute
of learning."[87]

These later statements tended to de-emphasize the
importance of the role of the Talented Tenth in the
debate. The Souls of Black Folk included a chapter
entitled, "Of Mr. Booker T. Washington and Others,"
presenting Du Bois' first full critique of Washington;
it is once again relatively balanced. He accepted the
notion of industrial training for the masses (at this
early period he did not criticize the sort of training
offered), and he joined with Washington in his advocacy
of thrift and patience.[88] He did, as he later claimed,
reject the leadership role of Washington, contending
that it represented a compromise with whites and was
not the result of a natural selection by blacks. And,

importantly, he rejected the emphasis on industrial
education to the exclusion of higher education for
the talented.[89] Finally, the most serious issue seems
to be Du Bois' rejection of Washington's handling of
political rights. Although he recognized occasional
attempts Washington made to directly face the problem
of racism,[90] he briskly condemned Washington's deemphasis of political power and civil rights. He thus
identified three paradoxes in Washington's thought
stemming from his position on rights and higher education: (1) The encouragement of black business enterprise is doomed to fail without the ability to defend
what is achieved through political power. (2) The
support for self-respect is undermined by "submission
to civic inferiority," and (3) the deprecation of higher
learning is coupled by the fact that industrial colleges
are staffed, to a large degree, by the college
trained.[91]

V

Even though this work concentrates on Du Bois'
social thought, it is most important to keep in mind
the social environment in which he operated. Racism
ranged from the incredibly vicious to the ridiculously
petty in a way that systematically denied blacks social
and economic status, and legal recourse. This, of
course, should be well known; a sample of Du Bois'
writings certainly underscores the pervasive everyday
effect of those social conditions. It went beyond
crippling poverty to include a humiliation and fear.
Du Bois clearly experienced all of this before finishing
college at Fisk, especially when he taught in a rural
Southern school.

The weapon that he tried to bring against all of
this was, by and large, knowledge. That he had great
faith in it, even in the face of the conditions that
existed, is obvious. The fact that it failed is perhaps
more obvious. The dispute with Washington brings out
the failure at the highest level: that is, even the
attempt to gain and propogate knowledge came under
attack by a social system which controlled the extent
of free inquiry at the university level. This clearly
hampered Du Bois and affected his belief that it was
best to give up his social studies at Atlanta.

The next chapter examines Du Bois' movement away
from knowledge as the key to social advance and toward

an economic plan designed to attack the source of the problem.

NOTES

1. Du Bois has been so charged: Francis L. Broderick, in his chapter entitled "Negro Chauvinism" appears to have claimed that Du Bois' thought involved a significant racist tendency which came to the surface after the depression: "The racist undercurrent now became the mainstream. Now when the depression made his hopes for integration seemed (sic) utopian, he turned easily to the secondary program which had always lurked just below the surface of his thought," W.E.B. Du Bois: Negro Leader in a Time of Crisis (Stanford, Calif.: Stanford University Press, 1959), pp. 168-169. Elliot M. Rudwick also suggested a racist strain in Du Bois. "For a long time Du Bois had denounced white critics for racism, but it was clear he learned a few lessons from them" Rudwick, W.E.B. Du Bois, p. 195.

2. W.E. Burghardt Du Bois, "The Conservation of Races," American Negro Academy, Occasional Papers, No. 2 (1897).

3. Ibid., p. 5.   4. Ibid., p. 7.

5. Ibid., p. 6.

6. W.E. Burghardt Du Bois, The Negro (New York: Oxford University Press, 1970), p. 13.

7. W.E.B. Du Bois, Dusk of Dawn: An Essay Toward an Autobiography of a Race Concept (New York: Schocken Books, 1968), p. 113.

8. Du Bois, "The Conservation of Races," p. 6.

9. Ibid., p. 7.   10. Ibid., pp. 7-8.

11. Ibid., p. 9.   12. Ibid.

13. Ibid.   14. Ibid.

15. Ibid., p. 10   16. Ibid., p. 12.

17. Clarence G. Contee, "The Emergence of Du Bois as an African Nationalist," The Journal of Negro History, 54 (1969), p. 51.

18. Ibid., p. 52.

19. Du Bois, "The Pan-African Movement," in W.E.B. Du Bois Speaks, p. 161.

20. Ibid., p. 162.

21. Du Bois, "The Conservation of Races," p. 13.

22. Ibid., p. 10.   23. Ibid., p. 7.

24. Ibid., p. 6.   25. Ibid., p. 9.

26. Josiah Royce, The Philosophy of Loyalty (New York: The Macmillan Company, 1928).

27. Josiah Royce, The Problem of Christianity, 2 vols. (New York: The Macmillan Company, 1913).

28. Josiah Royce, Race Questions, Provincialism and Other American Problems (New York: The Macmillan Company, 1908).

29. Royce, The Problem of Christianity, I, p. 139.

30. Ibid., II, p. 19.

31. Du Bois, "The Conservation of Races," p. 10.

32. Royce, The Problem of Christianity, I, p. xxvii.

33. Royce, The Philosophy of Loyalty, p. 116.

34. Ibid., p. 121.   35. Ibid., p. 126.

36. Royce, The Problem of Christianity, II, p. 341.

37. Du Bois, "The Conservation of Races," p. 9.

38. Ibid., p. 11.

39. Du Bois, The Negro, p. 6.

40. Thomas F. Gossett, Race: The History of an Idea in America (New York: Schocken Books, 1965), p. 3.

41. Ibid., p. 144.   42. Ibid., pp. 97-98.

43. Ibid., p. 110.   44. Ibid., p. 95.

45. Alexander Alland, Jr., Human Diversity (New York: Columbia University Press, 1971), p. 3.

46. Ashley Montagu, ed., The Concept of Race (London: Collier-Macmillan Limited), p. xiii.

47. Ibid., p. 6. Du Bois, "The Conservation of Races," p. 6.

48. Gossett, Race, p. 32-33.

49. Quoted in Gossett, Race, p. 70.

50. Gossett, Race, p. 67.

51. Du Bois, "The Conservation of Races," p. 6.

52. Ibid., p. 9.

53. Ibid., pp. 8-9; emphasis added.

54. Ludwig Gumplovitz, The Outlines of Sociology (Philadelphia: American Academy of Political Science, 1899).

55. Gumplovitz, The Outlines of Sociology, p. 135.

56. Ibid., p. 86.   57. Ibid., p. 140.

58. Ibid., p. 102.   59. Ibid., p. 140.

60. Ibid., p. 120.

61. W.E.B. Du Bois, "The Talented Tenth," (1903), in Julius Lester, ed., The Seventh Son (New York: Random House, 1971), I, p. 386.

62. W.E. Burghardt Du Bois, The Souls of Black Folk (Greenwich, Conn.: Fawcett Publications, Inc., 1961), p. 124.

63. Du Bois, "The Conservation of Races," p. 11.

64. W.E.B. Du Bois, The Philadelphia Negro: A Social Study (New York: Schocken Books, 1967), p. 311.

Du Bois' study was influenced by the growing empirical traditions of social studies in England. A dominant figure in the movement was Charles Booth who, in the 1880's, directed a systematic survey of London, which in its essentials was much like Du Bois', and the findings were published in the multivolumed edition, Life and Labour of the People, in London. Charles Booth, ed., (1892-1897), (rpt. New York: AMS Press, Inc., 1970). Jane Addams founded the well-known chicago settlement, Hull House, after observing Booth's work, and from her settlement the Hull House Papers and Maps, by the residents of Hull House, 1895 (rpt. New York: Arno Press, 1970) were undertaken in order to survey Chicago slum life. This project followed Booth's model. The influence on Du Bois of these works is apparent, for example, in the resemblance between the maps Du Bois presents in The Philadelphia Negro and those in the Hull House study. The influence of these surveys is noted by E. Digby Baltzell in his introduction to The Philadelphia Negro, p. xvii and by F.L. Broderick in "German Influence on the Scholarship of W.E.B. Du Bois," PHYLON XL (December, 1958), p. 369.

65. Du Bois, The Philadelphia Negro, p. 393.

66. Ibid., p. 317.   67. Ibid., p. 5.

68. Ibid., pp. 7-8.   69. Ibid., p. 392.

70. Ibid., p. 396.

71. W.E. Burghardt Du Bois, The Black North in 1901: A Social Study (New York: Arno Press and The New York Times, 1969), p. 46.

72. Ibid., pp. 28-29.

73. Du Bois, "The Talented Tenth," p. 390.

74. Du Bois, Dusk of Dawn, p. 58.

75. Du Bois, Autobiography, p. 197.

76. Du Bois, Dusk of Dawn, p. 65.

77. The Correspondence of W.E.B. Du Bois, Vol. II, p. 62.

78. W.E.B. Du Bois, ed., Some Efforts of American Negroes for their own Social Betterment (Atlanta: Atlanta University Press, 1898), p. 17.

79. W.E.B. Du Bois, ed., Economic Co-operation Among Negro Americans (Atlanta: Atlanta University Press, 1907), p. 11.

80. W.E.B. Du Bois, "Education and Work," (1930), in Julius Lester, The Seventh Son, I., p. 560.

81. Ibid., p. 566.

82. Du Bois, Dusk of Dawn, p. 70.

83. Ibid., p. 75.   84. Ibid., p. 74.

85. Ibid., p. 73.

86. A. Rampersad, The Art and Imagination of W.E.B. Du Bois, p. 93.

87. Ibid., pp. 93-94.

88. Du Bois, Souls of Black Folk, p. 53.

89. Ibid., p. 48.   90. Ibid., p. 44.

91. Ibid., p. 49.

CHAPTER III

THE ACTIVIST YEARS: 1905-1934

I

From 1897 to 1910 Du Bois worked at Atlanta
University as Professor of Economics and History, and
as Editor of the Atlanta University <u>Publications</u>.
Until about 1905 his activities can be characterized
by his efforts at social reform and racial leadership
through knowledge of social realities--those were years
of extensive social studies following the model presented in the doctrine of the Talented Tenth. Although
he engaged in public controversy before 1905, such as
his dispute with Booker T. Washington, his work was
mainly academic and nonpolitical. 1905 is selected as
the year in which he became a political activist not
because he then gave up systematic social research
(this occurred in 1910) but because he first became a
leader in an organized social movement, The Niagara
Movement.

The change from a social scientist to a political
leader and propagandist came as a result of several
factors. Perhaps the basis for such a change can be
found in his studies in Germany. There he claimed his
first awareness of the link between economic conditions
and political action.[1] While this relationship became
gradually clearer to him, he asserted that the connection only became thoroughly definite in his mind after
1910.[2] Even before he left teaching the significance
of economic realities was gradually forced upon him.
Looking back, he characterized world affairs during
the years he taught at Atlanta as filled with imperialism and racism.[3] Europe was expanding its power into
Africa and the United States sought to dominate the
economic life of Hawaii, Cuba, the Philippines, Panama,
Puerto Rico, Santo Domingo and South America: "All
this might have been interpreted as history and politics. Mainly I did so interpret it; but continually
I was forced to consider the economic aspects of world
movements as they were developing at the time. Chiefly
this was because the groups in which I was interested
were workers, earners of wages, owners of small bits of
land, servants."[4]

The significance of this change of emphasis is
greater than it seems at first sight. Early in his

life Du Bois placed his trust in historical progress
defined as cultural advance and guided by the knowledgeable elite. The most important feature of social
life was seen as cultural: the cultural elite could,
if capable, guide political decisions so as to strength-
en cultural attainment, and economic conditions could
then be manipulated, where necessary, in service of
deliberate, self-consciously adopted plans. All of
this came into question when economic conditions were
viewed as an overriding force in the life of nations
and individuals. Social problems began to look more
recalcitrant, the cultural elite began to look impo-
tent, and, even worse, cultural achievement no longer
appeared to be a sign of progress because such "progress" was consistent with and overshadowed by possible
economic decay. Du Bois thus began to define progress
in terms of economic and consequently political advance.
Coupled with this was an emphasis on economic production and a deemphasis on the cultural elite.

     A particular and dramatic event seems to mark a
clear initiation of the process of change. In 1899 a
black farm laborer from rural Georgia, Sam Hose, was
involved in a dispute with his employer who refused
to pay him. A fight resulted and the employer was
killed. Sam Hose fled; a lynch mob set after him,
aroused by the incorrect report that Hose had raped
the employer's wife. Du Bois believed that his studies
gave him some knowledge of this sort of case. So he
decided to explain the occurence to Joel Chandler
Harris, the editor of the Atlanta Constitution, in an
attempt to get the situation under control. On the
way to deliver his account he learned that Hose had
been lynched and that "some of his fingers were on
exhibit at a butcher shop which I would pass on my way
to town."5 In face of events like this the impotence
of reasoned argument supported by social scholarship
appeared most evident.

     Even though this event occurred years before Du
Bois shifted to political activism, it marked a dramatic beginning and came within the context of increasing
racism. Jim Crow legislation, lynching, racism and a
generally deteriorating social situation for blacks
marred the first decade of the twentieth century,
roughly corresponding to the period of the dominance
of Booker T. Washington. Du Bois gave his account
of the lynching of Sam Hose in Dusk of Dawn, and thus
delineated the proximate reason for his change of

emphasis: "Two considerations thereafter broke in upon my work and eventually disrupted it: first, one could not be a calm, cool, and detached scientist while Negroes were lynched, murdered, and starved; and secondly, there was no such definite demand for scientific work of the sort that I was doing, as I had confidently assumed would be easily forthcoming."[6]

Even as events weakened his faith in his studies, he realized the project he organized at Atlanta University was not being funded adequately, and so its survival was continually in doubt. And his social activities after his criticism of Washington stood to jeopardize his ability to generate funds by and large controlled by whites.

The full turn toward activism was pinpointed by Du Bois to one significant event. During the years of Washington's leadership an opposition movement was undertaken by the Boston black newspaper, the Guardian, edited by George Forbes and a former classmate of Du Bois' at Harvard, Monroe Trotter. Du Bois recognized Washington's power over the black community, a power that made it difficult for him to continue his social studies at Atlanta.[7] His 1903 critique of Washington in Souls of Black Folk marked a rather thoroughgoing break with Washington's position. However, Du Bois had not followed the style of acrimonious opposition to Washington adopted by Monroe Trotter. Du Bois tended to view the Guardian as extreme in its criticisms, but in 1905 the event occurred which led Du Bois into a leadership role against Washington. Washington was in Boston delivering a speech, and Trotter openly confronted him in order to force answers on questions of civil rights. This led to a jail term for Trotter. As Arnold Rampersad points out: "This act of humiliation against a man of his own class and general sympathies seems to have shaken him into confronting the power of the Washington following and the limits of his own influence."[8] Du Bois considered jailing unjustified and viewed it as the catalyst leading him to aid in the formation, with Trotter, of a political movement against Washington and for political and social rights. Du Bois decided to invite a number of prominent blacks to organize a political action group. Twenty-nine people responded to his invitation to meet in July, 1905, in Canada near Niagara Falls. Soon this "Niagara Movement" was incorporated with the following anti-Washington platform:

1. Freedom of speech and criticism.
2. Unfettered and unsubsidized press.
3. Manhood suffrage.
4. The abolition of all caste distinctions based simply on race and color.
5. The recognition of the principles of human brotherhood as a practical present creed.
6. The recognition of the highest and best human training as the monopoly of no class or race.
7. A belief in the dignity of labor.
8. United effort to realize these ideals under wise and courageous leadership.[9]

The following year the movement met at Harper's Ferry, and at Boston and Oberlin in succeeding years. Nothing especially momentous resulted, except perhaps in terms of the personal lives of those involved. For Du Bois, the movement probably cost, if indirectly, his position at Atlanta; his relations with those at Atlanta University became strained, partly because he was seen as a threat to their funding sources.

In 1909 a group of blacks and whites, including Du Bois, met in New York and founded the National Association for the Advancement of Colored People, "which without formal merger absorbed practically the whole membership of the Niagara Movement, save Trotter, who distrusted our white allies and their objects."[10] Du Bois became the Director of Publication and Research and began editing an enormously successful magazine, The Crisis, partly following in the pattern of two unsuccessful editing attempts, The Moon (1906) and Horizon (1907-1910). His editorial work, lasting until 1934, ended Du Bois' stay at Atlanta University and brought him to New York City. He observed, "My career as a scientist was to be swallowed up in my role as a master of propaganda. This was not wholly to my liking. I am no natural leader of men."[11]

Du Bois' movement toward public leadership follows from his growing recognition of the subordinate role of knowledge as a central force in society. This recognition stems from the affirmation of the centrality of economic and psychological conditioning. These viewpoints would not have been endorsed unless the futility and frustration of his academic studies had not become apparent. The viciousness of racism would not bend to careful scientific analysis; compounding this was the clear fact that the racist character of society stiffled even scientific inquiry. Predominately white universities dominating intellectual life were entirely unwilling to support such studies; even Du Bois' Philadelphia Negro was done in a hostile environment at the University of Pennsylvania--witnessed by the fact that he did not receive regular faculty status and that the study was commissioned with the intent of focusing on the bad effects of the black wards on Philadelphia's political organization. The poorly funded Atlanta studies, even given the efficacy of knowledge, could have achieved little in terms of developing a solution to racism. But the nature and extent of racism--its irrationality and ingrained nature--highlighted the relative impotence of scientific study.

For example, problems like that of Sam Hose were not about to be settled by calm analysis: the milieu in the South did not support such action. As editor of the Crisis Du Bois engaged in an anti-lynching campaign designed to pressure legislators into passing an anti-lynching law at the federal level. He helped to organize mass campaigns against lynching and he used the Crisis to publicize lynching, not in a sociological sense, but with dramatic accounts of the viciousness of the event. Rather than a careful sociological study, he offered a thorough and emotional exposé designed to bring about concerted action. This is the sort of thing Du Bois had in mind when he called himself a propagandist. And going beyond, he used the Crisis as a means of backing what he hoped would be a mass movement among blacks to form an independent position of economic power. His hope, albeit frustrated, represents a clear shift from his position as a social scientist to a position as social activist.

In brief, the social milieu around 1905 led Du Bois to abandon his early beliefs, and his growing recognition of economic and psychological determinism provided a logical support for the change. Consequently, the turn toward political activism was a new point of departure for Du Bois; his program of research, his reliance on the Talented Tenth, and his notion of race as cultural all seemed to be denied by his experience. Literature, art, law, and philosophy did not seem to predominate in human affairs, and advances in knowledge went along easily enough with deterioration in social life. For a pragmatist such lack of success suggested an abandonment of the program and a new attempt at

67

developing a power base capable of responding to the problem of racism. Yet no definite, fully worked out program or clear fundamental principles of group action existed in this period. Instead the years from 1905 to 1934 mark a pattern of development in which certain themes are worked through and accepted in increasingly extreme forms: (1) During these years he came progressivly closer to accepting a Marxian economic determinism, but he rejected the full Marxist doctrine. (2) He no longer placed faith in the Talented Tenth, but desired a more democratic egalitarianism. (3) Although vacilating on the issues of violence and war and peace, he tended toward a non-violent humanism. (4) He became more aware of global affairs and worked for a genuine Pan-Africanism.

II

The above characteristics of the period from 1905 to 1934 should make obvious the magnitude of change in Du Bois' social thought. Even though the link to a clear shift in social theory has not yet been established, it is evident that the early system had implications (e.g. the Talented Tenth and all that that involved) which became unacceptable to him; thus the theory of racial identity in "The Conservation of Races" had to be rejected. This period can be interpreted as being based on a theoretically revised concept of race, functioning much as the early concept did. Most of the period can be viewed as logically supported by the new concept of race, but this concept was not fully articulated until after the end of the period.

1934 was selected as the end of the period because it witnessed the end of Du Bois' leadership role in the N.A.A.C.P., and of his editorship of The Crisis. No conceptual break in his thinking occurred during that year. The concept of race logically dominating the years from 1905 until close to the end of his life was most fully presented in Dusk of Dawn, six years after the end of the period. Looking back from the 1940 statements, the logical relationships can be seen, but without that vantage point such an analysis would have been extremely difficult. So the years during which this notion of race explicitly developed cannot be determined with accuracy. However, an examination of a person's thinking is sometimes more fruitful if a position articulated at a later point can be shown to

68

be involved in an earlier position. This helps us to
understand why certain issues are considered important
and how certain issues can be fully defended. So without attempting to establish the time at which the
later concept of race became consciously operative in
his thinking, it is presented as a fundamental notion
in his social thought after 1905.

Perhaps the best way to approach the change in
his notion of race is through his closely related view
on racism. In "The Conservation of Races," racism
was identified as a "friction" between culturally
dissimilar groups. This reflects a concession to
social Darwinism which never occupied a strong role in
his thought. His more considered view on racism turned
on the negative factor of ignorance about the life-style
of other groups. This view of the cause of prejudice
suggests that racism could be combatted through an
appreciation and understanding of cultural differentiation. The concepts of racism and race were both heavi-
ly dependent upon the leading idea of the importance of
intellectual achievement; racial units were mainly
defined by unique cultural achievements; racism occurred when such achievements were not appreciated.
But as faith in the power of intellectual life waned,
Du Bois became suspicious of (1) the ability of knowledge to solve the problem of racism, and perhaps more
importantly, (2) the extent to which racism was caused
by ignorance. Du Bois apparently began to suspect that
race had a clearly different significance from what he
then believed to be the main ingredients of racial life.
And this element could be used to account for the tena-
cious character of racism. The new feature was the
economic life of a group; this feature, the material
as distinguished from the intellectual side of life,
became the new central element of race and racism.
The new view of racism traced dehumanization to the
economic structure of the slave system. Racism was
deeply entrenched in a long surviving economic system
in which blacks were portrayed as inferior with the
functional motive of facilitating economic gain.

The idea of an economic interpretation of racism
came to Du Bois from Marx. Du Bois began to accept
the theory that economic conditions mold social life
and cultural life. His thought began to shift toward
an acceptance of Marx's economic determinism. He
clearly stated this acceptance in Dusk of Dawn:
". . . I believed and still believe that Karl Marx was

one of the greatest men of modern times and that . . . economic foundations, the way in which men earn their living, are the determining factors in the development of civilization, in literature, religion, and the basic pattern of culture."[12] Again in his Autobiography: "I believe in the dictum of Karl Marx, that the economic foundation of a nation is widely decisive for its politics, its art and its culture."[13]

Marx's position is a form of the deterministic thinking growing in popularity after the stunning scientific advances of Newtonian physics. The deterministic model, in general, holds that every event is the way it is because of specific antecedent conditions and could not have been different. This principle was applied at the social level in various influential late nineteenth and early twentieth century positions. For example, on the biological level humans were characterized in a Darwinian fashion on the basis of the evolution of prehuman behavior. And on the psychological level Freudian psychology contended that human actions are determined by unconscious psychological forces, determined by the interaction, early in life, of basic antagonistic psychological structures.

Marx's "economic determinism" was by and large restricted to social institutions. His writings did not usually deal with individual determinants; he was mostly interested in historical changes in institutional life, based upon the economic changes bringing forward new patterns of life as exhibited in new historical periods. Thus, his position is also referred to as an "historical materialism." History, according to Marx, is in a process of movement in which one stage is transformed into another. These changes are patterned after a dialogue, or conversation. In a dialogue any view may be presented, let us call it X, by person A. Person B may deny the validity of X, or assert the truth of not X. In a genuine exchange, rather than a capitulation, both A and B might give up their views as mistaken and both might adopt a new view, Y, containing the partial truths of X and of not X. History was interpreted by Marx in a similar fashion, with an historical stage, like view X, firmly established, and then contradictory forces develop in that stage which eventually overthrow it and replace it with a new stage. The new stage, however, preserves the advances of the old stage. Because Marx modeled the movement of history after the dialectic, his view is also labeled a "dialec-

70

tic materialism."

Marx's dialectical materialism centers on material or economic conditions. The term "economics" refers to the way goods are produced, distributed and consumed. Different periods of history are distinguished by such economic conditions. Production in a large factory is different from small scale in-the-home production; distribution of goods on the basis of money gained from sale of labor or from profit is basically different from distribution on the basis of title (say to the lord of a manor) or by the direct fruits of one's own labor. Economic determinism rests on the doctrine that these sort of relations are the most important in any society and, further, economic conditions eventually mold every other social institution into conformity with the needs of these patterns. Thus, stages of history, with all their institutional relations, can be defined with nearly exclusive emphasis on economics. Perhaps the sharpest expression of this view can be found in Marx's early work, The Poverty of Philosophy: "Social relations are closely bound up with productive forces. In acquiring new productive forces men change their mode of production; and in changing their mode of production, in changing the way of earning their living, they change all their social relations. The handmill gives you society with the feudal lord; the steam-mill, society with the industrial capitalist."[14] This statement although unclear in ways, as is the entire doctrine of economic determinism, suggests a kind of technological determinism in Marx. "In acquiring new productive forces" seems to mean the same as acquiring new techniques of producing, and the reference to the handmill and the steam-mill seems to verify this interpretation because it suggests varying stages in technological competence as foundational.

In another passage we get a further insight into economic determinism through Marx's clear statement that intellectual enterprises are derived from economic life. He claimed that

> . . . we do not set out from what
> men say, imagine, conceive, nor
> from men as narrated, thought of,
> imagined, conceived, in order to
> arrive at men in the flesh. We
> set out from real, active men, and

> on the basis of the real life-
> process we demonstrate the develop-
> ment of the ideological reflexes
> and echoes of this life-process. . . .
> Morality, religion, metaphysics,
> all the rest of ideology and their
> corresponding forms of conscious-
> ness, thus no longer retain the
> semblance of independence. They
> have no history, no development;
> but men, developing their material
> production and their material inter-
> course, alter, along with this their
> real existence, their thinking and
> the products of their thinking. Life
> is not determined by consciousness,
> but consciousness by life.[15]

This passage should adequately show that Du Bois'
acceptance of a Marxian determinism is at odds with a
theory placing cultural development at the core of
history. Du Bois believed that historical materialism
partly explained the existence of racism and for this
reason a predominantly intellectual approach to the
problem did not succeed. Racism in its virulent form
had a relatively recent origin; using an economic
perspective it became easy to correlate the growth of
racism with the development of black African slavery.

Du Bois did not fully side with Marx on the
importance of economics. Marx believed that when one
economic period collapses a new set of institutions
would arise; these institutions are called the "superstructure." For Marx, most of a period's shared
conscious life, its beliefs, religion, and philosophy,
are part of the superstructure. He understood that
once established, the superstructure maintained a
certain independent life so that "hangovers" would be
retained in a period after the dissolution of another.
But Marx's economic theory is weak on explaining how
parts of the superstructure are retained. But racism
had a staying power, a continuing viciousness, that
could not be explained simply as part of a superstructure "lag"; racism involved much more than a
simple economic theory would account for. For example,
an economic view seems strained when attempting to
account for actions ranging from public lynchings to
petty meannesses such as refusing seats in certain
sections of buses and waiting stations. Perhaps

72

Du Bois' description of an event he observed typifies the blind irrationalism of racism: "I have seen a man--an educated gentleman--grow livid with anger because a little silent, black woman was sitting by herself in a Pullman car. He was a white man."[16]

To account for the rabid retention and entrenchment (after slavery ended) of racism, Du Bois added a Freudian note to his Marxian determinism. As slavery began to grow in importance it was "rationalized" or defended by slaveholders and those in slaveholding societies; the defense was designed to fight off the claims that owning slaves was immoral. They had to argue that slavery was neither against religion nor morality. The way used was to describe blacks as innately inferior, as children needing guidance, or as heathen needing reform. These were racist concoctions, but Du Bois thought they eventually became part of a collective unconscious through repetition from generation to generation. A kind of communal Freudian unconscious was blended with or, perhaps better, grafted on to an economic perspective; a collective, unconscious racism (beside conscious racism) eventually stood to defend base economic motives. ". . . I saw defending this bar not simply ignorance and ill will; these, to be sure; but also certain more powerful motives less open to reason or appeal. There were economic motives, urges to build wealth on the backs of black slaves and colored serfs; there followed those unconscious acts and irrational reactions, unpierced by reason, whose current form depended on the long history of relation and contact between thought and idea."[17]

The change in his concept of racism to highlight, as it does, the economic aspect of life as foundational suggests that he could no longer support the cultural concept of race. In 1940, Du Bois looked back and called for a re-examination of his early view: "One of the first pamphlets that I wrote in 1897 was on 'The Conservation of Races' wherein I set down as the first article of a proposed racial creed: 'We believe that the Negro people as a race have a contribution to make to civilization and humanity which no other race can make.'

"Since then the concept of race has so changed and presented so much of contradiction that as I face Africa, I ask myself: what is it between us that

73

constitutes a tie which I can feel better than I can
explain."[18]

He recognized his <u>lack</u> of cultural connection with
Africa, a point that, according to his early position
on racial differentiation, establishes a sharp and
unacceptable disunity. On the other hand, he felt a
tie with Africans. Perhaps this is one of the unex-
plained "contradictions" he referred to. He continued
to believe appearances, although obvious, are not especially important in themselves, so they could not be
relied on to establish a significant social connection
between Africans and Afro-Americans. The answer he
relied on was economic; more precisely he relied on a
similar interaction with economic conditions:

> . . . one thing is sure and that is
> the fact that since the fifteenth
> century these ancestors of mine and
> their other descendants have a
> common history; have suffered a
> common disaster and have one long
> memory. The actual ties of heritage
> between the individuals of this
> group, vary with the ancestors that
> they have in common and many others:
> Europeans and Semites, perhaps
> Mongolians, certainly American
> Indians. But the physical bond is
> least and the badge of color rela-
> tively unimportant save as a badge;
> the real essence of this kinship is
> its social heritage of slavery; the
> discrimination and insult; and this
> heritage binds together not simply
> the children of Africa, but extends
> through yellow Asia into the South
> Seas. It is this unity that draws
> me to Africa.[19]

This view of racial identity, based on economic
history instead of cultural traits, broadens the
notion of race to include vast groups of people, and
this establishes a Pan-Africanism in a way the former
view could not. He included the people of Africa,
Asia and the South Seas as being incorporated into the
same heritage. However, the extension leaves the
notion without any precise defining traits. He seemed
to recognize that his second concept, racial unity

established through economic exploitation, as compared with his early notion was indefinite because it lacked the cohesiveness of traits such as a common religion, law, language, etc. He claimed, "Perhaps it is wrong to speak of it at all as 'a concept' rather than as a group of contradictory forces, facts and tendencies."[20] A similar view of the grouping of people was held as early as 1920, which supports the claim made above that the 1940 view logically dominates much of his earlier work:

> There are no races, in the sense of great, separate, pure breeds of men, differing in attainment, development, and capacity. There are great groups,--now with common history, now with common interests, now with common ancestry; more and more common experience and present interest drive back the common blood and the world today consists, not of races, but of the imperial commercial group of master capitalists, international and predominantly white; the national middle classes of the several nations, white, yellow, and brown, with strong blood bonds, common languages, and common history; the international laboring class of all colors; the backward, oppressed groups of nature-folk, predominantly yellow, brown and black.[21]

In this passage Du Bois inserted something of the evolutionary flavor of the 1897 version, with history bringing a dissolution of color ties. Also in this statement the class analysis seems to be central with "race" occupying a secondary, almost tagged on, role. In the later view the occurrence of slavery and all it meant functions as a racially unifying trait apparently even more gripping than class structure economically defined. So in this sense Du Bois may be seen as vacillating between a class notion and a race notion.

The 1940 notion of race has its greatest emphasis on economic suffering, the sort of suffering that burdens the masses. Previously the emphasis was placed on the talented. The new concept of race spelled out a new goal, economic advance. While Du Bois previously insisted, for example in The Philadelphia Negro, on the recognition of class distinctions, he began later in his life to emphasize group solidarity and the absence of class structure in the black community.

> My own panacea of earlier days was
> flight of class from mass through
> the development of a Talented
> Tenth; but the power of this aris-
> tocracy of talent was to lie in its
> knowledge and character and not in
> its wealth. The problem which I
> did not then attack was that of
> leadership and authority within the
> group, which by implication, left
> controls of wealth--a contingency of
> which I never dreamed. But now the
> whole economic trend of the world
> has changed. That mass and class
> must unite for the world's salvation
> is clear. We who have had least
> class differentiation in wealth, can
> follow in the new trend and indeed
> lead it.[22]

The role of classes was important in Du Bois' thought from his first published work. But classes for him, while always partly economic in definition, had a leading cultural significance. That is, his main theoretical interest in class division was along cul- tural lines rather than economic lines. Economic determinism does not allow this sort of allocation of importance. Classes for Marx arise from and are de- fined by their relationship to economic conditions. This is succinctly stated in Engle's Anti-Duhring: "The materialist conception of history starts from the principle that production, and with production the exchange of its products, is the basis of every social order; that in every society which has appeared in history the distribution of the products, and with it the division of society into classes or estates, is determined by what is produced and how it is produced, and how the product is exchanged."[23] The conditions of production create and define classes in a society.

In various historical stages (e.g. feudalism) the class structure is complicated (e.g. lords and serfs, master craftsmen and journeymen) but wherever there are class differentiations there are differences of interests causing antagonism, whether latent or overt. A dominating class, in an attempt to protect its interests, oppresses the others and subjects them to its will using, as a means of oppression, dominant features of the superstructure: law, religion, morality, etc. For Marx, a key fact about the capitalist stage of history is that its class antagonisms have been simplified so that society is (with some minor exceptions) divided into two significant classes, the "bourgeoisie" and the "proletariat." Both are defined by their relationship to the means of production or the tools and equipment used to produce goods: "By 'bourgeoisie' is meant the class of modern capitalists, owners of the means of social production and employers of wage-labor; by 'proletariat,' the class of modern wage-laborers who, having no means of production of their own, are reduced to selling their labor in order to live."[24]

Classes, according to Marx, provide the moving force of history through their antagonistic relationships. Basically, the dialectic begins with a particular historical epoch with stable class relationships; when technical conditions develop changing those relationships, new conditions which "conflict" with the old way of doing things also develop. Marx considered them to be "contradictions" in the old system. For example, in the capitalist period, over-production in relation to money supply may lead to depression and, in fact, did so periodically. Yet the things produced fill social needs (are use-values) regardless of the money supply. The conflict between the use-value of a thing conflicts with its selling price (exchange value) with dire economic consequences. In Marx's analysis depression alters the balance of the two major social classes by forcing out smaller businesses and creating an increasingly large numerical difference between the two classes. Through various "contradictions," the power of the proletariat grows; when strong enough a revolution creates a new society. Eventually, for Marx, the result is a classless, non-exploitative, communist society, which, without class antagonism, ends the movement of history.

Du Bois did not accept Marx's theory of revolution because it omitted racial distinctions. But Du Bois did redefine classes along Marxian lines so that income alone was not a defining feature; instead the definition revolved around the relationship to capital. With this came the discovery that black Americans already form a

"classless" society and thereby have a great potential
for social advance. This is what he meant in the above
statement that blacks already achieved the unity of
class and mass. Du Bois eventually used this notion of
a "classless" black group to develop a notion of social
egalitarianism in opposition to his earlier elitism.

III

With the recognition that cultural achievement is
secondary in social life and that economic conditions
tend to mold culture, it is, of course, not plausible
to base social policy on an aristocracy of cultural
talent. The view that economic conditions predominates
tends to make all cultural class distinctions look
weak; the only class distinctions that fit into the
basic Marxian model are those centering on economic
classes. But by the nature of the economic system,
those classes that own capital are not more productive
than labor, indeed from the Marxian view they are less
productive. So with the ascendency of the role of
economic conditions in Du Bois' thought, we see the
downfall of classist thinking. In this period we find
him battling against social class distinctions; Du Bois
becomes a social egalitarian. This shows through in
his book, Darkwater (1920).

Although Darkwater is autobiographical in form, it
deals with five problems Du Bois considered crucial:
race, war, women's rights, the education of children,
and democracy. These problems were seen as inter-
linked, with capitalism playing a central role in
maintaining oppression. In each of these he placed
emphasis on the full development of the ordinary
person--all people should be able to develop to the
limits of their particular capacities. The result of
this was to underscore faith in a real, vital democracy,
as distinguished from his earlier flirtations with
aristocracy. Yet democracy is problematic insofar as
participation in the social decision-making process
seems to require certain minimum skills many might lack.

The problem of democracy, and, in part, of egalitarianism, comes into full focus in America with emancipation and Reconstruction. Du Bois claimed that after
emancipation Northern philanthropists saw an unusual
opportunity to test their faith in Democracy, including
an industrial democracy where employees have a voice in
matters of production. Blacks were not under the power

78

of northern industrial might; so with abundant land and staple crops available, chances for a successful, model democracy were seen as great.[25] And there was some progress: the 14th and 15th amendments, the development of a public school system in the South, and, he thought, the beginning of a large scale economic cooperative movement. But success itself lined up the opposition.

Against the movement stood farmers, former owners of slaves and Northern industrialists; all of these groups saw true freedom for blacks as a threat to their frontier. They used anti-color prejudice as a way of inducing whites to disfranchise blacks, to "Jim Crow" them, and to restrict the semblance of democracy to whites only. To do this, Du Bois insisted, it became necessary to mollify white workers with higher wages at the cost of super-exploitation of the darker people of the world. This did give a greater income to whites, but through racism it "in much greater proportion put wealth and power in the hands of the great European Captains of Industry and made modern industrial imperialism possible."[26]

While this was going on, European white labor grew in sophistication and power and, therefore, sought ways to understand and apply their new power to bring about democratic control of industry. The intent of reform was utilitarian: "the direction of individual action in industry so as to secure the greatest good of all."[27] The means were varied: socialism, Marxism, syndicalism; but behind many of these movements stood a kind of elitism. "Some Socialists openly excluded Negroes and Asiatics from their scheme. From this it was easy to drift into that form of syndicalism which asks socialism for the skilled laborer only and leaves the common laborer in his bonds."[28] (Here Du Bois suggests a path through which racism eventually engenders non-racial discimination; this developed into a general critique of western civilization in his later writing. This is fully explored in Chapter Six.)

The fundamental principle of elitism is that only the knowledgeable or skillful have a right to control-- whether control of government or of industry. But this, as reasonable as it may seem, is at least a partial abdication of democracy. Thus Du Bois proposed to reexamine "Democracy" to find out if it is justifiable to exclude the ignorant and inexperienced from social and

79

political rule.

Du Bois argued that restriction of the ballot for
the reasons of ignorance and inexperience, the sort of
shortcomings many believed to be present in Reconstruction governments, amounted to an attempt to limit power
to those who already have it; and besides, these argu-
ments, for him, unearth a kind of undemocratic illness
in the political body: "we say easily, for instance,
'The ignorant ought not to vote.' We should say, 'No
civilized state should have citizens too ignorant to
participate in government,' and this statement is but
a step to the fact: that no state is civilized which
has citizens too ignorant to help rule it. Or, in
other words, education is not a prerequisite to political control--political control is the cause of popular
education."[29] He believed that, in fact, experience
and education tend to follow from having a part in
elections because the vote tends, in the long run, to
guarantee the sort of social policy that makes all
people capable of participating in political control.
Further, democracy is the only way to insure justice
against rulers--a strong, capable ruler with devotion
to the people, he argued, is difficult to find.

Du Bois' shift from his principle of the Talented
Tenth was completed with the following amplification of
the above argument. It is often claimed that lack of
talent and ignorance ought to keep people from political power--but Du Bois contended that the knowledge
needed in the political process can only be found in
the people, even if ignorant. The best aristocracy (of
skill) suffers from a lack of knowledge of the needs of
the people "for in the last analysis only the man himself, however humble, knows his own condition."[30] To
exclude any group, notably blacks and women when Du
Bois was writing, from the political process is to exclude knowledge of the real interests and needs of these
groups. Du Bois gave as an example the exclusion of
women and concluded: "We have but to view the unsatisfactory relations of the sexes the world over and the
problem of children to realize how desperately we need
this excluded wisdom."[31]

Du Bois extended the argued-for principle of participation to industrial democracy: to the ownership
and control of the means of production. He threw his
support to the Marxian contention that democracy depends
on public ownership of capital goods and against those

who argue that the people do not know enough to make
this control effective. Control of machines is the
chief source of power over the average working person
and this ownership Du Bois attributed "as much to
chance and cheating as to thrift and intelligence. So
far as it is due to chance and cheating, the argument
for public ownership of capital is incontrovertible
even though it involves some interference with long
vested rights and inheritance."[32] But the question
remains as to whether the workers can make up for any
loss of thrift and ability that now rests with private
owners. Du Bois answered by crediting workers and
managers with the knowledge and skill that get goods
produced. And he thought that once the people understood this, public ownership becomes inevitable. This
position is consistent with the Marxist view that all
economic value follows from the labor-value put into
goods. In effect, Marx held that the profits that go
to owners do not in the main pay for anything such as
talent and thrift, but is that portion of the money
value created by labor which is not paid to them, a
system Marx chacterizes as "wage-slavery."

Du Bois believed that democracy needed to be extended to the industrial process, or, in other words,
to the real affairs that are vital in people's lives.
This would also make the political process more meaningful: "Politics have not touched the matters of
daily life which are nearest the interests of the
people--namely, work and wages; or if they have, they
have touched it obscurely and indirectly. When voting
touches the vital, everyday interests of all, nomina-
tions and elections will call for more intelligent
activity."[33]

Du Bois' egalitarian democracy carries him toward
socialism, which in its stronger versions involves
virtually complete public control of all production
and distribution. After claiming that at certain periods private control of industry may be needed to
stimulate production, he argued: "When . . . the inti-
cacy and length of technical production increased, the
ownership of these things becomes a monopoly, which
makes the rich richer and the poor poorer. . . . We
are rapidly approaching the day when we shall repudiate
all private property in raw materials and tools and
demand that distribution hinge, not on the power of
those who monopolize the materials, but in the needs
of the mass of men."[34]

81

In 1920 Du Bois believed that people in the United States wanted the elimination of class distinctions. But by and large this stand for equality was limited to white men. He observed that equality for white women faced greater reluctance, and black, brown and yellow people were virtually excluded. While the injustice of this is manifest, he added that such a world system, with the tensions and hostilities it builds, is unstable and will, eventually, lead to violence and war. His egalitarianism was thorough; it demanded the satisfaction of all human needs; and it took seriously the denial of cultural class-oriented distinctions. Further, he stated the view that labor ought to be done by everyone: "With Work for All and All at Work probably from three to six hours would suffice, and leave abundant time for leisure, exercise, study, and avocations.

"But what shall we say of work where spiritual values and social distinctions enter? Who shall be Artists and who shall be Servants in the world to come? Or shall we all be artists and all serve?"[35]

Du Bois' movement toward socialism began gradually. During his years at the University of Berlin he attended some meetings of the Social Democratic party, but these did not influence him very much.[36] In 1907 he labeled himself a "socialist of the path," which meant that he called for a greater public ownership of business, but he felt that many businesses were better off pursued privately. He concluded, "our natural friends are not the rich but the poor, not the great but the masses, not the employers but the employees. Our good is not wealth, power, possession and snobbishness, but helpfulness, efficiency, service and self-respect."[37]

It must be emphasized that Du Bois' movement toward economic determinism is mainly of major importance, during the years under analysis, for its impact on his theoretical stance on the nature of race and in his movement away from knowledge and the "Talented Tenth" as the way to racial advance. It did not, at this point in his development, have any decisive impact on his political affiliation. Du Bois was moving closer to the Socialist party at the beginning of this period; apparently he joined it in 1911 only to leave in 1912 so that he could support Wilson. Du Bois' vacillating attitude toward American socialist politics, ranging from firm support to harsh criticism, is well documented in Philip S. Foner's American Socialism and Black Americans: From the Age of Jackson to World War II. Foner traces Du Bois' attitude from his 1907 vague definition of himself as a socialist of the path to his challenge to socialists to stop ignoring blacks. "If American socialism cannot stand for the American Negro, the American Negro will not stand for American socialism."[38] Du Bois' vacillation, however, must be viewed in light of the ambiguous stand toward blacks taken by prominent socialists. For example, Foner points out that Eugene V. Debs took conflicting positions on social equality for blacks: he seemed at once to believe that socialists recognized the social equality of blacks and also claimed that blacks were socially inferior.[39]

Du Bois' "socialism" was designed to enable groups discriminated against to achieve equality. And his faith in equality (after the decline of the doctrine of the Talented Tenth) was built upon the view that talent had been, to a large degree, a matter of chance. To drive home the point Du Bois recounted the life of a great black composer-conductor, Samuel Coleridge-Taylor. Only through luck was he able to obtain the kind of training he needed. Du Bois remarked that what this man was able to achieve in Europe, with the help of chance, would have been even more improbable in America. Du Bois drew the socially significant conclusion: "We have a right to assume that hundreds and thousands of boys and girls today are missing the chance of developing unusual talents because the chances have been against them; and that indeed the majority of the children of the world are not being systematically fitted for their life work and for life itself."[40] Thus while many seem incapable of enjoying freedom unless others are "slaves," what he thought we really need is a maximum of human freedom and a minimum of human slavery for all.

Egalitarianism does not deny human differences; it denies that human differences deserve different social rewards. Human differences would perhaps be greater with Du Bois' brand of socialism because all would be allowed to attain their optimum development. This means more attention should be given to education and less to the activities that further degrade human beings.[41] Du Bois summarized his attitude:

> Today we are forcing men into educational
> slavery in order that others may enjoy
> life, and excuse ourselves by saying

the world's work must be done. We
are degrading some sorts of work by
honoring others, and then expressing surprise that most people object
to having their children trained
solely in their father's tasks.

Given as the ideal the utmost
possible freedom for every human
soul, with slavery for none, and
equal honor for all necessary
human tasks, then our problem of
education is greatly simplified:
we aim to develop human souls; to
make all intelligent; to discover
special talents and genius.[42]

The period being examined in this chapter, however,
was not completely devoid of a role for the talented.
The path toward equality involved development because
inequality, with its deprecating consequences, had
long prevailed. The talented were to use their gifts
to help bring about a maximum development for all. In
one of his infrequent references to the "Talented
Tenth," in this time period, Du Bois called for such a
group to labor toward economic opportunity: "It is our
duty then, not drastically but persistently to seek out
colored children of ability and genius, to open up to
them broader, industrial opportunity and, above all, to
find that Talented Tenth and encourage it by the best
and most exhaustive training in order to supply the
Negro Race and the world with leaders, thinkers and
artists.[43] This 1915 statement seems to fix talent in
a special and perhaps permanent social role, whereas
later on talent was either used solely to bring about
equality or it was made an end in itself without special institutional roles. The period covered in this
chapter is long, and so it is not surprising to see
a gradual development toward egalitarianism and to find
some carry-over, early in the period, from the views
partially dominated by the cultural elitism of "The
Conservation of Races."

The interpretation may be used to explain Du Bois'
answer to an inquiry by a college student about his use
of the "Talented Tenth." Apparently recognizing the
relative absence of the term from Du Bois' later writings the student asked, "Do you still believe that
special attention to the 'Talented Tenth' . . . is the

best method of approach to the task of improving race relations between whites and blacks in America?" Du Bois answered the letter:

> If I were writing today about 'Talented Tenth' I would still believe in the main thesis but I should make rather different emphasis. When I wrote in 1903 I assumed that educated persons especially among American Negroes would do two things: first, devote their main energy and talent to the uplift of the mass of the people; and secondly, recognize that their talent was not exceptional but should be continually enforced and increased by the talent among the masses. . . .
>
> Of course those two assumptions cannot be made at any time or among any people with complete assurance. Talented Negroes like other human beings are going to produce a large number of selfish and self-seeking persons who will not work for the best interests of the masses of the people. Secondly, there is always the temptation to assume that the few people who have gotten education and opportunity are the only ones who are capable or worthy of reaching the heights. As a matter of fact there is at least ten times as much talent undeveloped as there is in process of development."[44]

This statement, while starting with an apparent acceptance of his old doctrine, goes on to criticize it in line with the analysis above--that is that talent has a role, but without the connotation of a special class of persons. And his newer egalitarian emphasis is underscored by his reference to "at least ten times as much talent" in an undeveloped form. In his early writing the Talented Tenth formed a class--now ten times that, even allowing for hyperbole, makes nonsense of the notion of a Talented Tenth.

In _Darkwater_, his egalitarianism implies sexual
equality. In a moving chapter, "The Damnation of
Women," he examined, through the lives of four women,
what this sort of discrimination entailed. He believed
women should lead a life of economic independence, and
should be able to freely choose motherhood. This he
opposed to the _de facto_ status of women in 1920: "Only
at the sacrifice of intelligence and the chance to do
their best work can the majority of modern women bear
children. This is the damnation of women."[45]

So far we have touched on two of the campaigns in
Darkwater, racial and sexual equality. The third is
related and joins the others, for Du Bois, as the major
problems of the world: "The uplift of woman is, next
to the problem of the color line and the peace movement, our greatest modern cause."[46] In 1920 Du Bois
was very nearly a pacifist. He described war as murder
with an overriding economic intention. After calling
history economic history, Du Bois claimed that the main
business of dominant economic interests is war.[47] A
theme in Du Bois' writings from 1920 on is that this
war-business accrued from the attempt to make economic
gain on the backs of colonial subjects. Europe attained its apogee, he claimed, by thriving, through conquest, off the wealth, religion, political structure,
art and science of Africa, Asia and the Mediterranean
shores.[48] The use of colonial lands eventually became
a way to deal with European labor, which was unwilling
to suffer the sort of subsistance life Marx believed
to result from the economic laws of capitalism.
Through the exploitation of black labor at an exorbitant
rate, white European labor could receive a greater return on their labor; the conquest and colonization of
Africa was intended for profit, to be shared between
labor and capital. But the cost of such a conquest
was war: "The cause of war is preparation for war;
and of all that Europe had done in a century there is
nothing that has equaled in energy, thought, and time
her preparation for wholesale murder. The only adequate cause of this preparation was conquest and conquest, not in Europe, but primarily among the darker
peoples of Asia and Africa. . . ."[49]

In 1915 Du Bois laid out the scenario of war. The
attempt to gain wealth from Africa led to agreements
between Europeans to divide up colonial lands. As a
case of this Du Bois pointed to the Berlin Conference
of 1884, in which Germany gained control over seven

million Africans.[50] The brutal methods of control were not essentially different, he claimed, from the methods used by Great Britain, Portugal, France, Italy and Spain. Gradually, increasing areas of Africa came under European control. Again he insisted that exploitation of Africa was linked to the demands of European labor. This in turn built up patriotic ties that linked capital and labor and allowed for a united, national war effort: "Their national bond is no mere sentimental patriotism, loyalty or ancester-worship. It is increased wealth, power, and luxury for all classes on a scale the world never saw before."[51] The problem leading to European wars was that the wealth in Africa (which Du Bois thought was increasing[52]) was limited and rivalries over it developed between nations. This was especially important because many European nations exploited Africa when other areas were unaccessible. Asia was protected by the Asiatics and the Monroe Doctrine marked off South America.[53] He concluded: "The present world war is, then, the result of jealousies engendered by the recent rise of armed national associations of labor and capital whose aim is the exploitation of the wealth of the world mainly outside the European circle of nations."[54] The problem was exacerbated by an internal movement to keep labor in line by the threat to export capital (needed to maintain employment at home) to foreign lands. These threats engendered suspicion and hostilities among other nations, who viewed investment in foreign lands with suspicion.[55]

The same line of argument was presented in Darkwater: World War I "was primarily the jealous and avaricious struggle for the largest share in exploiting darker races."[56] This exploitation resulted in higher wages for European and American labor, and this required a huge capital investment in Africa and other colonized lands. And indeed the trade with Africa was extensive: "Annually $200,000,000 worth of goods was coming out of black Africa before the World War, including a third of the world's supply of rubber, a quarter of all of the world's cocoa, and practically all of the world's cloves, gum-arabic, and palm-oil."[57]

Africa also served as a market for processed goods. Du Bois viewed this activity as an attempt to build a permanent and modern industrial system designed for the benefit of non-Africans, and with the result of turning Africans into slaves.[58]

He proposed that, following a victory by the
Allies, granting Africa full independence should be
initiated by giving the German colonies their independence, thus freeing a million square miles and a
half million Africans. This would provide a small and
stable nucleus, relatively easily guided toward independence. Following this, other colonies such as those
occupied by Portugal and Belgium, could be freed.
England should soon follow by granting independence or
by working toward giving colonial nations an independent status "with a full voice in the British Imperial
Government."[59]

From all of this, the general condemnation of war
and the emphasis on the African roots of war, the
impression is that Du Bois would refuse to take sides
and simply reject any war effort of the United States;
but this did not happen. The hope he maintained was
that good could come out of World War I. That the war
raged was obvious; he seemed to want to make the best
of it. So he evaluated the past performances of various countries vis-a-vis their colonies. England and
France came out the fairest and the most capable of
change. (Again, we see a moralist note as opposed to
a pure economic view; on the other hand, this occurred
in 1915, early in Du Bois' move toward economic determinism.) Germany was characterized as "the most barbarous of any civilized people and grows worse instead
of better."[60] So he argued that if the Allies won,
the colonial nations would be at least as well off as
they were and perhaps things would even get better.

The hope that fighting in World War I would bring
blacks to a recognized equal status with whites extended, with more of a wish than good evidence, to the
United States: "Out of this war will rise . . . an
American Negro, with the right to work and the right
to live without insult. These things may not come out
at once; but they are written in the stars, and the
first step toward them is victory for the armies of
the allies."[61]

With this in support, Du Bois, in an editorial in
The Crisis, July 1918, called for American blacks to
support the Allies, against the Germans. In his famous
"close-ranks" appeal he asked, "Let us not hesitate.
Let us, while this war lasts, forget our special griev-
ances and close our ranks shoulder to shoulder with our
white fellow citizens and the allied nations that are

fighting for democracy."[62]

After the war ended, he set out to investigate the treatment black American soldiers received while in the Armed Forces. His conclusion, backed by detailed evidence,[63] was that black soldiers suffered serious and systematic discrimination and abuse. This signaled a disillusionment with the war and with its hoped for lessons: "A nation with a great disease set out to rescue civilization; it took the disease with it in virulent form and that disease of race-hatred and prejudice hampered its actions. . . ."[64]

Furthermore, hoped-for colonial reform did not come about. So in 1940 he looked back with regret over his "close ranks" appeal. His anti-war sympathies, although abridged at key times, seem on the whole to dominate. "I am less sure now than then of the soundness of this war attitude. I did not realize the full horror of war and its wide importance as a method of social reform. Perhaps, despite words, I was thinking narrowly of the interest of my group and was willing to let the world go to hell, if the black man went free. Today, I do not know; and I doubt if the triumph of Germany in 1918 could have worse results than the triumph of the Allies. Possibly passive resistance of my twelve millions to any war activity might have saved the world for black and white."[65]

IV

The view on war and peace, in Darkwater and other writings that fall around the middle of the period we are examining, was one of ambivalence. War was an evil, but other situations appeared to be even worse. The struggle with developing a policy toward warfare can be seen several years earlier in Du Bois' biography of John Brown, is, in part, an account of the beginnings of the Civil War. John Brown,[66] however, is a work which rests between the early years and the activist years, so while it is instructive in terms of his feelings toward war, its consideration in this chapter is partly out of place. Du Bois did view John Brown as one of his finest pieces, so it shall, nevertheless, be considered here.

John Brown (1909) is structured after Du Bois' early view of what he considered to be involved in writing good history. That is, it must be a work in

89

morality as well as in history, Thus in <u>John Brown</u> he asked moral questions: How can "force and violence . . . bring peace and good will?"[67] And, "If we are human, we must . . . hesitate until we know the right. How shall we know it? That is the "Riddle of the Sphinx."[68] And he came to the moral conclusion "that all men are created free and equal, and that the cost of liberty is less than the price of repression."[69] Thus he maintained something of a moral point of view, although without the moralizing tone of his earlier works, even after he began to accept economic determinism. That, indeed, is one of the problems of economic determinism, even in Marx. To what extent is an influencing force consistent with morally free action? Although Marx rejected "morality" as a tool of class domination, his writings are saturated with moral indignation over such things as the conditions of the working class in nineteenth century England. And his writings against what he considered to be utopian socialists only seems to make sense if we assume the ability to change in a conscious way, from mistaken to correct views. Such an ability to guide our own actions is at the core of the notion of moral responsibility.

While Du Bois continued to use moral discourse, the shift to an economic determinism came with a change in the type of moral evaluation made. That is, his moral injunctions once on the personal level, even including such things as personal hygiene, increasingly shifted toward broad social issues and away from talk of personal moral fibre of groups of people. Moral injunctions became related to functions of persons, as in their relations to the economic systém, rather than being related to personal worth.

While <u>John Brown</u> shows continuity with the <u>Suppression</u>, it centers around his ambivalence toward violence, as evidenced in Du Bois' attitudes towards World War I. But further, in <u>John Brown</u> he did, for the only time, draw specific conclusions about general and explicit moral principles reflecting on the problem of war.

The answer Du Bois offered to the "Riddle of the Sphinx" is a kind of ethical pragmatism stressing points of agreement among pluralistic views. Beliefs about the basic principles of morality vary from the principle that the good is what God orders to the utilitarian principle that the good is that which con-

tributes the greatest happiness to the greatest number.
Du Bois attempted to overlook such diversity on general
moral principles by concluding that there are "matters
of vast human import which are eternally right or
eternally wrong, [which] all men believe."[70] That is,
all reasonable people can agree that some particular
things are right or wrong. But in most cases answers
to moral questions are not simple because there is
right and wrong on both sides. So

> . . . life morality becomes always a
> wavering path of expediency, not
> necessarily the best or the worst
> path . . . but a good path, a safe
> path, a path of little resistance
> and one that leads to the good if
> not to the theoretical (but usually
> impracticable) best. . . . And yet
> we all feel its temporary, tentative
> character; we instinctively distrust
> its comfortable tone, and listen
> almost fearfully for the greater
> voice; its better is often so far
> below that which we feel is a
> possible best, that its present
> temporizing seems evil to us, and
> ever and again after the world has
> complacently dodged and compromised
> with, and skillfully evaded a great
> evil, there shines suddenly, a great
> white light--an unwavering, unflicker-
> ing brightness, blinding by its all-
> seeing brilliance, making the whole
> world simply a light and a darkness--
> a right and a wrong.[71]

To Du Bois, John Brown was such a light, claiming,
simply, "Slavery is wrong . . . kill it." Slavery
was one of those things that was simply wrong. "And
this men knew. They had known it a hundred years."[72]
Here is the sequel, in John Brown, to a hundred years
of compromise with evil documented in the Suppression;
a man who refused to compromise, no matter what the
cost. John Brown, in effect commenting on the lack of
justice in social institutions, claimed: '"Gentlemen,
I consider the Golden Rule and the Declaration of
Independence one and inseparable; and it is better that
a whole generation of men, women and children should
be swept away than that this crime of slavery should

91

exist one day longer.'"73

Du Bois took the opportunity of recounting Brown's hatred of slavery to condemn the institution as "the foulest and filthiest blot on nineteenth century civilization."74 And making the claim that four things make life worth living--movement, knowledge, love and aspiration--he added, "None of these was for the Negro slaves."75 Slaves themselves had three main options: to submit, fight or flee. To fight alone meant death and even in groups, although often tried, was futile. The easiest path was to flee through the underground railrod, which Brown aided.

Slave insurrections, like that of Nat Turner, began to take Brown's attention away from his every-day concerns and increased his boyhood dislike of slavery to the point of an all-out resistance--still, in 1839, a nonviolent resistance. He gradually turned to violence; Du Bois realized that precise reason for the change remained inaccessible: "Human purposes grow slowly and in curious ways; thought by thought they build themselves until in their full panoplied vigor and definite outline not even the thinker can tell the exact process of the growing, or say that here was the beginning or there the ending."76 Brown's passive resistance ended in 1855 when it began to appear as if Kansas would become a slave state. John Brown with four sons, a son-in-law and two others, killed five pro-slavery "border ruffians who were harrying the free state settlers. . . ."77 The result of the eventual battle initiated by Brown was that Kansas became free. The result of the eventual battle initiated by Brown was that Kansas became free. In ways that correspond to his reasons for his eventual support for World War I, Du Bois observed: "Free because the slave barons played for an imperial stake in defiance of modern humanity and economic development. Free because strong men had suffered and fought not against slavery but against slaves in Kansas. Above all, free because one man hated slavery and on a terrible night rode down with his sons among the Swamp of the Swan. . . ."78

The writing of John Brown came around the time of the founding of the Niagara Movement. The second meeting of that movement took place at Harper's Ferry, the site of John Brown's final raid. Du Bois realized at this time that knowledge was not the answer to social problems. In fact, part of the reason for calling the

92

movement was to counter the politics of Booker T. Washington, who used his power, thought Du Bois, to control the flow of information. Information and political power were thus connected; the reliance on information alone was futile. He began his conversion to action by invoking the memory of a man who had undergone analogous conversion. Yet Du Bois drew back from accepting the efficacy of violence. He joined in the resolution of the group at Harper's Ferry: "We do not believe in violence, neither the despised violence of the raid nor lauded violence of the soldier, nor the barbarous violence of the mob; but we do believe in John Brown, in the incarnate spirit of justice, that hatred of a lie, that willingness to sacrifice money, reputation, and life itself on the altar of right. And here on the scene of John Brown's martyrdom, we reconsecrate ourselves, our honor, our property to the final emancipation of the race which John Brown died to make free."[79]

Although he did not take on the violent path of John Brown, his was also a conversion to action. Brown shifted from non-violent resistance to violent strife. Du Bois changed from academic life to the life of public leadership. His book about Brown can be seen as a confirmation and admonition toward such a shift as required to solve the problems of black America. Brown represents the path of noncompromise and by recounting his life, Du Bois showed that passive roles are compromising roles.

After his conversion to violence, but before his raid on Harper's Ferry, John Brown attempted to enlist the aid of Frederick Douglass, but Douglass did not agree with Brown's attempts, believing that only national force could destroy slavery and knowing well the cost to any blacks who participated. Du Bois believed Brown's plan would have worked with full support of blacks; however, this he claimed, could not have been known at that time.[80] So with the minimum support of a small band of twenty-two men, including five or six blacks, on October 17, 1859, Brown captured the town and arsenal at Harper's Ferry. Those in his band, after bloody battle, were finally killed or captured, and on December 2, 1859, John Brown was executed.

Du Bois interpreted John Brown's raid as the single, most important event leading to the Civil War:

93

"The raid aroused and directed the conscience of the nation . . . A great throb of sympathy arose and swept the world. That John Brown was legally a lawbreaker and a murderer all men knew. But wider and wider circles were beginning dimly and more clearly to recognize that his lawlessness was in obedience to the highest call of self-sacrifice for the welfare of his fellow men."[81]

Various factors prompted Brown to action: a natural sympathy for his fellow men, underscored by religious conviction about responsibility, justice, and equality and sympathy with poverty. "And on all this was built John Brown's own inchoate but growing belief in a more just and a more equal distribution of property. From this he concluded--and acted on that conclusion--that all men are created free and equal, and that the cost of liberty is less than the price of repression."[82]

Relying on Brown's commitment to mutual aid, Du Bois scored the social Darwinists who interpreted Darwin's scientific work as positing essential and inevitable inequality, and the central role of struggle resulting in the survival of the strong. The role of the strong had been assigned to white Europeans with other races doomed to suffering and poverty. But Du Bois pointed to evidence that blacks have made great social strides even against almost overwhelming odds of adversity.

Instead of the prevalent interpretation of Darwinian evolution Du Bois offered an álternate view: Evolution and survival of the fittest suggested the idea of contributing to a group for group endurance. This social advance and freedom were on a far larger scale than a narrow individualistic freedom. "Freedom has come to mean not individual caprice or aberration, but social self-realization in an endless chain of selves; and freedom for such development is not the denial but the central assertion of the evolutionary theory. So, too, the doctrine of human equality passes through the fire of scientific inquiry, not obliterated but transfigured: not equality of present attainment but equality of opportunity, for unbounded future attainment is the rightful demand of mankind."[83] Freedom meant group development in the indefinite future.

White hegemony threatened such development because it proposed the rule of greed and degradation. "(I)t essays to make the slums of white society in all cases and under all circumstances the superior of any colored group, no matter what its ability or culture."[84] Du Bois claimed this had not succeeded, even with overwhelming superiority of arms, to control the world. In the South people claimed that the dropping of racial barriers "means contamination of blood and lowering of ability and culture."[85] The same sort of argument was used when class distinctions among whites were rigidly drawn in America; when these class boundaries on the whole were loosened, the result was increased ability and strength. In effect, equality of opportunity (left undefined by Du Bois) and democratic freedom "allow the best to rise in their rightful place."[86] And he added that with vertically drawn racial distinctions one faces an even greater division than with horizontally drawn class lines and thereby allows fewer chances for human betterment.

Du Bois' analysis of social Darwinism and class and racial distinctions tend to put John Brown in the category with his writings on the Talented Tenth, such as his early "The Conservation of Races." These works reject discrimination in its negative aspects while affirming a class distinction based on talent (instead of social condition). John Brown uses a similar "Darwinian" approach by claiming that competition allows the best to assume a rightful class position, and this position was seen as contributing to group advance. But this approach is muted by an otherwise strong appeal to equality of opportunity. So the work seems to stand as transitional, midway between the ideal of the Talented Tenth and the egalitarianism of Darkwater.

In attempting to show cause for eliminating social class barriers, Du Bois did not merely appeal to a benevolent Darwinism, but also contended that the world was growing smaller and that the darker people of the world, as they increasingly gain power, will use their power to fight against repression. "The price of repression will then be hypocrisy and slavery and blood."[87] He then asked what John Brown's message would be for people in 1909:

> . . . it is this great word: the cost
> of liberty is less than the price of
> repression. The price of repression

of the world's darker races is shown
in a moral retrogression and an economic waste unparalleled since the
age of the African slave-trade. What
would be the cost of liberty? What
would be the cost of giving the great
stocks of mankind every reasonable
help and incentive to self-development--
opening the avenues of opportunity
freely, spreading knowledge, suppressing war and cheating, and treating men
and women as equals the world over
whenever and wherever they attain
equality? It would cost something. It
would cost something in pride and
prejudice, for eventually a white man
would be blacking black men's boots;
but this cost we may ignore. . . .[88]

Du Bois also considered the exploitation that
occurred in the industrial system. He labeled as false
the claim that without exploitation production with
high efficiency could not be maintained. While advance
built on exploitation may increase production the real
cost of such production then becomes too great to bear:
"We have here a wonderful industrial machine, but a
machine quickly rather than carefully built, formed
of forcing rather than of growth, involving sinful and
unnecessary expense. Better smaller production and
more equitable distribution; and better fewer miles of
railways and more honor, truth and liberty; better
fewer millionaires and more contentment."[89] Du Bois'
sense of justice rebelled against the overriding demands
of efficiency.

The question remaining is, where did Du Bois stand
on violence? The book is about a violent movement and
a violent man, and seems to vindicate both. But he
drew back from an endorsement of such violence. "The
cost of liberty is thus a decreasing cost, while the
cost of repression even tends to increase to the danger
point of war and revolution. Revolution is not a test
of capacity; it is always a loss and a lowering of
ideals."[90] Yet the message seems to be that a major
compromise with evil leads to a John Brown. During
this period Du Bois equivocated over violence and war,
(as was the case throughout most of his life), striking
a pacifist tone, yet supporting World War I. And in
John Brown we find support for a violent movement, but

the support is reluctant.

V

John Brown ends by linking the treatment of blacks
in America to European exploitation of Africa. Even
in this early work, the theme of economic exploitation
surfaces much more strongly than in the early years.
The new concept of race seems to be in its initial
stages of development. A main implication of the new
concept is the clear link between Africans and Afro-
Americans, a link which led him to be increasingly
concerned with Africa and the Pan-African movement.
In 1915 Du Bois published his first study of Africa,
The Negro.[91] Designed to begin to counter the then
existing ignorance, fostered by prejudice, of the
history of the African continent, most of the book
deals with the geography, history and culture of Africa.
But in a Pan-African spirit, he included sections on
Black America and the slavery experience. The work
announces a coming Pan-African movement, built from
the tendency toward "a unity of the working classes
everywhere, a unity of the colored races, a new unity
of men."[92] Thus, Du Bois explicitly drew the status of
all labor to the status of black labor. As noted above,
he believed that European labor was being "bought off"
by increased wages at the expense of the super-exploitation of colonial people. What this meant was that
white European labor, although somewhat better paid,
remained exploited and without real justice and political power. So he claimed blacks were beginning to
say to these workers that, "so long as black laborers
are slaves, white laborers cannot be free."[93]

The Negro ends with the claim that a strong international brotherhood among blacks was slowly gathering
force. With their economic position as exploited, yet
being nonexploiters, Du Bois began to see for blacks a
role like that Marx envisioned for the proletariat:
that group became the major hope for a non-exploitative
world. Thus, "Most men in this world are colored. A
belief in humanity means a belief in colored men. The
future world will, in all reasonable probability, be
what colored men make it."[94]

Du Bois' involvement in the Pan-African movement
became increasingly intense. Ignoring the first Pan-
African Congress, he claimed in 1919 that the Pan-
African movement started after World War I ended when

97

the question of African reapportionment became crucial.
In February of the same year, Du Bois organized the
Second Pan-African Congress, convened in Paris, with 57
representatives from 15 to 16 countries. The Peace
Conference was simultaneously meeting, partly to resolve
the question of the disposition of Africa after the
defeat of Germany. He believed that the major powers
would welcome advice on this difficult question,[95]
and thus the Congress presented a list of resolutions,
mainly general in tone, to the Peace Conference. These
resolutions called for African control of Africa, for
equality, non-exploitation and the elmination of slavery (forced labor). They demanded the right of self-
representation, basic education, medical care, religious and cultural freedom, and equitable representation in the League of Nations.[96]

In the Manifesto of the Second Pan-African Congress, he assailed the actions of colonial powers toward natives and again struck the theme that present
conditions resulted from economic exploitation. The
unequal distribution of wealth in the world was condemned and international co-operation in government,
industry, and art was demanded.[97] The war experience,
with its horrors, suggested that the needed world
improvement would only come with genuine, international
respect: "This is a world of man, of men whose likenesses far outweigh their differences; who mutually
need each other in labor and thought and dream, but
who can successfully have each other only on terms of
equality, justice and mutual respect. They are the
real and only peacemakers who work sincerely and
peacefully to this end."[98]

The Third Pan-African Congress met in London,
Paris, and Lisbon in 1923. This meeting was less
successful than the 1919 Congress. A Fourth Pan-
African Congress was held in New York in 1927. In
1933, he urged American blacks to view their position
as linked to that of all other blacks. The unifying
theme is once again the common bond of discrimination.[99]
But Du Bois' faith that American blacks would generally adopt Pan-African sentiments and support the development of Africa proved mistaken.

VI

In 1934 Du Bois' editorship of The Crisis ended
in less than ideal circumstances. At this time he

98

was outwardly insisting on a form of segregation for blacks, a black economic cooperative in the United States. This caused antipathy among the Board of Directors of the N.A.A.C.P. On June 11, 1934, Du Bois resigned, claiming that the organization must recognize the need for a separate development, and that the organization lacked effective and purposive leadership. He claimed he had little influence with the office and did not wish to use The Crisis in a way that looked as though he "was washing dirty linen in public."[100]

As Editor of The Crisis Du Bois increasingly moved to a specific program for social action in the black community. He proposed the development of a segregated economic cooperative of world wide dimensions. The program falls within a socialist framework, and is, in effect, a rejection of a full Marxism. His plan was most fully presented in Dusk of Dawn in 1940. Between the time he left the N.A.A.C.P., and the publication of Dusk of Dawn, Du Bois sharpened his modified Marxism through the writing of what may be his greatest historical work, Black Reconstruction in America, 1860-1880.[101] The following chapter examines his "Marxian" account of Reconstruction, and his plan for a black economic cooperative.

NOTES

1. W.E.B. Du Bois, Dusk of Dawn: An Essay Toward an Autobiography of a Race Concept (New York: Schocken Books, 1968), p. 47.

2. Ibid., p. 41.   3. Ibid., p. 51.

4. Ibid., p. 53.

5. W.E. Burghardt Du Bois, "My Evolving Program for Negro Freedom," in Rayford W. Logan (ed.), What the Negro Wants (Chapel Hill, N.C., University of North Carolina Press, 1944), p. 53.

6. Du Bois, Dusk of Dawn, pp. 67-68.

7. Ibid., pp. 85-86.

8. Rampersad, The Art and Imagination of W.E.B. Du Bois, p. 912.

99

9. Du Bois, Dusk of Dawn, pp. 88-89.

10. Ibid., p. 95.   11. Ibid., p. 94.

12. Ibid., p. 303.

13. W.E.B. Du Bois, The Autobiography of W.E.B. Du
    Bois (New York: International Publishers, 1968),
    p. 290.

14. Karl Marx, The Poverty of Philosophy (New York:
    International Publishers, 1963), p. 109.

15. Karl Marx and Friedrich Engels, The German Ideology,
    Parts I and III (New York: International Publish-
    ers, 1947), pp. 14-15.

16. W.E.B. Du Bois, Darkwater (New York: Schocken
    Books, 1969), p. 32.

17. Du Bois, Dusk of Dawn, p. 6.

18. Ibid., p. 116.   19. Ibid., p. 117.

20. Ibid., p. 133.

21. Du Bois, Darkwater, p. 98.

22. Du Bois, Dusk of Dawn, p. 217.

23. Friedrich Engels, Herr Eugen Dühring's Revolution
    in Science (Anti-Dühring) (New York: International
    Publishers, 1939), p. 292.

24. Karl Marx and Friedrich Engels, The Communist
    Manifesto (New York: Appleton-Century-Crofts,
    1955), n.p.9.

25. Du Bois, Darkwater, pp. 136-137.

26. Ibid., p. 138.   27. Ibid.

28. Ibid.   29. Ibid., p. 139.

30. Ibid., pp. 142-143.   31. Ibid., pp. 143-144.

32. Ibid., p. 149.   33. Ibid., p. 150.

34. Ibid., p. 100.   35. Ibid., p. 104.

36. Du Bois, Autobiography, p. 168.

37. W.E.Burghardt Du Bois, "Negro and Socialism," Horizon, I (1907), p. 8.

38. Du Bois, New Leader, Febuary 9, 1929. Quoted in Foner, American Socialism and Black Americans, p. 357.

39. Foner, p. 111.

40. Du Bois, Darkwater, p. 205.

41. Ibid., p. 212.   42. Ibid., pp. 207-208.

43. W.E.B. Du Bois, "The Immediate Program of the American Negro," The Crisis, XI (April, 1915), p. 312.

44. Du Bois, Correspondence, Vol. III, pp. 131-132.

45. Du Bois, Darkwater, p. 164.

46. Ibid., p. 181.   47. Ibid., p. 37.

48. Ibid., p. 40.   49. Ibid., p. 46.

50. W.E.B. Du Bois, "The African Roots of War," (1915), in Julius Lester, ed., The Seventh Son: The Thought and Writings of W.E.B. Du Bois (2 Vols.) (New York: Random House, 1971), I, p. 453.

51. Ibid., p. 456.   52. Ibid., pp. 457-458.

53. Ibid., p. 458.   54. Ibid.

55. Ibid., p. 459.

56. Du Bois, Darkwater, p. 49.

57. Ibid., p. 63.   58. Ibid., p. 64.

59. Ibid., p. 67.

60. W.E.B. Du Bois, "World War and the Color Line," (1914), in Lester, The Seventh Son, II, p. 67.

61. W.E.B. Du Bois, "The Black Soldier," (1918), in Lester, The Seventh Son, II, pp. 72-73.

62. W.E.B. Du Bois, "Close Ranks," (1918), in Lester, The Seventh Son, II, p. 73.

63. See Lester, The Seventh Son, II, pp. 107-115.

64. W.E.B. Du Bois, "An Essay Toward a History of the Black Man in the Great War," (1919), in Lester, The Seventh Son, II, p. 156.

65. Du Bois, Dusk of Dawn, p. 255.

66. W.E. Burghardt Du Bois, John Brown (New York: International Publishers, 1962).

67. Ibid., p. 5.   68. Ibid., p. 338.

69. Ibid., p. 375.   70. Ibid., p. 339.

71. Ibid., pp. 339-340.   72. Ibid., pp. 340-341.

73. Ibid., p. 210.   74. Ibid., p. 76.

75. Ibid., p. 77.   76. Ibid., p. 93.

77. Ibid., p. 139.   78. Ibid., p. 143.

79. Du Bois, Dusk of Dawn, p. 92.

80. Du Bois, John Brown, p. 345.

81. Ibid., pp. 355-356.   82. Ibid., p. 375.

83. Ibid., p. 379.   84. Ibid., p. 380.

85. Ibid., p. 382.   86. Ibid.

87. Ibid., p. 383.   88. Ibid., pp. 383-384.

89. Ibid., p. 394.   90. Ibid., p. 395.

91. W.E. Burghardt Du Bois, The Negro (Oxford: Oxford University Press, 1970).

92. Ibid., p. 145.   93. Ibid., p. 146.

94. Ibid.

95. W.E.B. Du Bois, "My Mission" (1919), in Lester, The Seventh Son, II, p. 198.

96. W.E.B. Du Bois and Blaise Diagne, "The Pan-African Congress" (1919), in Lester, The Seventh Son, II, pp. 193-195.

97. Du Bois, "Manifesto of the Second Pan-African Congress" (1921), in Lester, The Seventh Son, II, p. 205.

98. Ibid., p. 201.

99. W.E.B. Du Bois, "Pan-Africa and New Racial Philosophy" (1933), in Lester, The Seventh Son, II, p. 206.

100. W.E.B. Du Bois, "Letter of Resignation from the N.A.A.C.P.," in Lester, The Seventh Son, II, p. 259.

101. W.E.B. Du Bois, Black Reconstruction in America: An Essay Toward a History of the part which Black Folk Played in the Attempt to Reconstruct Democracy in America, 1860-1880 (New York: Atheneum, 1970).

CHAPTER IV

BLACK RECONSTRUCTION

Black Reconstruction in America (1935)[1] best shows
Du Bois' relation to Marxism in the thirties. In it he
accepted much of the Marxian perspective and he rejected
or modified some significant doctrines. He took a
Marxian view of the determining effects of economic
conditions, but he added the notion of race as a factor
that often militates against the Marxian economic class
interest theory. This means that the notion of class
revolution is ineffective in ways that suggest the need
for a racially-oriented "revolution." Black Reconstruction is most important as a guide to Du Bois' basic
social thought in this period.

There are four main theoretical points:

(1) Throughout the work he approached the problems
of historical interpretation from a Marxian perspective.
Du Bois viewed the Civil War and the subsequent Reconstruction period as resulting from the clash of economic
systems and interests. The South was portrayed as a
quasi-feudal system, antithetical both in temperament
and in political motivation to the interests and demands
of the rising power of Northern industry.

(2) Du Bois focused on economic class interests,
both in the North and in the South, in an attempt both
to demonstrate the possibilities of a victorious,
unified proletariat movement in the South and to portray
the national and international implications of such a
movement.

(3) But his position was at odds with Marxism:
(a) The political and economic co-operation of Northern
industry was required to support Reconstruction; paradoxically, the political power of Reconstruction
governments was considered by him as an experiment in a
Marxian dictatorship of the proletariat. (b) At key
points he enlisted the support of moral imperatives (as
opposed to economical interests) as a prime motive behind the abolition movement. (c) The class structure
Du Bois used is more complex than Marx was willing to
admit. The concept of race, in Black Reconstruction,
takes a central role; although race was formed, as a
social category, from economic conditions, its tenacity
was further generated by a racist, partly subconscious,

cultural milieu. Such a subconscious environment maintained no such central role in Marx.

(4) The conclusions of Black Reconstruction tended to support Du Bois' reliance on a black economic co-operative movement. In it he attempted to document the failure of a truly democratic movement in the United States. The attempt to establish democracy through Reconstruction governments, in Du Bois' view, failed and failed in a pernicious way because power became concentrated in the hands of a most powerful "dictator"--the dictatorship of an expanding Northern capital.

On the whole, the book is a radical critique of the American political and industrial system. It is a critique in which race plays a central role, but it goes well beyond race, such that the system is condemned as a suitable environment for all labor. Black Reconstruction is pivotal in the change of Du Bois' social criticism from what was mainly a critique of the role southern blacks occupied in the social structure, to a call for a new industrial system.

The work also stands as an important, innovative historical approach to Reconstruction. In 1909 Du Bois proclaimed to the American Historical Association that the standard view of Reconstruction placed unwarranted blame on blacks and failed to recognize their achievements. His thesis was ignored; the then accepted stance, representing a prejudiced reading of history, continued until the 1940's. Du Bois' work thus stood against this tradition. Kenneth M. Stampp and Leon F. Litwack review this progress from the 1909 proclamation to present day studies:

> . . . Du Bois suggested that the increased tax burden had been necessary. . . , that the amount of corruption had been exaggerated, and that historians had virtually ignored the biracial bipartisan, and bisectional nature of such corruption. This was an extra-ordinary thesis to advance at a time when the Dunning School dominated the writing of Reconstruction history. . . . Some twenty-six years later, when he

published Black Reconstruction in
America, the American Historical
Review and most of the profession
chose to ignore altogether. . . .
In 1939 and 1940, two white
historians, Francis B. Simkins
and Howard K. Beale, called for a
more critical creative and
tolerant attitude toward Reconstruction. But it was not until
after World War II, and with young
scholars leading the way, that the
once cherished myths of Reconstruction were effectively challenged
and the complexities of the period
made much clearer."[2]

Although Du Bois' more sympathetic reading of the
period is supported today, his approach to Reconstruction remains far from full endorsement: he did place
his analysis in a controversial Marxist framework. A
Marxist approach is controversial enough, but the
nature of Du Bois' unusual use of Marx has itself been
the subject of speculation.[3] This puzzlement stems
from a variety of inconsistencies and inappropriate
use of Marxian doctrines which shall be examined in
this chapter.

Also, Du Bois' work has been criticized as
excessive in its visionary portrait of the possibility
of racial harmony and political democracy: Allen W.
Trelease concludes that Du Bois' hope for racial
democracy "was--alas--too utopian."[4]

With a balance viewed of the work's faults and
strengths, it seems safe to agree with Julius Lester
that "Black Reconstruction is one of his important
works. . . . Despite the criticsms, [it] remains the
best work . . . on the period from the black point of
view."[5]

I

From his earliest writings Du Bois insisted that
the presence of blacks in America formed a central
thread in its history and thereby in world history.
Black Reconstruction displays the same motif: It
begins with the claim that the existence of slavery in
the United States served as a perplexing anomaly to

the explicit foundational ideology of equality and
consent. It was not simply the case that slavery was
accepted without realizing the contradiction, but
indeed, efforts were made to rid it from the nation.
In The Suppression Du Bois reacted with moral indignation, but in 1935 he moved, almost entirely, to an
economic perspective. The early stance by the founding
fathers miscalculated the strength of the institution
of slavery because it did not accurately foresee
economic value of the slave.

     With this, in characteristic Marxian style, the
foundation of the conflict was fixed. For Marx, all
social institutions, including the important contours
of social power, were based on economic conditions.
Changing economic conditions created turbulences in
once stable systems. And here the tremendous increases
in the productive power of slave labor caused, in
Du Bois' view, serious conflict.

     Slavery, previously conceived as a dying institu-
tion, revived. But its revival was not without serious
problems. The main problem stemmed from its breach
of two economic systems. Slavery's growth was predicated on advancing manufacturing potential, including
its increased use of the product of the slave. But
this manufacturing system was capitalistic, using wage
labor; its interests were antithetical to the quasi-
feudal slave system.

     The Southern slave society was basically an
agricultural society but one with an exceptional
concentration of the ownership of the factors of production. Seven percent of the land owners, the large
planters, ruled politically and owned three million of
the nearly four million slaves. Their political power
was great, especially since slaves were counted as
three-fifths of a person for representation purposes.
But the political power of the planters was not equalled
by their personal life styles. Du Bois portrayed the
planter class as a kind of spoiled group, seeking
leisure and elaborate living without sufficient regard
to their business. Portrayed as lazy, Du Bois argued
that the planters were subject to price fixing by
northern merchants and manufacturers who, through their
diligence, combined to set the prices of the cotton
crop. He thus claimed that the planter class gave up
any chance to balance the industrial might of the
North. (37) (Numbers in parentheses refer to pages

in Black Reconstruction.)

The South feared the growing power of Northern industry, but according to Du Bois was incapable of responding to it. The course of action that could have abridged the increasing power of the North would have involved an upgrading of labor, black and white, through education, increased wages, industrial regulation, all in line with trends in the North. (38) Such a position would have permitted the modernization of production. But the position of being an owner of other people had its restraints: the status of the slave was rationalized on the grounds that they were incapable of anything but menial work; increased opportunity and political rights would run counter to the rhetoric of black inferiority. And in their lofty position as the "guardians" of culture and civilization, the planters felt neither sympathy nor community with poor whites.

The Northern industrialists tolerated political rights because they understood the changing nature of labor which increasingly demanded a skilled workforce. Appeasement in the North became economically necessary. Yet northern capital also understood the limits, in their own interest, of increased political liberty: "The North had yielded to democracy, but only because democracy was curbed by a dictatorship of property and investment which left in the hands of the leaders of industry such economic power as insured their mastery and their profits. . . . They remained masters of the economic destiny of America." (46) The Southern planter, on the other hand, completely disregarded the interests, both political and economic, not only of the slaves, but of the white masses.

Du Bois' analysis of the movement toward the Civil War followed Marxian lines: the clash was between two differing economic institutions. The South was attempting to preserve a dying economic order while Northern industry viewed the slave system, under the control of the planters, as backward and as a block to progress. Economically, however, the North could not let the South secede. The cotton crop had become too important and the North relied on the South as a market for manufactured goods. So the North ultimately engaged in war not to free slaves, or to keep Western territories as free, but in order to preserve the Southern market. (56)

Du Bois' analysis of the conflicts that paved the way to the Civil War was not limited to the capital owning classes. Black Reconstruction, of course, is tuned mainly to the role of blacks in the period. The mass of blacks before the war were slaves, some 4,000,000 people. Although Du Bois recognized that in some ways the slave was better off than Northern workers, mainly because of the sort security the system offered, providing food, care, old age "insurance," etc., the slave was still, judging from goods received, among the poorest "paid" workers in the world.

The poor whites in the South were by and large victims of the institution of slavery because they were forced to compete with landed monopolies and slave labor. Their economic and hence, by a Marxian analysis, their class interests rested with the abolition of slavery. Yet the poor white South supported the institution. They became, in effect, an armed camp positioned to police the slave population. This provided the means through which the class interests of the Southern poor whites were blunted from their own consciousness. It gave them some work and, through their vanity, made them believe that they had some common bond with planter in distinction to slave. They did not seek to end the system but in their illusion they hoped to become, eventually, part of it as a planter. As a result, "To these Negroes [the poor white] transferred all the dislike and hatred which he had for the whole slave system."(12) This statement indicates a willingness on Du Bois' part to offer psychological hypotheses which Marxists tend to avoid. And it shows that economic class interests did not unite the laboring classes in the South.

The next group Du Bois examined was the abolitionists, whom the conflict between slavery and American ideals produced. They became important in his analysis of Reconstruction and played a role in bringing about the Civil War in terms of adding to the South's perception of the North as a threat. Among their ranks were such important figures as William Lloyd Garrison, Charles Sumner, and Thaddeus Stevens, and they were joined by free blacks such as Frederick Douglass. These people represented what Du Bois calls "abolition-democracy." "The object and only real object of the Civil War in its eyes was the abolition of slavery, and it was convinced that this could be thoroughly accomplished only if the emancipated Negroes

110

became free citizens and voters" (184). Abolition-democracy, then, stood not simply for abolition, but for political rights and eventually for economic protection.

The final group Du Bois considered at length was Northern labor. The most significant features of Northern labor, again in violation of Marxism, were its unwillingness to see itself as a permanent laboring class and its desire to join those who exploit labor. (17) Du Bois thus opposed Marx's position that under capitalism the proletariat was increasingly conscious of their class interests and that this would lead them to rebel and not to an attempt to join in the exploitation.

While this seems to be his considered position, Marx did view class struggles as involving complications. For example, in the third volume of Capital, he wrote, "In England, modern society is indisputedly most highly and classically developed in its economic structure. Nevertheless, even here the stratification of classes does not appear in its pure form. Middle and transition strata even here obliterate lines of demarcation everywhere. . . ."[6] It would appear then that even for Marx the complexities of class structure could hinder consciousness of true interests and class unity. But Marx nowhere recognized the sort of thoroughgoing gap between real and perceived interests Du Bois found in the United States before the Civil War. Marx seemed to see at least a strong tendency toward class unity and an implicit awareness of true interests which would lead to a revolutionary overthrow of the oppressing class. For example, in the Communist Manifesto the proletariat are presented as understanding the falsity of the social "ideologies" urged to oppress them, "Law, morality, religion, are to him so many bourgeois prejudices, behind which lurk in ambush just as many bourgeois interests."[7] Also, the claim was made in the Communist Manifesto that the proletariat will succeed partly because it was aware of its interests: "All previous historical movements were movements of minorities. The proletarian movement is the self-conscious, independent movement of the immense majority, in the interest of the immense majority,"[8] While Marx believed there was a tendency toward self-awareness on the part of the proletariat, Du Bois believed that race indefinitely stalled such a movement. Even though Du Bois diverged from Marx, he retained the vocabulary of exploitation, identifying capital as gaining profits from unpaid labor, and not from entrepreneurship or cleverness. So he did not argue against a Marxian account of real interests, but only against the extent to which these interests were known.

II

According to Du Bois, then, the underlying cause of the Civil War was the presence of the black slave. He considered the slave system as "an oligarchy similar to the colonial imperialism of today, erected on cheap colored labor and raising raw material for manufacture." (237) In this the North had no complaint; the problem leading to war was one of conflicting interests within the scenario of exploitation: "If Northern industry before the war had secured a monopoly of the raw material raised in the South for its new manufactures; and if Northern and Western labor could have maintained their wage scale against slave competition, the North would not have touched the slave system. But this the South had frustrated. It had threatened labor with nation-wide slave competition and had sent its cotton abroad to buy cheap manufactures, and had resisted the protective tariff demanded by the North." (237)

Although Du Bois' interpretation of the origins of the Civil War was weighted toward an economic determinism, he quickly introduced a moral, political factor. Slavery was a moral wrong and a contradiction to democracy. While the moral wrong works its way to national disaster, the fruit of war was the surfacing of freedom. (237) Although this view of the moral dimension of the war recurs, his analysis of the movement of the war lacked any consistent moral thrusts, such as is found in his earlier works. So, the war instead was seen as beginning in economic conflict, with slavery as a moral issue taking a minor role.

But during the course of the war it became increasingly evident that the North had to deal with slaves if it expected to win. At first the slave could be ignored by both sides because both sides expected a short war, if any at all. The North expected whites to fight out of patriotism, especially in a short war; and "the South expected all white men to defend the slaveholders' property." (56) The

South did not expect a revolt among slaves, considering them in a sort of natural position.

But as the war dragged on slaves became a key ingredient to Northern victory: they were used as soldiers in place of unwilling whites, and, by leaving plantations in great numbers, they disrupted the economy of the South. Du Bois called this a "general strike" and believed that it cost a possible victory for the South. It is significant that Du Bois saw this as a strike, as a labor movement. (67) In this way, Du Bois laid claim to the contention that slaves, in contrast to poor Southern whites, understood their position as labor and acted according to that interest.

For Du Bois, the ending of slavery also ended the most glaring contradiction to American democracy. The promise of this was great: "At last democracy was to be justified of its own children. . . . At last there could really be a free common wealth of freemen." (125-6). He thus held the ending of the Civil War as the chance for a new epoch--as the groundwork for a true democracy through the purging of sin. The question of Du Bois' analysis is, Does the promise get fulfilled? Underlying this question is perhaps one more important: In what sense are we to take the promise of a new democracy? In dealing with this question Du Bois returned to the issues of democracy raised in Darkwater.

Beneath the details of the Civil War and Reconstruction runs, for him, a classical philosophical problem in political theory: How much real political and economic control ought to be in the hands of the masses? This is a problem because the masses normally apparently lack those qualifications often seen as necessary to assure the smooth functioning of the political order. The liberated slave was by and large uneducated and illiterate and nearly universally suspect in terms of the ability to independently conduct their own affairs. This was the case even in military service; the general opinion was that the slave was incapable of fighting. Many held that free contract labor was a system to which the slave could not adjust. The problem of democracy underscored by the social status of the slave became, for Du Bois, the most meaningful feature of slavery:

The true significance of slavery

113

in the United States to the whole
social development of America, lay
in the ultimate relation of slaves
to democracy. What were to be the
limits of democratic control in the
United States? If all labor, black
as well as white, became free, were
given schools and the right to vote,
what control could or should be set
to the power and action of these
laborers? Was rule of the mass of
Americans to be unlimited, and the
right to rule extended to all men,
regardless of race and color, or if
not, what power of dictatorship
would rule, and how would property
and privilege be protected? This
was the great and primary question
which was in the minds of the men
who wrote the Constitution of the
United States and continued in the
minds of thinkers down through the
slavery controversy. It still
remains with the world as the
problem of democracy expands and
touches all races and nations. (184)

The examination of Reconstruction was a partial
answer Du Bois gave to the problem: Reconstruction
was viewed as an experiment in democracy, as a test
case in which political rule was to a significant
degree given to the masses. It was only a partial
answer because the alternatives were limited: either
the masses ruled or else, by default, rule would be
left to wealth and not to an elite ruling for the
eventual rule of the masses. Du Bois seemed at times
to accept the latter as the ideal, but short of the
ideal, as reality dictates; the conclusion of the
study of Reconstruction is that the rule even of
illiterate labor is to be preferred to non-democratic
control of wealth.

In this sense, Reconstruction stands as a test of
the doctrine of the "Talented Tenth" as well: it
examines the extent to which the masses, through their
own representatives, can bring about the conditions
for their own betterment: the answer is a rebuke of
his earlier view and underscores his movement toward
a more egalitarian view.

114

The point of Du Bois' history then was to deter-
mine the effectiveness of mass rule and to examine the
methods employed to bring about such a rule. The
conditions in the United States from 1860-1880 were
seen as a model of world-wide arrangements in the
1930's. The position of the freed slave was considered
analogous to the "Third World" in relation to the highly industrialized world. So the extended point of the
study was to provide guidance in a world predominantly
filled with semi-literate and illiterate peasants
struggling for survival. (16)

In his analysis each attempt to educate and
organize the freed slave became a lesson. During the
Civil War the freedmen demonstrated various abilities,
both military and economic. For example, Du Bois
viewed the Freedmen's Bureau as a great success,
especially given the difficult circumstances of its
tenure. The lesson to be learned from the Freedmen's
Bureau supported full democratic participation. As
the Bureau carried out its functions, blacks became
increasingly a part of its operations by exercising
political power through petition and conventions.
"For the first time in history the people of the United
States listened not only to the voices of the Negroes,
friends, but to the Negro himself. He was becoming
more and more articulate, in the South as well as in
the North." (230)

The results of the efforts during the Civil War
to improve the conditions of freedmen were promising.
They also indicated the realities behind the efforts
at democracy. The freed slave was basically politically powerless: the building of democratic participation would, therefore, require external aid. And
that aid, to a great degree, depended on the economic
interests of Northern industrialists. On the other
hand, the moral and political power of abolition-
democrats also stood behind the slaves. But a necessary
condition for bringing these two sides together rested
with the actions and attitudes of the Southern aristocracy.

III

Around the time of the Civil War, Northern industry experienced rapid growth, and with it consolidation
of power in the hands of wealthy manufacturers, merchants and financiers. There were various reasons for

this, including war spending and inflated war currency.
But it was also a period of technological improvement
which added impetus to the consolidation of wealth;
industrial plants became larger and the use of steel
became a basis for the new industrial development.
The hostility between Northern industry and Southern
oligarchy leading to the Civil War, continued after
it, but in the new circumstance of pronounced inequality. While the Civil War witnessed an increase in
the power of Northern industry, it also meant a marked
decline in the power of Southern landowners. Not only
was production in the South grossly curtailed, but
Emancipation meant the loss of human beings counted by
the South as capital.

The surprising event Du Bois found here was that
in spite of new post-war power relations the Southern
oligarchs remained adamant in defiance of Northern
industry. After the war Northern industry expected to
use the South as a source of increased profit "by a
more intelligent exploitation of labor than was possible
under the slave system." (185) If Northern industry,
with its power, got what it wanted, the point seemed
to be that the experiment of Reconstruction would not
have begun. That is, Reconstruction was a reaction
by the North to the recalcitrance of the South after
the Civil War. The South did not accede: "It sought
to reestablish slavery by force, because it had no
comprehension of the means by which modern industry
could secure the advantages of slave labor without
its responsibilities." (185)

The real problem here was political--the political
interests of the North based on their economic needs
demanded a subservient South and rebelled against any
attempt at revised Southern political power:
"When . . . the South went beyond reason and truculently
demanded not simply its old political power but increased political power based on disfranchised
Negroes, . . . Northern industry was frightened and
began to move towards the stand which abolition-democracy had already taken; namely, temporary dictatorship,
endowed Negro education, legal civil rights, and
eventually even votes for Negroes to offset the Southern threat of economic attack." (185)

Du Bois thus set the stage for the ascendency of
Reconstruction: The forces that already favored true
emancipation of the freedmen, namely the abolition-

116

democracy, lacked the power to enforce their wishes.
The institution with power, Northern industry, did not
take a moral interest in the plight of blacks. Du Bois
vigorously characterized it as "the most conscience-
less, unmoral system of industry which the world has
experienced. It went with ruthless indifference towards waste, death, ugliness and disaster, and yet
reared the most stupendous machine for efficient
organization of work which the world has even seen."
(182) Yet Northern industry's interests were threatened; this made the alliance with abolition-democracy
an efficacious, egocentric move. Wealth and conscience united in temporary coalition.

Du Bois' account of the coalition behind Reconstruction involves a serious difficulty. The Reconstruction movement was examined as an experiment in
democracy. It was partly supported by the ideals of
men like Stevens and Summer and it approached, Du Bois
claimed, a test case of a Marxian dictatorship of the
proletariat. Yet behind all of this is the "unmoral"
strength of Northern industry. In short, moral ideal-
ism was put into effect by immoral egoism. There is
no proper a priori criticism of such a tension; but
it does signal a warning. The experiment in democracy
contained the promise of having a foundation which
actually ensured failure from the beginning. Du Bois
disregarded this; his point apparently was that, no
matter what the basis, the experiment did meet the
requirements of proletarian government. While taking
this stand, he clearly recognized its basis, and
showed that failure actually did eventually accrue
from the vicissitude of Northern industry.

IV

The force behind the birth of Reconstruction was
political--its initial success was based upon the
attempt of Northern industry to consolidate its own
growing strength and to strip the Southern oligarchy
of potential political power. But in his characteristically pragmatic manner, Du Bois took consequences
more seriously than initial motivation; so he concentrated on Reconstruction as a test case of democracy
because, despite its foundations, it was a situation
in which the representatives of Southern labor, both
black and white, held real political power. In this
role they wrote state constitutions and state laws,
and directed the allocation of revenue. So for him

the real significance of Reconstruction was as a test
of the ability of labor to rule itself over the
oligarchic power of the planter: "To a few far-seeing
leaders of democracy this experiment appeared in its
truer light. It was a test of the whole theory of
American government. It was a dictatorship backed by
the military arm of the United States by which the
governments of the Southern states were to be coerced
into accepting a new form of administration, in which
the freedman and the poor whites were to hold the
overwhelming balance of political power. As soon as
political power was successfully delivered into the
hand of these elements, the Federal government was
to withdraw and full democracy ensue." (345)

But as an experiment it was terminated too early
to reach its goal, and Du Bois suggested that partly
because of its military basis its results were pre-
dictably truncated; yet it remained the case that the
question of the extent to which labor could rule was
partly answered by Reconstruction. Du Bois speculated
that historically most have believed that the majority
are either too stupid or too corrupt to maintain effective political power. Then as civilization developed,
many began to realize that perhaps most people were
capable of such ability, but blacks were usually excluded from this class. However, he·asserted that in
the long run, all know that the mass must rule, if only

> by sheer weight of physical force. . . .
> But reason, skill, wealth, machines
> and power may for long periods enable
> the few to control the many. But to
> what end? The current theory of
> democracy is that dictatorship is a
> stopgap pending the work of universal
> education, equitable income, and
> strong character. But always the
> temptation is to use the stopgap
> for narrower ends, because intelli-
> gence, thrift and goodness seem so
> impossibly distant for most men. We
> rule by junta; we turn Fascist,
> because we do not believe in man;
> yet the basis of fact in this dis-
> belief is incredibly narrow. We
> know perfectly well that most human
> beings have never had a decent human
> chance to be full men. . . .

It is then one's moral duty to
see that every human being, to the
extent of his capacity, escapes
ignorance, poverty and crime. With
this high ideal held unswervingly
in view, monarchy, oligarchy, dic-
tatorships may rule; but the end
will be the rule of All, if mayhap
All or Most qualify. The only un-
forgivable sin is dictatorship for
the benefit of Fools, Voluptuaries,
gilded Satraps, Prostitutes and
Idiots. (382-3)

Du Bois would prefer a dictatorship _for_ the
proletariat but the next best situation is a dictatorship _of_ the proletariat. Although somewhat unclear on
this point, he seemed to agree with Sumner and Stevens
that a "Talented Tenth" is needed not for cultural
advance but to build an industrial democracy:
"[Sumner and Stevens] freely admitted . . . that while
it would be better to give the right of suffrage only
to those Negroes who were intelligent and particularly
those who by economic opportunity would amass some
little capital, nevertheless they felt that since the
South compelled them to choose between universal
suffrage and disfranchised landless labor in the
control of landholders and capitalists, with increased
political power based on the disfranchisement of labor,
the right of suffrage even in the hands of the poor
and ignorant gave better chance for ultimate economic
justice than their disfranchisement." (606; see p. 620)
At the time of Reconstruction the choice was between
such a second best dictatorship or continuing lack of
opportunity without significant power for the majority.

Despite its brevity and its failure to reach its
full potential, Reconstruction, in Du Bois' view,
still presented the opportunity to study an actual
test case of real movement to democracy. South
Carolina, the first Reconstruction state government
examined in the test, was recognized by him as falling
short of a dictatorship yet moving toward one. His
chapter is entitled "The Black Proletariat in South
Carolina;" in a footnote to the title he observed that,
"The record of the Negro worker during Reconstruction
presents an opportunity to study inductively the
Marxian theory of the State." Yet he backed away from
his original intention to label the chapter, "The

Dictatorship of the Black Proletariat in South Carolina," because "it has been brought to my attention that this would not be correct since universal suffrage does not lead to a real dictatorship until workers use their votes consciously to rid themselves of the dominion of private capital. There were signs of such an object among South Carolina Negroes, but it was always coupled with the idea of that day, that the only real escape for a laborer was himself to own capital." (381) Here again Du Bois recognized the experiment as only partial, yet the best available before the Russian revolution. (358) Oddly enough, even though he recognized that it did not form a genuine dictatorship, he did label it as a dictatorship throughout the text (see, for example, 358, 580, 622 and 690).

Du Bois thus proceeded to examine, in nearly two hundred pages of text, Reconstruction governments in each of the Southern and Border states, showing how the government was formed, the basic nature of the state constitutions, and problems and accomplishments of each. Some of these governments included large numbers of blacks, while in others blacks played only a minor role. The evaluation of each government tended to contain similar notes: effective constitutions were adopted; education was improved; railroad transportation was increased; corruption, although a general problem, was not as flagrant as often supposed; and financial mismanagement had been overstated and was mainly due to forces outside the control or Reconstruction governments. In short, considering their circumstances, these governments proved to be great successes.

His defense of Reconstruction in South Carolina and the other states is well documented and appealing, and does raise some questions that are most important to the purposes of this work. Du Bois, as noted below, considered Reconstruction, especially in South Carolina with its black majority, to be an inductive study in a Marxian dictatorship. Although he qualified this, he believed that it approximated such a test. The question then is the extent to which these governments formed such a dictatorship.

For Marx, the dictatorship of the proletariat deserved such a title because its purpose was the final destruction of the Bourgeoisie as a class. In this the proletariat would use the state's machinery against capital in order to wrest the means of production from capital. For Du Bois in Black Reconstruction, "dictatorship" did not seem to contain such a connotation. He claimed instead that a real dictatorship consciously used its votes "to rid themselves of the dominion of private capital." (381) Note here that this is to be done democratically through the voting procedure, a qualification absent in Marx. Further, when we turn to Du Bois for clarification of what was meant by eliminating the dominion of capital, the answer is ambiguous. The achievements of Reconstruction governments that Du Bois praised were reform oriented; they did not entail the destruction of the capitalist class. Also, he admitted that black leadership on the whole believed in capital and exploitation of labor. But he also claimed that black leadership was eventually pushed to the view that economic emancipation was needed. Here we may get insight into what Du Bois means by economic emancipation: "Thus the Negro leaders gradually but certainly turned towards emphasis on economic emancipation. They wanted the Negro to have the right to work at a decent rate of wages, and they expected that the right to vote would come when he had sufficient education and perhaps a certain minimum of property to deserve it." (351) His implied notion of economic emancipation as a decent wage rate with the right to vote differs dramatically from what Marx envisioned. Nevertheless when Du Bois lamented over the destruction of Reconstruction he understood the end of it as the triumph of capital and continuing exploitation of labor. So it remains doubtful that he intended to use the term "dictatorship" to imply the destruction of capital; he seems instead to have advocated a partial control over capital through democratic procedures. It is unfortunate then that Du Bois used the appeal to a Marxian experiment for what, in his own analysis, was in no clear sense a dictatorship. And this view of Du Bois' analysis omits the origin of the power of Reconstruction governments in Northern capital, a contingency most at odds with Marxian dictatorship of the proletariat.

V

The circumstances that led to the fall of Reconstruction were complicated; many forces were vying for political power with a resulting weakening of the alliance that kept it together. Indeed Reconstruction governments functioned within a turmoil of interests variously attempting to wrest power from the military and from newly enfranchised blacks. Reconstruction, then, was set in a stage of struggle for political power. The first clear manifestation of the lack of power in the Reconstruction governments came into focus over the issue of land redistribution.

Du Bois insisted that blacks during Reconstruction were beginning to understand that their political power could only make their lives substantially better if it was used for economic advance. In this sense he viewed them as pregressive: "In their conception of the ballot as the means to industrial emancipation, they were ahead of the Northern labor movement." (361) It has been noted that in the context of the accomplishments of Reconstruction governments, economic emancipation meant reformist social improvement. But he spoke differently when viewing the potential and inchoate aspirations of blacks during Reconstruction. These exhibited a tendency toward the desire to overthrow capitalism as an economic system. Du Bois himself seemed to view, contrary to his account of its accomplishments, Reconstruction as the only sound opportunity during the period to overthrow the political power of the capitalists. The freedmen expressed, in a more limited way, a similar concern in their demand for land. The right to land became the rallying point about which blacks agitated. (368) Blacks did increase their landholding after the Civil War; but this was mainly done through individual efforts aided by the cheap post-war price of land. (603) The fact that no great land redistribution took place indicated a lack of power on the part of blacks. Their traditional allies, abolition-democracy, did not offer firm support for redistribution. They themselves largely owned significant property; except for people like Sumner and Stevens, they did not consider it democratic to confiscate property.

The freedman's lack of power, dramatized by their inability to secure land redistribution, led to attempts at alliances. Other classes in the South, lacking power and wealth, also struggled for allies in efforts to gain dominance. The South thus became the ground of a contest over ultimate rules with several main participants in addition to the freedmen: Northern industry, represented in the South by the carpetbaggers, Southern white labor, and the defeated planter class.

The class oppositions here were complicated. The

unity a Marxian would expect, following class lines based on economic interests, would be between poor Southern white and black labor. But traditional rivalries and lack of social contact kept these groups apart. Instead of seeking unity with white labor, blacks first attempted to gain help from their former masters: "The best of the planters, those who in slavery days had occupied a patriarchal position toward their slaves, were besieged not only by their own former slaves but by others for advice and leadership. If they had wished, they could have held the Negro vote in the palm of their hands." (611) But once again, the intransigence of the planters, evidence earlier by their inability to accept economic innovation, made them incapable of making an effective response. They avoided any compromise over political power for blacks and insisted on "hard regular toil, vague and irregular wages. . . ." (612)

The move toward the planters and not toward a reconciliation with labor went deeper than simple traditional revalries; it uncovered the pro-capitalism and pro-individualism which was at first exhibited by the freedmen. The leaders of the freedmen received what education they had on the New England capitalistic, individualistic model. Their only clear economic demand pertained to the redistribution of land. This predilection for capital and their traditional trust of those they identified with emancipation eventually led the freedmen to turn to the carpetbaggers who represented Northern industrial capital.

Class struggles, so important in Du Bois' analysis of Reconstruction, became troublesome at this point and offered an opportunity for Du Bois to amend the Marxian perspective from which he operated. A Marxian pattern would place classes together according to economic interests, that is, the role classes perform in the productive process. And for Marx, as already observed, the laboring class is more or less aware of their true interests based on their position in economic arrangements. Thus Marx predicted the unity of labor. On this model one would expect that labor, North and South, black and white, would join forces as the opportunity presented itself, and that capital, in its defeated form in the South and its dominant form in the North would reach reconciliation. This would spring from Southern initiatives at compromise with the new industrial order. But labor was split by

123

racial considerations; Southern white labor attempted to join forces with the planter. With this in mind, Du Bois explicitly denied the validity of the theory of working class unity by adding his own concept of racism:

> The theory of laboring class unity rests upon the assumption that laborers, despite internal jealousies, will unite because of their opposition to exploitation by the capitalists. According to this, even after a part of the poor white laboring class became identified with the planters, and eventually displaced them, their interests would be diametrically opposed to those of the mass of white labor, and of course to those of the black laborers. This would throw white and black labor into one class, and precipitate a united fight for higher wages and better working conditions.
>
> Most persons do not realize how far this failed to work in the South, and it failed to work because the theory of race was supplemented by a carefully planned and slowly evolved method, which drove such a wedge between white and black workers that there probably are not today in the world two groups of workers with practically identical interests who hate and fear each other so deeply and persistently and who are kept so far apart that neither sees anything of common interests. (700)

On the other hand, wealth was also unable to present a unified front. In order to destroy the power of Southern aristocrats, Northern industry formed an alliance with willing blacks through the carpetbaggers. "But both capitalists and laborers were split in two; there was hatred and jealousy in the ranks of this new prospective capitalist class, and race prejudice and fear in the ranks of the laborers." (609-610)

The situation as set up was unstable. A unity of perceived interests between Northern capital and Southern planters was feasible; the division between these two groups was not as deep seated as the division between the races. Furthermore, the Southern planting class could not realistically hope to revert to their former style of life. A coalition with the North held out the hope of regaining some of their lost power. However, the alliance between Southern blacks and Northern industry was precariously based on Northern self-interest, which in the long run was likely to suffer under what Du Bois saw as the increasingly radical perspective of Southern blacks. The delicacy of the balance suggested an eventual turn from policies that favored blacks. And deep-seated racial animosities virtually secured the absence of an effective labor alliance that was the only realistic hope of maintaining such policies.

Two serious developments added to the delicate balance maintaining political power for blacks: first, a growing corruption permeating Northern industry and, second, the panic of 1873. Northern industry attempted to use Reconstruction as a means to weaken the power of the planter and thereby set up industry in the South based on the Northern model. Northern industry, according to Du Bois, worked through the carpetbaggers. But these people were steeped in corruption and greed for power. The problem of corrupt carpetbaggers was perceived as coincident with widespread corruption in Northern industry. After the Civil War the power of Northern industry was greatly expanding; this opened possibilities for great individual gain. Du Bois claimed that a corrupt scramble for power followed. The government, through its financing of essential ingredients of industrial development, such as the railroad network, became a part of the debilitating corruption which Du Bois described in the harshest terms: "It broke down old standards of wealth distribution, old standards of thrift and honesty. It led to anarchy of thieves, grafters, and highwaymen. It threatened the orderly processes of production as well as government and morals." (581)

A reaction to this corruption eventually built. This reaction, in effect, contained two prime elements: first, it argued for the need to reinstigate honesty and efficiency in business. But second, and more important, it recognized that new, large-scale industry

required new techniques, indeed a new form of control.
Thus a new and more efficient industrial leadership
took over, in the name of honesty, from the old robber-
barons. "The dictatorship of property, as represented
by the wild freebooting from the close of the war to
the panic, had proven to many minds that free competition in industry was not going to bring proper control
and development." (583)

According to Du Bois, the new industrial leadership supported a more powerful dictatorship: "the
new plan was to concentrate into a trusteeship of
capital a new and far-reaching power which would dominate the government of the United States." (583) Du
Bois called this new dictatorship a new "feudalism"
because of its monopoly over raw materials such as
iron, oil and coal, and its domination over rail
transportation. With this, the new feudalism could
control manufacturing. "The new feudalism was destined
to crush the small capitalist as ruthlessly as it
controlled labor, and even before the panic of 1873,
it was beginning to consolidate its power." (584)

Du Bois' view was that the people of the country,
the electorate, were incapable of dealing with this
new industrial development. Because of lack of intelligence, provincial attitudes and bigotry, they were
unable to guide new industrial wealth to the advantage
of the workers. So they needed a dictatorship under
the talented and dedicated, presumably, again, people
like Summer and Stevens. So we find a further example
of the strained quality of Du Bois' analysis: his
dedication to the masses and their ultimate right to
rule coupled with the deprecation of their ability and
their need for a watchful dictatorship of the talented.
But the vacuum of power after the Civil War was not
filled by a benevolent dictatorship, but by the "super-
dictatorship" of self-interested industry.

The efforts of the new dictatorship at securing
acceptance and control was nearly total:

> Great corporations, through their
> control of new capital, began to estab-
> lish a super-government. On the one
> hand, they crushed the robber-barons,
> the theives and the grafters, and
> thus appeased those of the old school
> who demanded the old standards of

> personal honesty. Secondly, they
> made treaty with the petty bour-
> geoisie by guarantying them reason-
> able and certain income from their
> investments, while they gradually
> deprived them of real control in
> industry. And finally, they made
> treaty with labor by dealing with
> it as a powerful, determined unit
> and dividing it up into skilled
> union labor, with which the new
> industry shared profit in the
> shape of higher wages and other
> privileges, and a great reservoir
> of common and foreign labor which
> it kept at low wages with the
> threat of starvation and with
> police control. (584)

The movement toward such effective control was
facilitated by the harsh depression of 1873. In this
crisis the appearance of a new, strong leadership pro-
moting growth, efficiency and security evoked the
favorable responses even from socialist unions. (596)
The panic, then, became the opportune time for a new
form of industrial control. In the panic the government with its corruption appeared as the enemy; so it
appeared progressive to attack its graft. This became
the chance for the South to divest itself of Reconstruction. The white South named blacks as the source
of corruption in Reconstruction governments. In
effect, they linked the corruption in industry with
corruption in Reconstruction and found that the experiment in democracy was the root of the evil. The ultimate conclusion was the disfranchisement of the
freedmen.

With the change in the control of the industrial
system in the North came a changed attitude on the
part of both the carpetbaggers and the planters, which
weakened the basis of Reconstruction governments. "The
carpetbag reformers moved toward an alliance with the
planters with an understanding that called for lower
taxes and the elimination of graft and corruption."
(623) In order to ensure the end of Reconstruction,
the planters were willing to agree not to reinstigate
old attacks against the tariff, banks and the national
debt. (686)

The period after 1873 was suitable for the overthrow of Reconstruction. The South had the nation's
sympathy in face of the alleged corruption, and the
labor vote was racially split. In some places this
allowed for white majorities to unify and suppress the
black voters. In other places, such as Mississippi in
1874, violence was used to force blacks into submission.
Finally, explicit agreements to end the Reconstruction
experiment were worked out. "On the 26th of February,
1876, there were three conferences. The outcome was
an agreement. The Republicans guaranteed that Mr.
Hayes, when he became President, would by non-inter-
ference and the withdrawl of troops allow the planter-
capitalists, under the name of Democrats, to control
South Carolina and Louisiana." (692) The Democrats,
for their part, promised law and order. Thus, in one
way or another Reconstruction was virtually destroyed
after 1876. The main reason behind its disestablish-
ment, Du Bois believed, was that the experiment in
Democracy always lacked a secure, altruistic power-base.

   After Reconstruction blacks were systematically
disfranchised. Race hatred increased and the pseudo-
scientific doctrine of racial inferiority became strongly entrenched. But these were only partial effects--
perhaps even more vicious, in Du Bois' view, were the
implications of the general acceptance of the new dictatorship. The arrival of this dictatorship meant that
labor supported the dictatorship of capital, and with
it the excessive exploitation of imperialism. With
charges similar to those that dominated the opinions
of the last period of his life, Du Bois attacked the
new system:

               This meant a tremendous change
          in the whole intellectual and
          spiritual development of civiliza-
          tion in the South and in the United
          States because of the predominant
          political power of the South, built
          on disfranchised labor. The United
          States was turned into a reactionary
          force. It became the cornerstone of
          that new imperialism which is subject-
          ing the labor of yellow, brown and
          black peoples to the dictation of
          capitalism organized on a world
          basis; and it has not brought nearer
          the revolution by which the power of

capitalism is to be challenged, but
also it is transforming the fight
to the sinister aspect of a fight
on racial lines embittered by awful
memories. (631)

The meaning of the failure of Reconstruction in
the South, for Du Bois, was the failure of American
democracy and the advent of an American industrial
imperialism growing rich partly from the exploitation
of colonial lands. And this imperialism was made most
vicious and hard to overcome because it was predicated
on cultural and racial differences between people. The
new industrial system thus paved the way for American
exploitation on a wide scale: "Here is the real modern
labor problem. Here is the kernel of the problem of
Religion and Democracy, of Humanity. Words and futile
gestures avail nothing. Out of the exploitation of the
dark proletariat comes the Surplus Value filched from
human beasts which, in cultured lands, the Machine
and harnessed Power veil and conceal. The emancipation
of man is the emancipation of labor and the emancipation of labor is the freeing of that basic majority of
workers who are yellow, brown and black." (16)

Du Bois again took a Marxian view. Although Du
Bois did not mention Lenin, there are several ways in
which he more clearly parallels Lenin's reforms of
Marxian thought than Marx's position. One theme in
Lenin in opposition to Marx is the notion that the
working class is not aware of its own interests.[9] Labor
was, for example, easily enthralled by nationalism while
Marx claimed labor was internationalist in outlook. Du
Bois similarly argued that labor accepted racism to
their own detriment. Secondly, Lenin insisted on the
need for an elite group to control labor and foment
revolution.[10] Du Bois, while unclear on the role of
an elite, suggested that the uneducated masses would
have been better off under a benevolent dictatorship
of men like Stevens and Summer working for the ultimate
control (when this became practicable) of the masses.
And thirdly, Du Bois, with Lenin, saw labor in advanced
countries as sharing in the exploitation of the third
world.[11]

The turn from democracy to imperialism Du Bois
perceived was made possible by the panic of 1873. Like
Marx, Du Bois saw that an economic crisis crippling the
system signals the need for change and has the potential

of becoming the lever of change. Such was the case in 1873, even though the panic led to an unacceptable system. In 1935, as Black Reconstruction was published, the nation was caught in another serious depression which meant, to him, that the system of exploitation was itself in need of and ready for change. The change he hoped for was to be guided by the ideals he saw as operative in Reconstruction: "The world wept because within the exploiting group of New World masters, greed and jealousy become so fierce that they fought for trade and markets and materials and slaves all over the world until at last in 1914 the world flamed in war. The fantastic structure fell, leaving grotesque Profits and Poverty; Plenty and Starvation, Empire and Democracy, staring at each other across World Depression. And the rebuilding, whether it comes now or a century later, will and must go back to the basic principles of Reconstruction in the United States during 1867-1876--Land, Light and Leading for slaves black, brown, yellow and white, under a dictatorship of the proletariat." (634-35)

Although Du Bois believed that Reconstruction could serve as a model for future change, he understood that such a use was hampered by the fact that Reconstruction had been presented by historians in a distorted manner. The last chapter of Black Reconstruction, "The Propaganda of History," is a systematic condemnation of the writing of the history of the period. Du Bois claimed that the then prevalent view turned blacks into ignorant, lazy and extravagant sources of bad government during Reconstruction. Most histories presented Reconstruction as a costly mistake, and information contrary to this view was ignored. History thus was used as an anti-black tool, rather than as a scientific search for the truth. Du Bois offered his work in opposition to the dominant theories and hope that the materials he presented would plainly establish the true story of Reconstruction. Yet he viewed himself as standing alone against the majority which simply could not believe that blacks were full human beings. He concluded: ". . . in propaganda against the Negro since emancipation in this land, we face one of the most stupendous efforts the world ever saw to discredit human beings, an effort involving universities, history, science, social life and religion." (727)

Du Bois' analysis of Reconstruction is most significant, in terms of its theoretical stance, in its use
and modification of Marx. His use of Marx set the main
threads of the analysis as economic, with class structures and economic development used as the basis for
virtually all that occurred in the period. Also, the
terminology he used, terms such as "exploitation" and
"proletariat," are from Marx. But his use of Marxism
is limited; indeed at this point in his career he was
not a Marxist. Several points clearly, and self-consciously, separate the two: Du Bois added the notion
of race to economic categories. Race, while based, in
the final analysis, on economic realities, was maintained through cultural or psychological forces. Du
Bois bridged economic determinism with psychological
determinism, a move traditional Marxists abhor. In
this way class analysis could not simply be economic.
As a corollary, the proletariat was seen as ignorant
of its own interests and thereby in need of leadership,
much as Lenin advised.

Black Reconstruction must be considered an ambiguous work. It uses the language of revolution, but in
its infrequent appeal to concrete changes, it seems
more reform oriented. It is hard to tell what sort
of specific advances Du Bois had in mind. Of course,
the work was written about a particular historical
period in which the possibilities were limited and he
may have felt bound by historical parameters. Further,
he may have envisioned the "revolution" as taking a
number of years to develop its anti-capital aims behind increasingly aware leadership.

The role of leadership in Black Reconstruction is
at once similar to yet distinct from his early notion
of the "Talented Tenth." In 1935 talent had the task
of leadership--but with the aim of bringing all to the
level at which full industrial control could be democratically divided. And the leadership was mainly
economic leadership, not leadership ultimately dedicated to their own achievements.

Du Bois' partial rejection of Marxism continued
until near the end of his life. The next chapter
examines the rejection in more detail. Black Reconstruction, while it rejects Marx, also presents a
wide-reaching critique of American capitalism. Capi-

talism is considered non-democratic, tremendously
powerful, and imperialistic. He took seriously the
relationship between American economic activities and
the people in the world united under his revised concept of race. This viewpoint was present in his analysis of the cause of World War I; but in Black Reconstruction he explicitly extended the analysis to the
conditions operative in everyday life. The structure
of capitalism causes continual misery and deprivation
to the world's darker people. Du Bois' final years
manifest a deepening concern over this observation, a
concern that eventually drew his interest, by and
large, away from the American black community and
caused him to take up citizenship in Ghana, his home
at the time of his death. But his immediate response
to the Great Depression was a plan for an alternate
economic system, at first in the United States and,
eventually, in the world. The plan he had was to start
with a black economic cooperative in the United States.
The black cooperative was Du Bois' most detailed plan
for social amelioration, and thus it shall be explored
at length in the following chapter. Coming during the
depression, it contains analogies to the possibilities
opened by the panic of 1873. This time, however, Du
Bois hoped that democracy would prevail. In effect,
he hoped that reform would be the result of lessons
learned from Reconstruction.

NOTES

1. W.E.B. Du Bois, Black Reconstruction in America:
    An Essay Toward a History of the Part Which Black
    Folk Played in the Attempt to Reconstruct Democra-
    cy in America, 1860-1880 (New York: Atheneum,
    1970); numbers in parentheses refer to pages in
    this text.

2. K.M. Stampp and L.F. Litwack (eds.), Reconstruction:
    An Anthology of Revisions and Writings (Baton
    Rouge, La.: Louisiana State University Press,
    1969), pp. 221-222.

3. Herbert Aptheker, Afro-American History: The
    Modern Era (New York: Citadel Press, 1971), p. 56.

4. A.W. Trelease, "Who Were the Scalawags," in
    Stampp and Litwack, eds., Reconstruction, p. 322.

5. Lester, The Seventh Son, I, p. 114.

6. Karl Marx, Capital: A Critique of Political
    Economy, Vol. III, The Process of Capitalistic
    Production as a Whole. Edited by F. Engles (New
    York: International Publishers, 1967), p. 885.

7. Karl Marx and Friedrich Engels, The Communist
    Manifesto (New York: Appleton-Century-Crofts,
    1955), p. 21.

8. Ibid., emphasis added.

9. V. I. Lenin, "What is to be Done" (1902), in J. E.
    Connor (ed.), Lenin: On Politics and Revolution
    (Indianapolis, Ind.: The Bobbs-Merrill Company,
    Inc., 1968), p. 53.

10. Ibid., p. 65.

11. See V. I. Lenin, "Imperialism, The Highest Stage of
    Capitalism (1916)," in Connor (ed.), Lenin, pp.
    111-148.

CHAPTER V

ECONOMIC COOPERATION

Black Reconstruction shows the extent to which
Du Bois both agreed and disagreed with the orthodox
Marxist theory. His major point of disagreement was
the addition of race. Race maintained a central role
in the analysis of the Reconstruction period. Such a
theoretical difference would lead to different prescrip-
tions on the sorts of actions that can be effective in
leading to better social organization. Marx advocated
a working-class revolution; Du Bois, aware of the
vertical split in that class, could entertain no such
revolutionary hopes. Instead he adopted a plan thought
to be realistic because it revolved around both race and
class. Instead of advocating a revolution, he proposed
a black economic cooperative; this was his second
attempt at the formulation of a racial community capable
of solving the dilemmas of social life.

Du Bois believed that his work in establishing a
black cooperative was one of the most important contributions of his life. In 1940 he claimed that his
three most important post World War I activities were
his work on Pan-Africanism, his encouragement of
artistic activities among blacks, and his speculation
on economic cooperation. And his effort toward economic rehabilitation through economic cooperation was
thought by him to be the most fundamental and prophetic
of the three.[1] His high regard for the theory of economic cooperation, however, has not been shared by
those who have studied Du Bois' writings and was rejected by many of those who had worked with him.[2]
Even more devastating, the plan completely failed at
the practical level. But the facts that his plan
generally lacked support and ultimately was discarded
do not demonstrate that the plan was unreasonable or
poorly constructed, as is often argued. The plan was,
in fact, to a good degree, a careful, rational and
realistic plan for the economic betterment of a minority group especially during a severe depression.

I

His plan for economic cooperation was meant to be
flexible enough to respond to varying situations. He
never gave a complete and detailed description of his

135

theory; rather, he gave a complete rationale, a general description, and a fairly complete program for the initial steps in its development. A general outline of his theory is found in Dusk of Dawn, but one must include material from The Crisis in order to get a more thorough view of the basics of Du Bois' concept.

The economic cooperative Du Bois proposed followed some of the main tenets of the proven course of European cooperation, with one essential difference, namely the added dimension of race. His plan called for a segregated racial economic cooperative, insofar as this was feasible.[3] Because of segregation blacks were predominantly a consumer group without a capitalist class; the cooperative would begin by organizing neighborhood groups as consumers. These groups would buy wholesale food and manufactured goods from white owned plants already established to provide lower prices to consumer groups. But discrimination existed in the white establishments, and thus blacks could not have become an effective part of a general consumer cooperative movement. Instead they would have to form their own wholesale and manufacturing organizations.

The first step in setting up a large-scale, well organized cooperative movement would be the establishment of local cooperative stores stocking food, clothing and household goods. In order to open a store, the required capital would be raised by selling stocks at low cost to those already profiting from wholesale buying. Each shareholding member would have one vote, would receive a fixed interest on shares, and would receive returns from profits based not on shares but on the total amount of purchases.[4] Du Bois believed that local cooperative stores could be established in cities with black populations of 10,000 or more.[5] As the number of local consumer societies increased, and thus their total sales, the point would come when these could unite to form a wholesale society and eliminate some dependence on white economic power.

As the consumer cooperative grew into a series of wholesale societies, the demand for knowledgeable leadership would arise. Du Bois knew that the leadership must be capable, honest and inspired if the cooperative was to succeed. But, furthermore, the cooperative must always remain consumer oriented; thus the leadership must be under the democratic control of the membership, which can be accomplished only if the leadership is willing to teach the principles and methods of cooperation to the masses. This educational process must be continued, Du Bois maintained, until mass ownership would be able to use their votes knowing "exactly the principles and persons for which they are voting."[6]

Once local consumer cooperatives had joined together into wholesale societies and the essential leadership had been established, then the cooperative could expand from the consumption sector to the production sector. Consequently, blacks could begin to use their already partially segregated economy in a planned, rational way by reorganizing and employing their productive capabilities. Du Bois claimed that blacks already supplied a significant part of their food, clothing, home building, repair, books, and personal services such as hotels and restaurants.[7] Black workers could have fulfilled almost all building, growing and repairing needs; what was required in the cooperative was "A simple transfer of Negro workers, with only such additional skills as can easily be learned in a few months. . . ."[8] As the consumers' and producers' cooperative grew, more and more workers would be incorporated into its production and distribution network. Careful planning would be required to develop the organization necessary to overcome detrimental geographical distribution and to provide the centralization and the relocation necessary for large scale manufacturing. But once achieved, the services of the racial cooperative could continue to expand, for example, schools could be improved by providing the best possible teaching and equipment.[9] He called for a centrally planned hospital system and a program of socialized medicine. Blacks, he insisted, must do something about crime and improve legal defense provisions. In short, he advocated a program of socialization of all professional services including the establishment of banks along the lines which would allow them to give needed credit and social services.[10]

Du Bois' racial cooperative was to be organized according to the needs and desires of the consumer and not with regard to the profits of the producer. The program would provide modest yet sufficient salaries; mass and class, he hoped, would unite in common economic effort. Exploitation of labor, risk and profit would have to be avoided by gearing production to the already expressed demands of the consumer, and by selling at

the price of actual cost. Unemployment among blacks
would have to be eliminated by the success of the cooperative.

The group economy Du Bois envisioned was to be
accomplished by a series of steps each of increasing
centralization and utilization of existing productive
capacity. His cooperative was to be built without
government aid and mainly without dependence on the
general economy. He clearly intended to organize a
racial cooperative solely within the black community,
but one based on the principles that had spawned
relatively successful cooperative movements from
Russia to England.[11]

For Du Bois cooperation seemed to be a form of
socialism; thus, in 1935, he could proclaim his increased faith in socialism and his diminished confi-
dence in the talented: In a letter to a critic Du Bois
claimed: "You believe in Socialism as I do. You think
however, that Socialism is coming through the leadership of the workers led by a few men of intelligence
like yourself. I believe in the same thing, but I
believe that the intelligent leaders need not be con-
fined to a few like you, but can spread through the
young Negroes when they are properly taught."[12]

Du Bois believed that the use of segregation to
establish a strong group economy would eventually destroy discrimination and segregation. This would
result because: (1) With economic support from the
cooperative blacks would have a better vantage point
from which to wage a campaign (like that of The Crisis
and the N.A.A.C.P.), against racism,[13] and (2) it
would provide an excellent model of an effective organization such that the rest of society would eventually
want to join the movement, and thereby accept an integrated way of life. Du Bois' hope was forcefully
stated, "We have a chance here to teach industrial and
cultural democracy to a world that bitterly needs
it."[14]

Du Bois' point of view about a separate economy
was not intended as an exercise in any black nationalism based on exclusionary ideal but instead was intended as a short term practical proposal: This is
clear in one of his last statements on economic cooperation contained in a 1940 letter: "my growing
conviction has been since the depression that the
fundamental problem facing American Negroes is securing

138

a place in American industrial life. I am certain that if they simply wait to get their share in any change of plan and reorganization of economic life in America the so-called race problem will show itself by making their entrance into this economy late and uncertain. . . . For that reason I want Negroes to begin intelligent planning for themselves, not of course, for a separate economy but for the purpose of seeing how far their own efforts can help them toward economic security. . . ."[15]

This statement clearly shows the absence of an ingrained black nationalism in his social thought. On the other hand, this late statement on a separate economy seems to be only a partial endorsement of the full blown cooperation he had proposed earlier. Here he seems to be advocating a partial effort serving as a test of planning that may be successful short of the consumers' and producers' cooperative outlined before 1940. This statement, then, may represent a subtle change in his thinking before the notion of cooperation more or less completely disappeared from his writings.

II

The fullest and most mature statement of racial cooperation came in Dusk of Dawn (published in 1940); but he had given significant attention to some form of economic cooperation even before 1900. Those early views show the extent to which his outlook on social participation changed. It also shows how Du Bois examined the social foundation necessary for any successful social movement. He considered cooperation (in varying forms) to have been a well established practice in the black community and he believed an entrenched cooperative spirit existed. This suggested that past tendencies could be molded into a thoroughgoing reform effort. He also thought that previous conscious and unconscious cooperative practices formed a potentially powerful economic network; this, he eventually believed, could be used to bring about an effective cooperative in a brief period of time.

Du Bois' most complete statement on economic cooperation in Dusk of Dawn was the product of many years of work on the subject, beginning with the Atlanta University study of 1898, Some Efforts of American Negroes for Their Own Social Betterment.[16] His earliest statements on cooperation in the Atlanta University

139

Publications included many activities significantly
differing from the later socialistic concept of cooperation. Yet these activities were important to the
later plan because they indicated an historical spirit
of cooperation needed for the plan's success. "Cooperation" was used in the Atlanta Publications as the
generic term for two sorts of group activities among
blacks, charity and public oriented business; such
group activities were considered superior to individual
efforts, especially in education, property accumulation
and home owning.

        Cooperation among blacks, Du Bois pointed out,
had undergone a substantial history which had brought
about many different institutions and techniques of
group effort. He began the history of cooperation
among Afro-Americans by turning back to the African
tribal life. He maintained that tribal life was organized on a communistic basis in which "no individual can
be poorer than the tribe."[17]

        American slavery held over communal traits from
Africa,[18] but also kept blacks from the sort of economic competition based on an individualistic social
Darwinism he viewed as antithetical to cooperation.[19]
Furthermore, slavery witnessed what Du Bois called
"a kind of quasi co-operation," consisting in the "buying of freedom by slaves or their relatives."[20] Another
direct effect of slavery on the tendency toward cooperation was the charity performed by slaves for slaves.
Even though slaves depended on masters for relief from
suffering, slaves did help each other "in the line of
adopting children and caring for the sick. The habit
of adoption is still wide-spread and beneficent."[21]

        The church was, in his opinion, the foundation of
cooperative efforts. It was the center in slavery of
'economic activity as well as of amusement, education
and social intercourse."[22] Also, the church in slavery
days became the organizing center of many insurrections:
". . . we must find in these insurrections a beginning
of co-operation which eventually ended in the peaceful
economic co-operation."[23] A more prevalent form of
rebellion was the underground railroad. As Northern
states became increasingly free, "we find that the
spirit of revolt which tried to co-operate by means of
insurrection led to widespread organization for the
rescue of fugitive slaves among Negroes themselves. . . ."[24] Du Bois believed that the underground

railroad must have involved at least partially conscious cooperative organization: It was too systematic to be accidental, and there was widespread knowledge of the best paths, places and times for escape. Consequently, he claimed, without full explanation, that efforts in support of the underground railroad led to "various co-operative efforts toward economic emancipation and land-buying. Gradually these efforts led to co-operative business, building and loan associations and trade unions."[25]

This is "co-operation" in a most limited sense when related to a full economic cooperative. Here Du Bois' tracing of the cooperative spirit among blacks seems an ad hoc clutching at any sort of evidence available, no matter how tenuous. Perhaps such conclusions ultimately made Du Bois naive about the extent to which cooperation would be a natural appendage onto existing inclinations.

Although Du Bois traced the cooperative spirit to the African and the early slavery experience, he contended that "a study of economic co-operation among Negroes must begin with the Church group."[26] He viewed the church as pivotal between African and Afro-American experience and he considered the Church as the main functional unit of social life: "The Negro Church is the only social institution of the Negroes which started in the African forest and survived slavery; under the leadership of the priest and medicine man, afterward of the Christian pastor, the Church preserved in itself the remnants of African tribal life and became after emancipation the centre of Negro social life. So that to-day the Negro population of the United States is virtually divided into Church congregations, which are the real units of the race life."[27] As blacks became Methodists and Baptists, discrimination forced them to become established as separate and economically independent of the white churches. This was crucial in the history of cooperation: the church became the first large scale group among blacks which was economically self-sustained and self-governed. Furthermore, he saw the church as the main source of economic charity among blacks.

The significance of the church went well beyond the organized effort at benevolence; it became the foundation for various other cooperative efforts. Du Bois explained: "Out of the churches sprang two

141

different lines of economic cooperation:

    1.   Schools.

    2.   Burial societies.

From the burial societies developed sickness and death
insurance, on the one hand, and cemeteries, homes and
orphanages, on the other. From the insurance societies
came banks and co-operative business."[28]

Du Bois located various types of cooperative
societies providing social benefits for blacks, including orphanages, hospitals, and cemeteries, each
built from the problems caused by segregation and
discrimination. Du Bois saw two other types of beneficial societies as fundamentally important and difficult to distinguish: One was the insurance society
and the other was the secret society such as the Masons,
the Knights of Pythias, the Odd Fellows, etc. Secret
societies often provided insurance and benefits against
sickness and death, which, in his view, was a sort of
cooperative business. But perhaps more importantly
Du Bois insisted that they went beyond the churches,
because they tended to put the talented in leadership
roles.[29]

His support for the role of talent suggests a
sharp distinction between his early and later concept
of cooperation. In early works he was writing within
the framework of the "Talented Tenth" as the advance
guard of racial reform. Thus, cooperative leadership
was not to be under democratic control; leadership must
dictate from their talented position above the masses.
Du Bois was quite clear on this point: a race recently
emancipated from slavery could not be expected to have
reached a point at which democratic participation in
cooperative effort could be expected. Strong individual leadership, consequently, was necessary to overcome
the disadvantaged group status.[30] The "Talented Tenth"
must be in firm control. These views were obviously
at odds with his later statements on cooperation in
which democratic organization was the foundation of a
meaningful effort and leadership was obliged to teach
any unusual methods to the masses.

The secret societies, which produced necessary
leadership capabilities, sprang directly from beneficial societies which were directly associated with

churches. Secret societies kept the rituals and oaths of the church, but were an advance from church activity in terms of their business-like practices. Beneficial societies also gave rise to other forms of cooperative business. His category of cooperative business is perhaps the most instructive insofar as they proximate the structure of his later concept of cooperation. Du Bois listed three categories of cooperative business: (1) Productive cooperation, (2) cooperation in transportation, and (3) distributive cooperation.[31]

The early form of cooperation was not socialistic. This is helpful in identifying his turn toward socialism in his later years. The nature of cooperation in the early writings was capitalistic, as his examples indicate: One example offered of a successful black productive cooperative was the Coleman Manufacturing Company established in 1897. The company soon employed 200-230 people but Coleman, its leader, died within seven years, and the company was purchased by whites. This seems to be an example of a cooperative only in the sense that several people organized, ran it and hired only black workers. Again we see Du Bois using cooperation in an ad hoc manner. Neither of the other two forms of cooperation seem to be genuinely cooperative; instead they appear to be either partnerships or stock companies designed to make profits for blacks and to serve the black community. But even if these businesses were cooperative only in a truncated sense, they are interesting because they suggest both the economic substructure in the black community and the racial exclusiveness of Du Bois' mature plan. He pointed out in his early work that the major successes of black cooperative business had been due to pressures of race prejudice.[32] Du Bois, as early as 1898, was hinting at the effects of prejudice on business in terms of building, out of necessity, a separate economic foundation controlled by blacks.

Perhaps the closest Du Bois came in the Atlanta University Publications to a notion of cooperation like that in Dusk of Dawn was in his discussion of a group economy presented in one of the final publications, The Negro American Artisan (1912), two years after he began as the editor of The Crisis. He defined a group economy as consisting in "such a co-operative arrangement of industries and services within the Negro group that the group tends to become a closed economic circle largely independent of the surrounding white world."[33]

143

Du Bois explained that many black businesses catered
almost exclusively to black trade.

> So far has this gone that today in
> every city of the United States
> with a considerable Negro popula-
> tion the black group is serving
> itself with religious ministration,
> medical care, legal advice and
> education of children; and to a
> growing degree with food, houses,
> books and newspapers. . . . Rep-
> resenting at least 300,000 persons,
> the group economy approaches a
> complete system. To these may be
> added the bulk of the 200,000
> Negro farmers who own their farms.
> They form a natural group economy
> and they are increasing the scope
> of it in every practical way.[34]

Du Bois viewed these 300,000 people at the economic
forefront of the black economy as "independent of
prejudice and competition."[35] The central question for
Du Bois then became, "How far can the Negro develop a
group economy which will so break the force of race
prejudice that his right and ability to enter the
national economy are assured?"[36] In The Crisis, he
attempted to answer this question by developing a
theory of socialistic, racial cooperation and by proposing concrete steps for the implementation of his
plan.

                        III

       Du Bois' editorship of The Crisis (1910-1934)
marked the apogee of his social leadership. As editor
he persistently revised, explained and advocated his
notion of economic cooperation. His presentation of
a racially segregated cooperative began with the idea
of using segregation to overcome economic and social
disadvantage. His first defense of a segregated
effort appeared in an editorial entitled "Blessed
Discrimination" in 1913 which declared his contempt
for the evil effects of segregation, but, further,
indicated his intent to turn its disadvantage to advantage. He pointed out that thousands of businesses
such as drug stores, grocery stores, insurance societies and daily newspapers had been established precisely

because there had been discrimination. He continued, "In a sense The Crisis is a capitalized race prejudice."[37] He quickly added that discrimination was not a veiled blessing "save in a few exceptional cases."[38] Segregated schools were poor in quality, businesses were poorly run, newspapers were a "sad lot" and sickness and disease were often the outcome of segregation. He concluded, "Race discrimination is evil, it forces those discriminated against to a lower standard and judges them by a higher."[39] Yet, he went on to say, almost in the spirit of Booker T. Washington, that "if in any place and time race hatred is so unreasoning and bitter that separate schools, cars and churches are inevitable, we must accept it, make the best of it and turn even its disadvantages to our advantage. But we must never forget that none of its possible advantages can offset its miserable evils, or replace the opportunity, the broad education, the free competition and the generous emulation of free men in a free world."[40] This conforms to the attitude Du Bois took in Dusk of Dawn in which segregation was used to destroy segregation in a planned building of a model, workable economy. He took the same pragmatic attitude in 1913: Racial discrimination is an evil eventually to be destroyed, but one which could be turned to advantage as the means of its own destruction.

Some early writing in The Crisis serve as precursors of his later plan, yet even after 1910 the notion of cooperation was congruent with capitalistic development. In "The Immediate Program of the American Negro," (April 1915) Du Bois presented a five point plan for the eventual elimination of the problems faced by Afro-Americans. ". . . (1) economic co-operation, (2) a revival of art and literature, (3) political action, (4) education and (5) organization."[41] He explained that economic cooperation meant that wealth must be used for social ends, and that the ownership of small individual amounts of property and money must be supplemented by cooperation in "production and distribution, profit sharing, building and loan associations, systematic charity. . . ."[42] However, Du Bois' use of the term "cooperation" was vague in terms of the type of cooperation he meant and how it would be implemented. It becomes clear that in the early years of his editorship, he used "cooperation" as a term which may refer to capitalistic corporate ownership but with a public conscience. In July 1914 he explained that "If the Negro was a large capitalist . . . he

could reap great advantage . . . by buying up . . .
depressed property. Some day, through widespread
cooperation, colored people will learn to do this."[43]
In the same editorial Du Bois hinted at a plan of
action by suggesting that organizations such as the
Negro churches and the YMCA buy strategic plots of
land. He saw groups which were dedicated to philanthropy and public works (even if spiritual) as primary
examples of cooperation.

His interest in philanthropy led Du Bois to a
business ethic based on the concept of service. He
remarked in 1911 that "The test . . . of enterprise is
doing for men the things they ought to have done for
them, when we consider not simply their present desires,
but their future welfare."[44] Business ought not to be
based on the expectation of maximum profits. Du Bois
admonished the Negro Business League to "emphasize
business life among Negroes today as a philanthropy,
as a means of group employment and group gain, not for
making millionaires, but for making a large class of
well-to-do citizens."[45] This statement was in interesting contrast with his later views. Here class
structure was emphasized--the solution to the problem
was in terms of developing the inchoate middle class
among blacks without emphasis on eliminating the class
of poor blacks. The Dusk of Dawn statement strived to
destroy the antagonisms of a class structure by providing economic equality at a decent level.

Around 1918 "cooperation" ceased to refer to a
charitable black corporate ownership. In that year he
advertised a cooperative notion containing features
clearly defining a socialistic cooperative. In an
editorial entitled "The Rochdale Pioneers," he described the 1844 attempt in England to begin a cooperative store.[46] Yet this early mention of the
Rochdale Pioneers was only the barest outline of cooperation and lacked his eventual rationale.

His efforts as Editor showed not only a persistent
effort to clarify and explain the nature of cooperation
in general and racial cooperation in particular, but
he also tried to convince the black community that it
was in their interest to adopt its principles as the
solution to their problems. For example, in 1917 he
offered a twofold defense of cooperation: First the
old form of industrial organization, he believed, was
failing and a new form was coming. Blacks should not

146

attempt to plan around the old form of "individual exploitation." Second, he emphasized the peculiar condition of blacks that made success in cooperation particularly likely. This point goes to the basis of his concept of race based on group loyalty, to the importance of the absence of economic class differentiation and to the economic necessity for cooperation: "Slowly and with great difficulty this new spirit is going to work itself out in the white world; but if we American Negroes are keen and intelligent we can evolve a new and efficient industrial cooperation quicker than any other group of people, for the simple reason that our inequalities of wealth are small, our group loyalty is growing stronger and stronger, and the necessity for a change in our industrial life is becoming imperative."[47] In the same editorial Du Bois stressed the need for a separate "industrial machine" for blacks so that self-improvement within the group may prevent victimization at the hands of white employers. He thus introduced the notion of cooperative production rather than simply consumer cooperation; but this aspect of cooperation remained relatively dormant until Dusk of Dawn.

He continued to underscore the absence of economic classes (in the Marxian sense) among blacks throughout his years as Editor. In 1921 he criticized the application of a class structure to Afro-Americans, and he pointed to the practical split between white and black workers even though both were theoretically part of the proletariat. He went on:

> Then consider another thing: the
> colored group is not yet divided
> into capitalists and laborers.
> There are only beginnings of such
> a division. In one hundred years
> if we develop along conventional
> lines we would have such fully
> separated classes, but today to a
> very large extent our laborers
> are our capitalists and our capi-
> talists are our laborers. Our
> small class of well-to-do men
> have come to influence largely
> through manual toil and have
> never been physically or mentally
> separated from the toilers. Our
> professional classes are sons and

daughters of porters, washerwomen
and laborers.[48]

Du Bois viewed this absence of a strong economic
class structure as a democratic basis which, with the
aid of interclass (mainly cultural classes) sympathy,
was the foundation for the introduction of a new
industrial democracy. When this happens, he insisted,
"we may not only escape our present economic slavery
but even guide and lead a distraught economic world."[49]

A 1919 issues of The Crisis included an article
by James Peter Warbasse, the President of the Cooperative League of America. Warbasse explained the
fundamentals and methods of cooperation and documented
the success of various European cooperative movements.[50]
A few months before publishing Warbasse's article, Du
Bois stressed that the best way to explain cooperation
was by way of quoting Warbasse and proceeded to offer
selections from a pamphlet by him. These selections
underlined a feature of cooperation essential to Du
Bois' purpose, that is, that cooperation is "nonpolitical".[51] This was essential for the success of a
racial cooperative because any movement dependent on
government aid would run into the continuing force of
government racism. In short, the government was not
to be trusted. He found in cooperation a successful
movement which had been organized solely on social
lines without government support. Further, the movement had proved successful even though the entire population did not participate, indicating the possibility
of success for the black population independent of
whites as well as the state. Du Bois' addition to
Warbasse's outline, beyond details, mainly concerned
the added racial dimension, and the manner in which
race provided the force, appeal and economic basis for
a successful movement.

Du Bois provided the first concrete proposal for
the implementation of cooperation among blacks in
September 1917. He suggested that cooperative stores
selling groceries, clothing and fuel could be organized with determined effort in cities with a black
population of 10,000 or more.[52]

In September 1918 Du Bois called a meeting to
organize the Negro Cooperative Guild.[53] The meeting
was attended by twelve representatives from seven
states who proposed to hold annual meetings, study

cooperation and "form a central committee for the
guidance and insurance of . . . stores."[54] A month
later he announced that the Negro Cooperative Guild
intended "to spend the year 1919 encouraging as many
American Negroes as possible to study modern consumers'
cooperation."[55] But the movement was almost a complete
failure; a few stores and businesses were established,
only to fail.[56] Du Bois recognized that cooperation
was not especially successful in the United States,
neither among blacks nor whites. But he blamed this
lack of success on insufficient knowledge of its principles and on fraudulent schemes. Many of his efforts
in The Crisis were intended to overcome that lack of
information.

With the lingering of severe depression in the
1930's, he paid more attention to general economic
conditions and to the history of cooperation. He fore-
saw the beginning of a radical change in the industrial
system which imposed a duty on blacks to organize for
the coming form of industry. "The fact is that the
change is inevitable. No system of human culture can
stand world war and industrial cataclysm repeatedly,
without radical reorganization, either by reasoned
reform or irrational collapse."[57] To answer the problem of industrial decay, he invoked the teachings of
well known figures in the development of socialist
thinking, Robert Owen and Charles Fourier. Du Bois
seemed to view himself as being so much in the spirit
of Fourier that he called for the establishment of
"garden cities," in order to develop "a progressively
self-supporting economy that will weld the majority of
our people into an impregnable, economic phalanx."[58]
He knew that many similar socialistic proposals had
failed in the past, but he directed his critics to the
success of cooperation in Denmark, Vienna and Russia;
he also bluntly claimed that "production is already
gone cooperative with technocratic control, oligarchic
ownership and built on Democratic stupidity under a
plutocracy."[59] To further defend his ideas against
critics, he appealed to the strong social basis of the
black community; this he believed to be an advantage
in establishing a cooperative. First, blacks had a
greater motive than past cooperators who were fleeing
poverty: blacks were also escaping murder, insult,
and "social death."[60] Furthermore, "We have an instinct
of race and a bond of color, in place of a protective
tariff for our infant industry. We have, as police
power, social ostracism without; and behind us, if we

will survive, is Must, not May."[61] Those traits were
needed to replace the power of a state and the dictatorship of the proletariat. Blacks neither had a
state nor formed a majority, thus they had to depend
on group solidarity.

One of his last statements on cooperation as
Editor of The Crisis was an explicit attempt to relate
economic cooperation to the Pan-African movement. In
"Pan-Africa and New Racial Philosophy" (November,
1933), he claimed that a common economic bond of
scarcity united American blacks with Africans, so that
whatever may have been true of Afro-Americans with
regard to the necessities and possibilities of cooperation applied even more forcefully to a world-wide
black movement. Together all blacks could raise and
produce everything they needed and desired. This
movement extended in principle to all exploited darker
people: "It is, therefore, imperative that the colored
peoples of the world, and first of all those of Negro
descent, should begin to concentrate upon the problem
of their economic survival, the best of their brains
and education. Pan-Africa means intellectual understanding and cooperation among all groups of Negro
descent in order to bring about at the earliest possible time the industrial and spiritual emancipation of
the Negro people."[62]

Du Bois' program for economic cooperation was not
followed; his emphasis on segregation became an increasing embarrassment to many of those in leadership
roles in the N.A.A.C.P. Finally, when Du Bois resigned
as Editor he charged that the N.A.A.C.P. failed to live
up to the new economic duties imposed on it by the
great depression. And he accurately assessed his lack
of success with cooperation within the N.A.A.C.P. with
the claim that, "My program for economic readjustment
has been totally ignored."[63] This, however, did not
keep him from presenting cooperation, in Dusk of Dawn,
as the only realistic solution to the problems blacks
faced.

IV

One of the primary tasks of Dusk of Dawn was the
formulation of a concept of race capable of uniting
people with diverse cultural backgrounds. This attempt
formed a key link in Du Bois' program of economic
cooperation: the economy he proposed was to be, by

150

and large, segregated and organized by a clear, rational plan for self-improvement. The sort of plan Du Bois envisioned required the unity of all blacks, even though cultural groups within the larger group were often at odds. Thus a uniting force was required; the force of persuasion Du Bois appealed to was race. He concluded that even though the establishment of united effort in economic cooperation would be difficult, there were chances for success:

> In the African communal group, ties of family and blood, of mother and child, of group relationship, made the group leadership strong, even if not always toward the highest culture. In the case of the more artificial group among American Negroes, there are sources of strength in common memories of suffering in the past; in present threats of degradation and extinction; in common ambitions and ideals; in emulation and the determination to prove ability and desert. Here in subtle but real ways the communalism of the African clan can be transferred to the Negro-American group. . . .[64]

The unity and singleness of purpose required for the success of a social economy were to come from the common history of Afro-Americans, an essential ingredient in his revised concept of race. He used the concept of race partly to overcome the problem that blacks lacked unity because of cultural differentiation.

While part of the overall problem was cultural disunity, there were two other sides to the problem blacks faced as defined in Dusk of Dawn: segregation and economic deprivation. Together all three formed the double environment facing blacks. "The Negro American has for his environment not only the white surrounding world, but also, and touching him usually much more nearly and compellingly, is the environment furnished by his own colored group."[65] The theme of the double environment permeates much of Du Bois' writings; its clearest presentation is in Souls of Black Folk.[66] On the black counter-balancing side of the double environment of his early writings was the

151

"Talented Tenth;" later this group was seen as, by
and large, resentful of the segregated or black part
of their environment. Those with greater educational,
cultural, and financial advantages, were forced by
segregation into what was characterized as bitter
contact with the average person, and they often tried
to discriminate themselves from "ordinary" blacks.[67]

Thus two sides of the problem were interlocked--
cultural differentiation and segregation contribute to
bitterness and hostility. But the underlying cause of
these social problems was economic deprivation. "Above
all the Negro is poor: poor by heritage from two
hundred forty-four years of chattel slavery, by emancipation without land or capital and by seventy-five
years of additional wage exploitation and crime peon-
age. . . . The Negro worker has been especially hard
hit by the current depression."[68] Even with the
ending of the Depression Du Bois projected "that not
more than two percent of the Negro families in the
United States would have an income of $2,500 a year
and over; while fifty-eight percent would have incomes
between $500 and $2,500."[69]

Low income contributed to a variety of problems;
poor housing, high death rate, crime and obviously
poor education accounted for much of what Du Bois took
to be the low cultural standing faced by blacks. Consequently, the three aspects of the problem were thoroughly linked. Du Bois summed up with the harsh statement that "The Negro of education and income is jammed
beside the careless, ignorant and criminal."[70] This
made the situation in terms of class structure different from that among whites. For blacks in 1940, Du
Bois argued, "the poor, ignorant, sick and anti-social
form a vast foundation, that upward from that base
stretch classes whose highest members, although few
in number, reach above the average not only of the
Negroes but of the whites."[71] And the "class structure
of the whites, on the other hand, resembles a tower
bulging near the center with the lowest classes small
in number as compared with the middle and lower middle
classes; and the highest classes far more numerous in
proportion than those among blacks."[72] We must note
here that Du Bois was examining cultural class distinctions among blacks as a problem, and not, as in his
early days, as a way toward a solution.

Any solution to the problem needed to be in terms

152

of solving all three aspects: what was required then, was allegiance to the concept of race (group solidarity), the end of economic and hence cultural deprivation, and the solution to the difficult effects of segregation.

Du Bois proceeded to examine and criticize in terms of these three criteria the various solutions offered. Many younger blacks, he maintained, tried to avoid the appearance of segregation and attempted "to join the political and cultural life of the whites."[73] But this usually failed; whites did not accept them and blacks tended to avoid their company. On the other hand, some attempted to withdraw completely from whites by exclusively associating with blacks in existing organizations. This failed by resulting in provincialism and declining cultural contacts. Between these two extremes Du Bois found a continuous gradation of alternatives. But in each case the problem was reinforced: "In practically all cases the net result is a more or less clear and definite crystallization of the cultural elements among colored people into their own groups for social and cultural contact."[74] Du Bois omitted the more obvious: none of these proposed solutions generally ameliorated economic hardship.

Various paths to increased economic well being had been offered. Many proposed that blacks build their own class-dominated social, economic and religious institutions. Du Bois contended that in 1940 this was actually going on in an unplanned way, but on a small level involving small groups joining together and forming new communities mainly on the basis of cultural ties. He insisted that this sort of class oriented movement was counterproductive; it would direct effort and energy "not simply into social advance, but in the vast and intricate effort to duplicate, evolve and contrive new social institutions to maintain their advance and guard against retrogression."[75] At this point he explicitly rejected his early concept of cultural advance through the "Talented Tenth." His new belief was that culture did not maintain an upper class, instead wealth and political influence tend to maintain the upper end of the class structure. Thus a development of a cultural class structure, as in the doctrine of the Talented Tenth, would not further the cultural or the economic conditions of the average black. Besides, economic conditions would not allow the development of a class system paralleling that of whites. Blacks could not match the gradations of wealth in the white community nor the political power necessary to manipulate wealth, and they would not get help from the whites who recommended this plan.

Another proposal had been the use of moral suasion, continuing demands, and physical force in a campaign of agitation for equality. But he asserted that the sort of effective campaign needed was too expensive for a poor group, and, furthermore, agitation had rested on two ungrounded assumptions, both held by him earlier in his life. First, that "race prejudice is a matter of ignorance to be cured by information; and on the other hand that much discrimination is a matter of deliberate devilty and unwillingness to be just."[76] He thus revised his view of racism. The significance of racial distinctions was based on economic exploitation and demanded a doctrine of inferiority that became internalized and mainly subconscious. Du Bois accounted for his view by claiming that he learned it from the "new psychology." "My own study of psychology under William James had pre-dated the Freudian era, but it had prepared me for it. I now began to realize that in the fight against race prejudice, we were not facing simply the rational, conscious determination of white folk to oppress us; we were facing age-long complexes sunk now largely to unconscious habit and irrational urge. . . ."[77] A situation such as this required time and patience for rectification, but the problem was so pressing that time could not be afforded. Hence, merely to agitate without simultaneously establishing an economic base was to lose.

Another form of action which he claimed appealed to the proud and served as a last resort was the "back to Africa" movement. Such plans were merely last resorts because, proximately speaking, they failed the test of reality; he thought that by training, education and habit blacks were unsuited to the life of the pioneer. Also the industrial expansion of Europe "made colonies in Africa or elsewhere about the last place where colored folk could successfully seek freedome and equality."[78]

The positions Du Bois criticized up to this point all fell into the category of traditional solutions espoused by leaders such as Booker T. Washington and

Marcus Garvey, or groups such as the N.A.A.C.P. Most were socially or culturally oriented or were directed to the status quo. Du Bois' solution was at basis a radical economic plan; so the real competition for his cooperative came from alternative plans which were basically economic. He took opposition to three alternate economic approaches: communism, the labor union movement, and the capital-labor strategy.

Du Bois called the communist solution a program for a majority, not a minority. The exploitation historical materialism located in the capitalist era was against an increasingly powerful majority. Blacks, however, formed a minority alienated from the white society, including white workers. He was in some sense a Marxist, yet, as Black Reconstruction shows, the approach Du Bois used contained an essential difference from that of Marx: race was the gap between two sections of the American proletariat. In fact, he maintained that the cleavage between white and black workers was greater than the split between workers and capitalists. He concluded that the "color blindness" of communism obviated its analytical capacities and falsified its vision of revolution. "This philosophy did not envisage a situation where instead of a horizontal division of classes, there was a vertical fissure, a complete separation of classes by race, cutting square across the economic layers."[79]

Probably the greatest influence of the communist party on blacks, Du Bois related, was to accentuate the working class status of blacks and hence to indicate the need to associate with the white labor movement. However, in 1940 Du Bois stated that blacks found the same patterns of discrimination generally in America to be present in the AF of L and the CIO. To counter the problem of discrimination in the ranks of organized labor, Du Bois suggested support for a United Negro Trades modeled after the United Hebrew Trades, which would eventually allow blacks a chance to enter the labor movement with their own organized power as a base. This form of action, he emphasized, would be consonant with his "plan to use the segregation technique for industrial emancipation."[80]

Finally, he explored the proposal that advised blacks to join with labor, but insofar as possible to enter into the ranks of capitalists by becoming employers. Du Bois called this "a sophisticated attempt to

155

dodge the whole problem of color in economic change. . . ."[81] This plan did not face the forthcoming changes in the structure of capitalism he was convinced would come, and it overlooked the difficulty blacks faced in unions and in securing capital and credit.

As was indicated earlier Du Bois intended to use the concept of race as the main social support for his economic cooperative; but he also provided an economic basis as a support for his plan: his contention, asserted during the Depression, that capitalism must undergo fundamental changes in order to survive, led him to the conclusion that the new wave of economic organization would follow the model of consumer oriented production and distribution as proposed in his cooperative plan. He clearly believed that implementing his plan would be justified by the movement of the entire economy toward socialism.

Economic cooperation was selected by Du Bois as a solution because he believed it could solve the internal problems of Afro-Americans, but, furthermore, he felt it conformed to the general requirements of overall economic and social conditions. This fit with his emphasis on the double environment facing blacks; on one side was the white world and on the other, the inner group.[82] Any solution which did not contend with both sides would be only a partial solution. So it was important to Du Bois that his plan be assessed in terms of how it fit into the entire social setting.

His appraisal of economic and social conditions in the late 1930's led to various conclusions significant to his plan for cooperation. First, he insisted that the American class structure, in which income and monopoly dominated state and industry, was breaking down. In short, the great depression witnessed the collapse of capitalism.[83] He believed that this collapse was basically a result of the organization of industry around the producer; future reorganization, he envisionsed, would compensate for this weakness by organizing around consumer needs.[84] It followed that the future of industrialism lay in the support of a consumers' movement such as Du Bois proposed, and he intended blacks to be in the forefront of the new economic structure.

A racial consumers' cooperative was viewed as

sound economically because it based production on consumer needs and not on the profit motivation of the
producer. So whether or not the larger economy
changed to a consumer orientation, the racial cooperative would be following good economic practice. Furthermore, Du Bois agreed with the Marxian contention
that economic conditions were the main determinant of
social institutions.[85] This general principle indicated that the primary solution to any social problem
ought to be economic, and the major considerations
about the surrounding environment ought to be guided
by economic analysis. Hence, Du Bois considered his
theory of cooperation to be based upon realistic and
practical rather than utopian consideration.

V

Cooperation, then, was the plan Du Bois conceived
as best meeting the internal and external demands of
the situation blacks faced. That the plan was not
accepted does not demonstrate that it could not have
succeeded. Perhaps the most damaging argument against
the plan's possibility for success is that he did not
foresee the adoption of new economic policies by the
government which protected this country from severe
depression for over thirty years. However, even this
does not prove that his plan, were it put to operation,
would have failed. Even Du Bois knew the plan would
meet difficulties; he was realistic enough to know that
his proposal would require a degree of discipline and
sacrifice which might prove to be too great.[86]

Even though Du Bois overemphasized the past cooperative spirit among blacks, the plan was well defended.
The development of the idea took Du Bois over forty
years of social investigation and theoretical study.
Implicit in his approach to cooperation was a sound
method for developing solutions to social problems,
especially to the problems of minority groups. The
first step in his method was to survey and clearly
define the problem in order to establish the initial
and essentially negative standards for weighing possible
solutions. This step involves the development of an
exacting statement of the various aspects and ramifi-
cations of a problem in terms which will form the first
criteria for an acceptable solution. In trying to
understand the problems of blacks, Du Bois found that
his analysis of the problem as one of cultural division,
segregation and economic deprivation provided a three-

fold criterion which he could use to judge the merits
of the continuum of solutions presented in his day.
No solution was acceptable unless it dealt with all
three aspects of the problem. Also, he found that
the threefold problem must be viewed from both within
and outside the group, thereby adding a further dimension to his criterion. Consequently, a clear statement
of the problem provided the means of rejecting incom-
plete or flaccid solutions. This first step places
the method in a strongly empirical and pragmatic framework which is antithetical to solutions proposed solely
on the basis of ideological commitment. Thus Du Bois
was unwilling to accept the Marxian solution of proletarian revolution simply on the basis of his own
belief in certain Marxian principles, because such a
solution would not deal with all the aspects of the
problem as he saw it. Nor was he willing to accept
the solution of black capitalism on the ground that it
would have benefitted his own social class and status.

While the first step in the method provides initial
criteria by which proposed solutions should be rejected,
it also begins to suggest the possible general outlines
of a realistic solution. However, more is required for
the formulation of a workable plan than simply a definition of the problem. The second step in Du Bois'
method provided him with positive criteria for evalu-
ating possible solutions. This step required that the
history and cultural heritage of a group be examined
so that the accepted solution would be consistent with
the historical tendencies and the current strengths
and weaknesses exhibited by that group. A proposed
solution might be theoretically acceptable in terms
of the negative criteria, that is, the solution might
in fact be designed to solve the problem which analysis
revealed but it might be the sort of program that would
simply be foreign to the traditional values or behavior
patterns of the group. Thus there needs to be some
indication that the group will respond favorably to the
plan and that the group possesses the required characteristics to make the plan work. Du Bois' plan for
solving the problem facing blacks required a spirit of
cooperation and the presence of an economic base in
the black community. He found a cooperative spirit
permeating Afro-American history, and he found that
blacks already had a partly established group economy.
Therefore he proposed racial economic cooperation as
a method which would take advantage of the strengths
of the black community and tend to overcome its weak-

nesses. He found strength in the concept of race identity and in the group's classless economic structure, and he believed that the weakness of cultural division and of segregation could be overcome through the appeal to racial loyalty and through the expedient use of segregation.

The third point in the method is extremely important and introduces a future-oriented perspective. Du Bois attempted to demonstrate that his plan was in harmony with social developments that would affect the problematic situation in the future. His point was that any plan worthy of adoption must be in harmony with relevant predicted social developments. He believed that the essential development would be a change in the economic structure away from the dying capitalism of the Depression era towards a socialized cooperative economy. Proposing a black cooperative was in line with this expected future since blacks would not only be a part of it but could be leaders. Black capitalism, on the other hand, would have to be rejected as antithetical to the expected future.

Finally, Du Bois' method was based on the assumption that the foundation of most social problems were economic. He came to this view for various reasons, one of the most important being his belief that racial prejudice was rooted in slavery as an economy system.[87] But in terms of his method for dealing with social problems, this view operated as the explicit premise that in defining the problem and organizing a solution, economic considerations must be primary. For example, Du Bois viewed the classless economic structure of the black community as a more powerful social factor than the cultural division within the community. And partly as a result of this view, he proposed an economic solution which would be strongly supported by the substructure of a group economy and which would take advantage of expected economic developments.

Proposed solutions to social problems are obviously never foolproof and conclusive means to test them are rarely available. However, Du Bois' method was meant to eliminate those suggestions which were Utopian or alien to the group, those based solely on ideology or social commitment, those which were not future-oriented, and those which failed to give economic factors their due weight.

Du Bois' plan was not successful: it was never adequately tested. After 1940 little mention was made of economic cooperation. In fact, Du Bois never again proposed a detailed large-scale social program for blacks. His attention turned instead to various other pursuits, developed in a way which seems to represent more of a search for alternatives than for a plan of action. Many of his earlier concerns, however, remained intact after Du Bois left The Crisis. He continued to develop his socialistic ideas, he became increasingly interested in Africa, and he consistently advocated peace.

NOTES

1. W.E.B. Du Bois, Dusk of Dawn: An Essay Toward An Autobiography of a Race Concept (New York: Schocken Books, 1968), p. 280.

2. Francis L. Broderick in W.E.B. Du Bois: Negro Leader in a Time of Crisis (Stanford: Stanford University Press), p. 178, contended that the plan for economic cooperation was an inevitable failure because it was "built on a racial chauvinism which the race would not sustain." Elliott M. Rudwick in W.E.B. Du Bois: Propagandist of the Negro Protest (New York: Atheneum, 1969), p. 196, saw Du Bois' theory of cooperation as a mark of his "frustration at being in a no-man's land and groping desperately for an exit." Julius Lester's lengthy Introduction gave cooperation only the briefest mention in The Seventh Son: The Thought and Writings of W.E.B. Du Bois (2 vols.) (New York: Random House, 1971), I, pp. 87-88. Du Bois recognized that his plan was not accepted. In his letter of resignation as Editor of The Crisis he lamented that "My program for economic readjustment has been totally ignored." W.E.B. Du Bois, The Crisis, XLI (August, 1934), p. 245.

3. Du Bois, Dusk of Dawn, p. 215.

4. Part of this outline comes from James Peter Warbasse's article "The Theory of Cooperation," The Crisis, XV (March, 1918), p. 221.

5. W.E.B. Du Bois, The Crisis, XIV (September, 1917), p. 215.

6. Du Bois, Dusk of Dawn, p. 213.

7. Ibid., p. 198.   8. Ibid., p. 210.

9. Ibid., p. 201.   10. Ibid., p. 214.

11. For a brief description of cooperation in Europe, see Harry W. Laidler, History of Socialism (New York: Thomas Y. Crowell Co., 1968), Chapter 41.

12. Du Bois, Correspondence, II, p. 102.

13. Du Bois, Dusk of Dawn, pp. 193-194.

14. Ibid., p. 219.

15. Du Bois, Correspondence, p. 233.

16. W.E. Burghardt Du Bois (ed.), Some Efforts of American Negroes for Their Own Social Betterment (Atlanta: Atlanta University, 1898).

17. W.E. Burghardt Du Bois (ed.), Efforts for Social Betterment Among Negro Americans (Atlanta: University, 1909), p. 10.

18. Du Bois (ed.) Some Efforts of American Negroes for Their Own Betterment, p. 43.

19. W.E. Burghardt Du Bois (ed.), The Negro Artisan (Atlanta: Atlanta University, 1902), p. 22.

20. Du Bois (ed.), Economic Cooperation Among Negro Americans (Atlanta: Atlanta University, 1907), p. 149.

21. Du Bois (ed.), Efforts for Social Betterment Among Negro Americans, p. 11.

22. Du Bois (ed.), Economic Cooperation Among Negro Americans, p. 24.

23. Ibid.   24. Ibid., p. 26.

25. Ibid.   26. Ibid., p. 54.

27. Du Bois (ed.), Some Efforts of American Negroes for Their Own Social Betterment, p. 4.

28. Du Bois (ed.), Economic Cooperation Among Negro Americans, p. 73.

29. Du Bois (ed.), Some Efforts of American Negroes for Their Own Social Betterment, p. 17.

30. Du Bois (ed.), Economic Cooperation Among Negro Americans, p. 11.

31. Du Bois (ed.), Economic Cooperation Among Negro Americans, p. 157. He claimed, however, that productive cooperation was rarely successful "as the history of cooperation among all nations proves. . . ." Ibid., p. 159.

32. Du Bois (ed.), Some Efforts of American Negroes for Their Social Betterment, p. 24.

33. Du Bois (ed.), The Negro American Artisan (Atlanta: Atlanta University, 1912), p. 40.

34. Ibid.,   35. Ibid., p. 142.

36. Ibid., p. 129

37. W.E.B. Du Bois, The Crisis, V (February, 1913), p. 184.

38. Ibid., p. 185.   39. Ibid., p. 186.

40. Ibid.

41. W.E.B. Du Bois, The Crisis, IX (April, 1915), p. 312.

42. Ibid.

43. W.E.B. Du Bois, The Crisis, VIII (July, 1914), p. 128. Emphasis added.

44. W.E.B. Du Bois, The Crisis, II (June, 1911), pp. 64-65.

45. W.E.B. Du Bois, The Crisis, VI (October, 1913), p. 290.

46. W.E.B. Du Bois, The Crisis, XV (January, 1918), p. 115.

47. W.E.B. Du Bois, The Crisis, XIV (August, 1917), p. 166.

48. W.E.B. Du Bois, The Crisis, XXII (August, 1921), p. 152.

49. Ibid.

50. W.E.B. Du Bois, The Crisis, XV (March, 1918), pp. 221-224.

51. W.E.B. Du Bois, The Crisis, XV (November, 1917), p. 9.

52. W.E.B. Du Bois, The Crisis, XIV (September, 1917), p. 215.

53. W.E.B. Du Bois, The Crisis, XVI (September, 1918), p. 215.

54. W.E.B. Du Bois, The Crisis, XVI (October, 1918), p. 268.

55. W.E.B. Du Bois, The Crisis, XVII (November, 1918), p. 10.

56. Du Bois, Dusk of Dawn, p. 280.

57. W.E.B. Du Bois, The Crisis, XL (April, 1933), p. 93.

58. Ibid.   59. Ibid.

60. Ibid., p. 94.   61. Ibid.

62. W.E.B. Du Bois, "Pan-Africa and New Racial Philosophy," The Crisis, XL (November, 1933), p. 247.

63. W.E.B. Du Bois, The Crisis, XLI (August, 1934), p. 245.

64. Du Bois, Dusk of Dawn, p. 219.

65. Ibid., p. 173.

66. W.E. Burghardt Du Bois, The Souls of Black Folk (Greenwich, Conn.: Fawcett Publications, Inc., 1961), p. 17.

67. Du Bois, Dusk of Dawn, pp. 179.

68. Ibid., p. 181.

69. Ibid., p. 182.

70. Ibid., p. 185.

71. Ibid., p. 183.

72. Ibid.

73. Ibid., pp. 186-187.

74. Ibid., p. 187.

75. Ibid., pp. 188-189.

76. Ibid., p. 194.

77. Ibid., p. 296.

78. Ibid., p. 196.

79. Du Bois, Dusk of Dawn, p. 205.

80. Ibid., p. 207.

81. Ibid.

82. Du Bois, Souls of Black Folk, p. 17: "The Study of the Negro Problems," Speech on November 19, 1897, American Academy of Political and Social Science, in Lester, The Seventh Son, I, p. 244; Dusk of Dawn, p. 173.

83. Du Bois, Dusk of Dawn, p. 198.

84. Ibid., p. 208.

85. Ibid., p. 303.

86. Ibid., pp. 209-210.

87. Dusk of Dawn is, in part, a chronicle of the considerations which led him to the adoption of this Marxian perspective.

CHAPTER VI

SOCIALISM, PEACE AND AFRICA

Du Bois' proposal for a black cooperative hinged on several views: (1) the absence of an economic class-structure in the black community, (2) the coming decay of capitalism during the Great Depression, and (3) his rejection of communism. During the last period of his life, roughly from 1941-1963, all three came under revision, and his plan was rejected. The rejection of his cooperative left him without a program; he never developed another program for social advance. He did make a series of brief suggestions and eventually, toward the end of his life, he accepted communism, as the only real solution to the world's problems. But the positions taken during these years were vague and sketchy; even his adoption of communism was ambiguous on central points.

After 1940, as the attention he paid to economic cooperation diminished, his efforts turned increasingly to two interrelated topics: Africa and world peace. His interest in Africa followed naturally from his later concept of race: the perceived bond of economic exploitation brought him to a close theoretical bind with the people of Africa and so a greater practical concern for African problems. His Pan-African movement took on new meaning insofar as it became truly centered in Africa, but this drew his interest away from racial matters in the United States. Africa also maintained a central role in the question of war and peace. His part in the peace movement around the time of World War II and into the fifties, revived his view, adopted in the 1920's, that World War followed from African exploitation and that peace would come only if African exploitation ended.

His writings on Africa in the 1940's prompted a thoroughgoing critique of capitalism in the United States and Western Europe. But even with his overwhelmingly negative appraisal of the United States, he hesitated in espousing communism. He maintained a reformist attitude toward the United States until he was in his nineties; he hoped for an extension of Roosevelt's New Deal so that the country could move toward socialism guided by the electorate.

The period considered in this final chapter in-

cludes more than 20 years, during which he occupied
several different posts. In 1934 he resigned from
the N.A.A.C.P. and went back into academic life, to be
unexpectedly retired in 1944. He returned to the
N.A.A.C.P. as Director of Special Research, but had
little authority and mainly pursued his own interests;
in 1948 problems with the executive secretary, Walter
White, lead to Du Bois' dismissal by the Board.[1] After
his dismissal he remained in New York City as co-chairman of the Council on African Affairs, worked for
various peace movements and visited Russia and China.
In 1961 he moved his permanent residence to Ghana to
direct work on a proposed <u>Encyclopedia</u> <u>Africana</u>. He
died in Africa in 1963.

I

A major change in the final period of his life
involved his eventual acceptance of communism (late
in his life) and his movement toward increasing concern
over Africa; this exhibited a concomitant shift in
attitude about the American black community. The
examination of this period begins by examining in detail the reasons for rejecting, in the beginning of
the period, a complete Marxian perspective. These
reasons crystalize his attitudes toward the black
community at least until the early 1940's. The eventual shift to the adoption of Marxism can then be read
as a rejection of the validity of the criticism he made
and as a re-evaluation of the class-status of the black
community.

The May, 1933 issue of <u>The</u> <u>Crisis</u> contains one of
Du Bois' fullest statements on theoretical Marxism;
although brief, his statement underscores his objections to it. He began by identifying what he took to
be the essentials of Marxism: economic determinism,
class struggle, the labor theory of value, exploitation
of labor in surplus value,[2] and the inevitableness of
a revolution ending exploitation and allowing for the
distribution of goods and services according to need.

Du Bois was unwilling to evaluate doctrines such
as the labor theory of value and the theory of surplus
value; he simply claimed that there were known logical
and theoretical difficulties in Marx. Nevertheless,
Du Bois explicitly agreed that economic reorganization
was crucial, especially in light of the Great Depression. He added, in agreement with the basic philosoph-

ical thrust of the labor theory of value that, "Labor . . . is the sure foundation of value and whatever we call it--exploitation, theft or business acumen--there is something radically wrong with an industrial system that turns out simultaneously paupers and millionaires and sets a world starving because it has too much food."[3]

After acknowledging his sympathy with Marxism, he proceeded to identify two main problems: (1) The role of intra-class struggle had been largely ignored by Marxism. For example, while blacks were part of the proletariat, there was a split between the white and black proletariat in the United States. But Du Bois here was not simply satisfied with locating the split; he went on to claim, in effect, that greatest abuse of blacks was at the hands of the white proletariat rather than the capitalistic structure; and ignorance was no excuse: ". . . the bulk of American white labor is neither ignorant nor fanatical. It knows exactly what it is doing. . . ."[4] The criticism goes to the heart of the Marxist view of a unity of economic interest overriding other and less important interests. Here Du Bois had a non-economic, psychological motivation (racism) overtaking economic unity of interest (yet he recognized this unity as a valid real interest),[5] and by denying that this took place in ignorance, closes a possible way of defending the primacy of economic interest. This gap in the proletariat, as noted earlier, was used to explain events in the Reconstruction period.

His second criticism was based on a development in capitalism since the death of Marx: Capitalism had become world-wide in structure. The tremendous technical expansion in production had created a new working class of technologists and managers "forming a working aristocracy between the older proletariat and the absentee owners of capital."[6] These and other workers were able to invest small amounts of money which made them, even if only in their own minds, partners in capitalism. And through their savings, a powerful class of financiers, standing between capital and labor, had grown up to further complicate the class structure. Furthermore, the common laborer in the main wanted to become rich by exploiting his fellow workers. This characterization of the laborer as exploiter was facilitated by their identification with a particular ethnic group in opposition to other groups: "Thus in America we have seen a wild and ruthless scramble of labor groups over each other in order to climb to wealth on the backs of black labor and foreign immigrants."[7]

Du Bois located a second influence on white labor that also mitigates the Marxian analysis: world-wide imperialism had used grossly substandard pay and conditions in underdeveloped regions to gain excess profits in order to bribe the "white workers by high wages, visions of wealth and the opportunity to drive 'niggers.'"[8] Such a position is, in its essentials, in line with Lenin's revision of Marxism. Claiming that western capitalism used imperialistic exploitation of foreign labor as a way of amassing wealth, Lenin added, "Obviously, out of such enormous superprofits (since they are obtained over and above the profits which capitalists squeeze out of the workers of their 'own' country) it is possible to bribe the labor leaders and upper stratum of the labor aristocracy. And that is just what the capitalists of the 'advanced' countries are doing: they are bribing them in a thousand different ways, direct and indirect, overt and covert."[9] Lenin also examined the expanding role of financial institutions as part of the final stage of capitalistic development.[10] With these similarities between Du Bois and Lenin one questions why Du Bois did not mention Lenin. The apparent answer to this is found in his Correspondence (Vol. III) in which he asks H. Aptheker (in a 1954 letter) for source material to follow-up his reading Lenin's "imperialism." Aptheker comments that Du Bois studied Lenin late in his life;[11] this would, of course, explain the absence.

Du Bois concluded that while Marxism was by and large valid for Europe in the 19th century, it must be modified for use in the United States. He did not explain the details of the modifications, which would appear to be so extensive as to amount to a rejection of Marxism; he did, however, claim in his closing sentence, that, "In the hearts of black laborers alone, therefore, lie those ideals of democracy in politics and industry which may in time make the workers of the world effective dictators of civilization."[12] This statement indicates that the "reform" in Marxism should at least involve the sort of attempt at reform suggested by Lenin: A world proletariat must be identified and distinguished from the exploiting proletariat of Western countries. In this world proletar-

168

iat Du Bois would appear to locate peoples in lesser-developed countries and virtually all blacks in the United States.

Although these weaknesses were stressed, Du Bois still considered himself to be in essential agreement with Marxism "that eventually land, machines and materials must belong to the state; that private profit must be abolished; that the system of exploiting labor must disappear; that people who work must have essentially equal income; and that in their hands the political rulership of the state must eventually rest."[13] But he quickly added that socialism had no automatic power over racism.

Du Bois not only examined Marxism from a theoretical perspective but also took issue with the practical political affairs in organized communist movements. In the 30's he had little praise for the American Communist Party. In 1936 he advised against blacks joining the Party: "The Communists of America have become dogmatic exponents of the inspired word of Karl Marx as they read it. They believe, apparently, in immediate, violent and bloody revolution, and they are willing to try any and all means of raising hell anywhere and under any circumstances. This is a silly program even for white men. For American colored men, it is suicide."[14] In 1931 he critcized the radical movement in the United States, including socialists and communists, by claiming that it was only concerned about white labor and thereby usually ignored black labor.[15] Beyond this, Du Bois charged that American Communists were willing to use blacks as "shock troops" to be cruelly and publicly harmed by the structures of capitalism in order to expose its evils to the American people. Du Bois made this charge in obvious anger against the treatment by American Communists of eight young blacks in the Scotsboro case. In that case he claimed that Communists attempted to undermine the N.A.A.C.P.'s defense of the youths with propaganda slogans which he felt would effectively deny the defendants any possibility of a fair trial.[16]

These issues were raised against the American Communist Party and do not apply to all communists and should not be read as contradicting his generally favorable attitude toward Russia following his first visit in 1926. In fact, Du Bois' praise for Russia was usually elaborate. Commenting on his 1926 visit, he stated: "The marks of war were all over Russia--of the war of France and England to turn back the clock of revolution. Wild children were in the sewers of Moscow; food was scarce, clothes were in rags, and the fear of renewed Western aggression hung like a pall. Yet Russia was and still is to my mind the most hopeful land in the modern world."[17]

With the decline in capitalism during the Great Depression and with the absence of a class structure in the black community, Du Bois offered cooperation as the only solution to racial problems. But when America moved into World War II, Du Bois' attention turned toward it and away from cooperation. Economic recovery in the United States seems to have played a part in his near omission of cooperation of his writings after 1940.[18] He apparently believed that if the plan did not catch on during the crisis years of the depression, its chances during a recovery period were virtually zero.

Attention to the war meant, for Du Bois, a renewed interest in Africa. In fact, after 1940 the percentage of his writings about <u>American</u> blacks dropped greatly-- Africa, Russia, China, and the Peace movement occupied his most significant efforts. He began to believe that the American black community contained a significant class structure, that the hope of the world rested with the communistic countries and with the colonial lands, and later in his life, that communism must be accepted in the United States.

II

The turn in attention to Africa, colonialism, imperialism and war dominated his work until his death in 1963. However, the seeds for this turn were well planted in Du Bois' thought from his earliest essays. As previously stated, his original concept of race, although asserting a link between Afro-Americans and Africans, made the link difficult to maintain; indeed the cultural life of Africans and Afro-Americans appeared to be quite different. The later concept of race, on the other hand, established a strong link between these groups, as was intended. That is, the later concept of race solves a problem in the earlier concept. When taken seriously, in fact, the ties Du Bois considered significant were most clearly present in colonial lands and were to some degree less mani-

170

fest among Afro-Americans during the forties.

The concept of race centers attention on Africa
because Africa was the center of the slavery, exploitation and suffering Du Bois referred to. Because
"race" was linked to economic exploitation, the
strongest racial ties were in those places where problems were greatest. These places, around the time of
World War II, were identified as the colonies. In
Color and Democracy (1945) Du Bois put the matter in
straightforward terms: "Colonies are the slums of the
world. They are today the places of the greatest concentration of poverty, disease, and ignorance. . . ."[19]

In an attempt to explore the significance of race,
Du Bois attempted, in the 1940's, to show the link
between European and American life and slavery and
colonialism. Both of these involved Africa: "In
modern times two great world movements have hinged on
the relation of Africa to other continents: the
African slave trade, which transferred perhaps ten
million laborers from Africa to America and played a
major role in the establishment of capitalism in
England and Europe based on sugar and cotton; and the
partitioning of Africa after the Franco-Prussian War
which, with the Berlin Conference in 1884, brought
colonial imperialism to flower."[20] In 1944 Du Bois
argued that the slave trade up to the 19th century
"was the greatest social event of modern history."[21]
Various reasons, besides the enormous drama of the
suffering and loss of life it involved, seemed to
provide evidence in support of this claim.

First of all, Du Bois believed that slavery provided the major support for the accumulation of capital
and thereby for the development of modern industry.
In The World and Africa he credited Marx with pointing
out capitalism's foundation in slavery.[22] In support
of this thesis, Du Bois surveyed the triangular trade
as the method by which England pursued capital investment. The products of slavery (sugar, tobacco, and
cotton) allowed England to become a manufacturing
country and spurred the development of new industrial
techniques. The profits from colonial trade allowed
for accumulation of much of the capital used to finance
the Industrial Revolution. At this point in his analysis, he approvingly quoted from Eric William's
Capitalism and Slavery, which followed Marx in claiming
that capital development in Great Britain mainly stem-

med from slavery and the slave trade. (Indeed, much of Du Bois' brief statement was nearly directly from Williams.) Du Bois quoted Williams' citation of Bourne's claim identifying the British Empire as a "'magnificent superstructure of American commerce and naval power on an African foundation.'"23

According to Du Bois, the fundamental factor allowing for the development of large-scale industry, as opposed to small-scale medieval production, was the nature of the raw materials supplied by the slave system. Previously, the commerce that did exist was in exotic luxuries, but the products produced by slaves were used for mass consumption: "The result of this labor was an economic organization by which the middle-classes of the world were supplied with a cheap, sweetening material derived from sugarcane; a cheap luxury, tobacco; and finally and above all, a cheap and universal material for clothing, cotton."24

The result of the development of capitalism was an enormous increase of Great Britain's power, especially in relationship to Africa and Asia.25 Great Britain's ability to dominate the world stemmed from her industrial development supported by slavery.

Aside from supporting capitalism, slavery proved to be important, in Du Bois' view, because of its impact on the sensibilities of Europeans and Americans. His position was that it created a callousness about human rights and human dignity. At the time when the notion of human rights was advanced in philosophical doctrines (such as in the theory that government is validated by the consent of the people and in the view that human action is to be evaluated by the happiness it produces for all humans), these notions of human rights were not applied to most of the world's peoples. This led to conflicts between thought and action. He observed: "I believe that the trade in human beings between Africa and America, which flourished between the Renaissance and the American Civil War, is the prime and effective cause of the contradictions in European civilization and the illogic in modern thought and the collapse of human culture."26 Much of his effort after 1940 was devoted not to a programmatic approach to reform but to an investigation of the "contradictions" in Western culture.

During the time of slavery Europeans developed a

problematic attitude toward wealth. Wealth became regarded as a kind of end-in-itself instead of a service to humans. For Du Bois, the slave trade initiated the "modern change from regarding wealth as being for the benefit of human beings, to that of regarding human beings as wealth."[27] In short, slavery ushered in an overriding sense of greed; the acquisition of wealth became the main object of labor. Human labor was looked on as valueless in itself, as degrading and to be avoided when consistent with accumulating wealth. The degardation of labor reduced the perceived status of human dignity in the laborer. Respect for humanity was thereby lost.[28] The age of slavery, then, witnessed a significant growth of greed based on vast new accumulations of wealth. The result of the degradation of labor was, in his view, twofold: (1) The struggle for social improvement in the condition of labor in Europe was hampered. Despite the fact that labor's share of the new wealth grew and despite newly won political freedoms, the movement toward economic and political equality became more difficult because of the supposed position of labor as justly inferior.[29] (2) The rationalization of the cruelty of slavery linked, for the first time, "color to race and blackness to slavery and degradation."[30]

Du Bois saw slavery as blocking a movement toward respect among humans; he thus tried to relate both the development of revolt in the laboring classes and the communistic movement to African slavery.

> from the early Christian communism and sense of human brotherhood which began to grow in the Dark Ages and to blossom in the Renaissance, there came to white workers in England, France, and Germany the iron law of wages, the population doctrines of Maltus and the bitter fight against the early trade unions. The first efforts at education and particularly the trend toward political democracy, aroused an antagonism of which the French Revolution did not dream. It was the bitter fight that exacerbated the class struggle and resulted in the first furious expression of communism and attempt at revolution. The unity of apprentice and master,

the Christian sympathy between rich
and poor, the communism of medieval
charity, all were thrust into the
new straight-jacket of thought;
poverty was the result of sloth and
crime; wealth was the reward of
virtue and work. The degraded
yellow and black peoples were in the
places which the world of necessity
assigned to the inferior; and toward
these lower ranks the working classes
of all countries tended to sink save
as they were raised and supported by
the rich, the investors, the captains
of industry.[31]

Du Bois thus broke with Marx's more rigid view
that all periods exhibit fundamental class opposition.
Du Bois seemed to read history as displaying a movement
toward class reconciliations until the slavery movement.
Marx claimed, in a well known passage of the Communist
Manifesto that "Freeman and slave, patrician and
plebian, lord and serf, guildmaster and journeyman, in
a word, oppressor and oppressed, stand in constant
opposition of one another, carried on in an uninter-
rupted, now hidden, now open fight. . . ."[32] It is
not so much that Du Bois denied an opposition between
classes, but that he apparently asserted a precapital-
istic movement toward an amelioration of the opposition.

Consequently, the loss of life and cruelty of
slavery had effects that went beyond the treatment of
Africa. But costs to Africa were enormous. The dis-
ruption caused by the death or deportation of some
100 million people over the centuries was significant
in itself. But it also meant the development of tribal
wars and the general retardation of African development.[33]

The slave trade eventually stopped, Du Bois
insisted, not solely because it was viewed as cruel
and inhuman, but mainly because it became unprofitable
and new types of investment leading to colonialism
proved more profitable. ". . . new fields of investment and profit were being opened to Englishmen by the
consolidation of the empire in India and by the acquisition of new spheres of influence in China and elsewhere. In Africa, British rule was actually strength-

ened by the anti-slavery crusade, for new territory
was annexed and controlled under the aegis of emancipation."[34]

III

Slavery gave way to colonialism and economic
imperialism. Africa became a source of cheap raw
materials produced by poorly paid indigenous labor.
Through the years the main efforts of Europeans, Du
Bois claimed, was to search for new ways to exploit
Africa. At first gold and diamonds were the main
concern; but gradually Africa became valuable for
other important resources: vegetable oils, copper,
tin, manganese, vanadiam, cocoa, rubber, cotton, etc.[35]

The effort at investment in Africa was dominated
by an excess rate of profit and by conditions which
made European labor less profitable: "Profit in home
industry is being increasingly limited by organized
labor; by the demand for higher wages and shorter hours;
by limitation of the labor of children and women; and
by other devices for diverting the profit of the in-
vestor and property-owner to the income of the wage-
earner."[36]

The greed of colonialism eventually led to World
War.[37] At this point Du Bois centered on the depression as a proximate cause. He remarked, "Make no
mistake, war did not cause the Great Depression; it
was the reasons behind the depression that caused war
and will cause it again."[38] He was not at all clear
about the causes of depression. He seemed to view it,
much as many socialists do, as the result of a lack
of social planning or as a periodic breakdown in the
market equilibrium. Yet this is related to imperialism.
The relationship between depression, imperialism and
war, although unclear in Du Bois' origins, seems to be
as follows: Lack of large-scale social planning of
the sort supported by socialism, leads to depression.
Socialism thus offers a solution to recurrent economic
crises. But imperialism divides nations in their greed
over colonial possessions, fosters war in colonial
lands[39] (and so world wars) and through its racism and
brutality, causes a "moral pollution." "Under this
veil, cheating, lying, murder and rape, force, decep-
tion, bribery, and destruction, become methods of
achieving imperial power, with few questions asked."[40]
And under these conditions socialism is untenable:
"The questions of Egypt and India, Kenya and Palestine,

175

make it impossible for Ramsey MacDonald, Lord Olivier, Sidney Webb and many others to follow out their Socialistic principles."[41] The solution mainly sought to economic crises in the West, then, was not social planning with human welfare as its object, but increased profits through further exploitation. In sum, the exploitation of colonial lands blocked a socialistic solution to depression.

This analysis of the causes of world war, constant in Du Bois from the 1920's, is similar to Lenin's view; it is another point of intellectual compatibility between Lenin and Du Bois. In 1917, Lenin wrote: "Both the Germans and the Anglo-French bourgeoisie are waging the war for the plunder of foreign countries and the strangling of small nations, for financial world supremacy and the division and redivision of colonies, and in order to save the tottering capitalist regime by misleading and dividing the workers of the various countries."[42]

War and peace were clearly related in Du Bois' perspective on colonialism and economic imperialism. Virtually all other major social problems were also related to slavery, colonialism and imperialism because so many situations were saturated with doctrine of racial superiority. So he pleaded that world peace would come only after racial peace came. He hoped that this would be recognized with the end of the trauma of World War II. He argued that post-world war planning, in order to secure peace, must deal with the sorts of problems exacerbated by the notion that some people are naturally superior to others. During the war Du Bois surveyed the major questions that needed to be dealt with when the fighting ended: The major problems were defense, full employment, economic distribution of raw materials and manufactured goods, the abolition of poverty, and the general improvement of health.[43] He claimed that "race-thinking," by which he meant "racism," diminishes the chances of solving any of these.

First of all, racism limited the scope of reform to the predominantly white sections of the world. This meant that problems remained essentially untackled for most of the people of the world. Racism essentially perverted those institutions in the West which were called upon for solutions within Europe and America. Hence, no meaningful solution even within capitalistic countries was possible. The social sciences, for example, had been used, he believed, as a tool to validate racism and thus tended to lose their ability to ascertain the truth about social relationships.[44] And the truth was needed to effect reform. In political organization, the maintenance of racism created political oligarchy and hampered democracy. In America the absence of black voters gave greater power to Southern Whites who exercised a disproportionate share of power with which to block social reform.

As an example of the way racism tended to invalidate social science inquiry, he pointed out that colonialism was not properly studied by economists. Race injustice, prolonging economic inequality, upset the economist's ability to deal with economic realities head on. "Organized industry has today made the teaching of the elementary principles of economic thought almost impossible in our schools and rare in our colleges; by outlawing 'Communistic' propaganda, it has effectively in press and on platform almost stopped efforts at clear thinking on economic reform."[45]

By and large, then, the problems Europe and America faced were viewed as the long-range results of slavery, racism and imperialism. Du Bois viewed the central problems in a sort of Marxian way, identifying them as "contradictions" in the social structure. For example, the "Golden Rule" stood beside the use of force "to keep human beings in their appointed places." The "White Man's Burden" was accompanied "by the actuality of famine, pestilence, and caste." Lip, service was paid to democracy while "the mass of people were kept so poor, and through their poverty so diseased and ignorant, that they could not carry on successfully a modern state or modern industry." And the peace movement of the 19th century turned its back on the almost continuous "wars . . . waged to subjugate colonial peoples."[46]

Du Bois' rejection of capitalism in the West was nearly thorough, and at its basis stood the drive for profit. Profit, not welfare, was the motive of capitalism; the ideal was the rich man, and this created a "spiritual slavery."[47] He concluded that America needs to foster industrial organization for equality, welfare, to move toward an end to racism and war, and to recognize the interdependence of all people.

177

Apparently DuBois believed that anxiety prevalent over the maintenance of peace and questions about the status of colonies provided an opportunity for reform. Consequently, he sought to influence the initial talks at Dumbarton Oaks which eventually led to the development of the United Nations. His message was that a disregard for the colonies equaled a plan for war instead of for peace.[48] He criticized the Dumbarton Oaks conference because it ignored the colonies taken from Germany. This, in effect, meant that these colonies would be assumed as part of already existing empires.[49]

Du Bois' appeal was, in the main, to democracy, equality, and the avoidance of war between world powers. Besides these, however, he suggested that colonial areas will eventually rebel if they are not properly treated: "Have the present masters of the world such an eternal lien on civilization as to ensure unending control? By no means; their very absorption in war and wealth has so weakened their moral fiber that the end of their rule is in sight. Also, the day of the colonial conquered peoples dawns, obscurely but surely."[50]

IV

At the end of World War II it did not seem that the Western countries would change their attitude toward Africa and Asia. This and Du Bois' fundamental rejection of the life style and attitudes of Europeans and Americans made any reformist plan seem futile. Nevertheless, he did not take up a revolutionary attitude. He seemed to maintain the belief that America was not ready for a communist movement, for the sorts of reasons already given, and that colonial lands were only potentially rebellious, and so, more proximately, what was required was a change of attitude on the part of imperial powers. The fact that he did not advocate specific, radical change placed Du Bois in what we might call a negative period; after 1940 his main insights and the bulk of his writing were mainly concerned with exposing global problems.

There were scattered positive proposals after 1940, but none appeared as a seriously developed plan and one in particular seemed to be ad hoc and virtually counter to his usual attitude. Du Bois in the main was non-religious and sometimes even hostile to religion because he viewed it as standing in defense of exploitation.[51] Yet in 1945 organized religion was briefly presented as the only means to attain the motivation required to aid the struggle of those in exploited lands: ". . . it is all too clear today that if we are to have a sufficient motive for the uplift of backward peoples, for the redemption and progress of colonials, such a motive can be found only in the faith and ideals of organized religion; and the great task that is before us is to join this belief and the consequent action with the scientific knowledge and efficient techniques of economic reform."[52] This approach viewed the amelioration of colonial conditions as requiring a philanthropic effort directed mainly by Europeans and Americans.[53] Organized religion was not advocated again; later on he implicitly rejected the basis of such a view because Africans were placed in a central position in their own development. And even before looking to religion (in an article published a year earlier), Du Bois approved a policy whereby the world proletariat could partially use their own power and thus by-pass appeals to philanthropic aid. After calling for a consumers cooperative on an international scale, he quixotically stated: "A union of economic liberals across the race line, with the object of driving exploiting investors from their hideout behind race discrimination, by freeing thought and action in colonial areas is the only realistic path to permanent peace today."[54] This union would be aided, he claimed, by an international mandates commission, presumably under an organization like the United Nations, "with native representation, with the power to investigate and report, and with jurisdiction over all areas where the natives have no effective voice in government."[55]

The point is that in the 1940's it is not only difficult to find a well defined positive plan, but even difficult to find a consistent attitudinal direction. His views were vague and sometimes contradictory. For example, his attitude toward Russia in 1945 was ambivalent; it seems that he considered Russia to have been in a transition period from war to peace from which it was possible for her either to adopt a policy of exploitation or to become the hope of the world.[56] Du Bois maintained a strong interest in Russia for many years and especially stated an admiration for her attempts to provide education for the masses and to solve the problems of its racial diversity. But he did not offer a scenario on how a progressive Russia

would benefit the people of Asia and Africa--aside
from an implicit suggestion that Russia might help
the Chinese Communists.[57]

Du Bois, in this period, rejected capitalism,
supported socialism and believed that Communism was
inevitable.[58] Yet he maintained the view, perplexing
in light of these attitudes, that "There is still a
chance for the capitalist nations to set their houses
in order, and to show that neither Socialism nor its
extreme, Communism, is necessary for human happiness
and progress."[59] Part of the problem here may rest
with the definition of terms. "Communism" and "Socialism" have no clear, universally accepted meanings and
therefore are used in different ways by different
authors. Fortunately, Du Bois gave what seems to have
been his idea of the defining features of both:

> The Progressives and Socialists
> propose in general increased
> government ownership of land
> and natural resources, state
> control of the larger public
> services and such progressive
> taxation of incomes and inherit-
> ance as shall decrease the
> number and power of the rich.
> The Communists, on the other
> hand, propose an entire
> sweeping away of the present
> organization of industry; the
> ownership of land, resources,
> machines and tools by the state,
> under incomes which the state
> limits. And in order to intro-
> duce this complete Socialistic
> regime, Communists propose a
> revolutionary dictatorship by
> the working class, as the only
> sure, quick and effective path.[60]

Part of the problem in determining how the United
States and Europe can be reformed while maintaining
capitalism can be solved through the last sentence of
the above definitional note. Communism is defined as
a species of socialism. So the reform of capitalism
may be socialistic and avoid an extreme variety of
socialism as unnecessary. Du Bois' language here is
perplexing but it does seem abundantly clear that in

180

spite of the above statement, during this period he was a socialist.

Furthermore, part of this paradox is solved by his view that capitalism was being slowly reformed through socialistic measures, especially in the United States under the presidency of Franklin Roosevelt, whom Du Bois supported during all four terms.[61] During most of the 1940's economic conditions were improving in the United States. Apparently for this reason Du Bois was not especially concerned about internal economic improvement; with evidence of social progress, such as the Roosevelt years provided, he could turn the preponderance of his attention to the "Third World" and to American foreign policy. He apparently maintained the belief that, given gradual improvement at home, the main responsibility of the United States was to aid in an improvement in the conditions of colonial and quasi-colonial lands. Such improvements did not necessarily involve (at least in the 40's) any precipitous change toward socialism. Regardless, he did view reforms as socialistic, and most of what he said was from a socialistic perspective. Yet any attempt at a complete clarification of his apparently contradictory statements seems futile.

V

The last years of Du Bois' life, from 1949-1963, were not especially productive in terms of presenting an overall, positive plan for social amelioration. In 1949 Du Bois was 81 years old. He no longer held a teaching position; he was forced out of the N.A.A.C.P. and then held a relatively unimportant position as a co-chairman of the Council on African Affairs (until 1955). His affirmative position on cooperation was never accepted and he lacked a firm, positive program from which to approach either African or American problems. His position on socialism was indefinite, and, as we have seen, bordered on the contradictory. Nevertheless, in a sense, Du Bois' last years are marked by a greatness of character and of insight. His public activities make this especially obvious: Besides his work for the Council on African Affairs, he served as chairman of the Peace Information Center in 1950--an activity that led to his trial and acquittal as an "unregistered foreign agent." He ran for the United States Senate in 1950 and received 224,599 votes in New York state's election.[62] He consistently supported full human rights for those persecuted during the McCarthy era[63] and he worked to have the United Nations examine the issue of civil rights for black Americans.[64] During the fifties, Du Bois stood for world peace and disarmament which, in the McCarthy era, was tantamount to crime. He stood for social justice, meaning that the rich countries had a responsibility to give up some of their wealth so that others would not starve; in the days when abundance for all seemed reasonable, this was a kind of heresy. Today with global issues clearly in the informed consciousness, such a view, to many, takes the guise of sound, practical wisdom.

This period was marked by three concerns: Peace, socialism, and Africa. From 1949 through, say, 1959, his main crusade, and the only thorough positive thrust apparent after 1940, was for world peace; peace to Du Bois, however, entailed progress and justice. So his emphasis on peace meant, for him, a movement toward socialism. Peace also meant African advance.

Early in his career Du Bois struggled with the morality of the social use of war and violence. In The Suppression and John Brown war was considered an evil, resulting from the compromise with evil. As such, war became an unfortunate but a "necessary evil" or, in other words, a morally acceptable social policy. Du Bois' support of the American effort in World War I was on the same level; but in Darkwater he lamented his decisions to support the war claiming that no real good stemmed from its horrible losses. It seems safe to say, then, that Du Bois stood opposed to large-scale war except in the most extreme circumstances. Even though this position is perhaps relatively extreme, he moved even further from it toward a total condemnation of war. In spite of the above, in looking back at his early position on war he identified himself as one who glorified war: ". . . my attitude toward the problems of peace and progress slowly became revolutionized. Formerly I had assumed with most folk that the path of human progress lay necessarily through war, and that if the colored peoples of the world and those of America ever secured their rights as human beings, it would be through organized violance against their white oppressors."[65] He claimed, further, that in 1911 the thought of a black army thrilled him.[66] These claims are unsupported by his published writings.

Regardless, by the 1950's Du Bois began to place most of his energies in the peace movement. This seems, in retrospect, to be the only concrete activist move he had open to him. Without a university or an N.A.A.C.P. position, he had no effective leadership role in the civil rights struggle. His realization that Africa must be guided by Africans made it improper for him to seek significant leadership role in Africa; and without an overall program, the peace movement provided a specific goal with an opportunity to occupy a forum that was broad enough to include the topics of African progress, the corruption of capitalism, and the need for a socialistic state.

There are four basic reasons Du Bois presented as conclusively establishing his pacifism. The first was utilitarian: The costs of war far exceeded its benefits. The costs of war had obviously accelerated with the introduction of atomic weapons. Even before their introduction war proved expensive. Indeed, Du Bois said he achieved a greater feeling for peace after viewing a prostrate Germany and Russia in 1928: ". . . I began to realize that under modern conditions such means to progress were self-defeating. With modern techniques in world war, there could be no victory. The victor was, in the end, as badly off as the vanquished. Reason, education, and scientific knowledge must replace war."[67] While the cost of war was growing, the gains from war had never, even in the past, been worth the cost: ". . . we realize that there is scarce a victory formally claimed by war, which mankind might not have gained more cheaply and more decently and even more completely by methods of peace."[68]

The second reason, like the first involved the costs of war. In effect, war itself and the prepara- tion for war had opportunity costs: other socially beneficial projects required labor and materials that tended to be used up by the military. The cost of war was thus a blockade to progress. For example, he compared the money spent on the military to the money spent on what he viewed as a crucial ingredient in social progress, education: "We are now wasting $40,000,000,000 a year for more wars and we owe $284,000,000,000 for past wars. In sixty years we have spent only $14 billion for education."[69] In effect, war amounted to social impoverishment. Du Bois claimed that the military posture of the United States

183

"forces other nations to fight and asks you and me to impoverish ourselves, give up health and schools, sacrifice our sons and daughters to a Jim-Crow army and commit suicide for a world war that nobody wants but the rich Americans who profit by it."[70] In short, without peace public welfare programs and equality were not possible: "Peace on earth today is a must for us. We need it for survival, for accomplishment, for equality with the best of earth's people."[71] In this way, Du Bois identified those in the peace movement as standing for world uplift rather than simply maintaining the negative goal of ending hostilities.

His third reason was not independent of the second; actually it is a specification of it. War, Du Bois believed, was linked to the efforts of the American corporate structure to fight what they saw as the growing threat of socialism. War benefits some businesses directly, for example, those that make munitions. But more generally, he maintained that American business used war and the threat of war to maintain and extend world business interests: "American business . . . is desperately trying to maintain and restore where possible the essentials of colonialism under the name of Free Enterprise and Western Democracy, and is plunging the world into destruction with false ideals and misleading fears."[72] The main aim of the United States business was its attempt to keep the world from socialism by using force abroad and fear of Russia at home.[73] Du Bois insisted that Russia was not a threat to peace and viewed as propaganda the attempt to so portray her.[74] His faith in Russia's desire for peace extended so far that he chided America for not giving Russia the plans of the atomic bomb.[75] On the other hand, United States policy was characterized as that of a warmonger. Truman was compared with Hitler as one of the greatest killers of the twentieth century. "Without expressing a world of public regret he killed 150,000 Japanese men, women, and children. . . ."[76] Eisenhower was presented as boasting in a public hearing that "We can lick the world."[77] Thus, war was, according to Du Bois, the policy instrument used to keep the world from socialism.

Finally, Du Bois' longstanding doctrine that war and colonialism are essentially linked led him to believe that support for peace implied support for the independence of colonial lands. The only way to bring peace was to abort the causes of war. War, he consistently maintained, thrives on the desire for wealth gained at the cost of exploited people. He contended that the causes of war were still present in the world in terms of the raw materials needed for industry, and these were produced in tropical lands by people of color living in abject poverty.[78] War comes from rivalry over these products; and from the continuing effort to dominate foreign labor. (The beginning of the American involvement in Viet Nam and Loas was presented as such.)[79] Du Bois succinctly stated the case: "There are today at least eighteen main causes of World War and no one of them is Russia. On the contrary, they are the great groups of essential raw material, and the land and labor necessary for their production, which the leading nations of the world need for their industry and their standard of living."[80]

This fourth reason led to the great problem facing Americans and Western Europeans: ending war meant giving up title to the wealth of others. This would have been difficult--a changed style of living was required: Colonial trade, he insisted, was much more profitable than domestic industry; thus capital rushed to those foreign sources.[81] Greater profits, which allowed American business to provide a rising standard of living for the average American[82] raised a moral demand: "Suppose it proved true that if we had fewer automobiles, fewer nightclubs, and fewer mink coats-- if this self-denial on the part of certain Americans would prevent world war and give Chinese children enough to eat, would we be willing to make the sacrifice?"[83]

Du Bois' main message was that the greed of the United States and Western Europe stood behind the causes of war and used the fear of war as a propaganda tool against socialism. Powerful Americans thus had a stake in war and were hostile to peace. He viewed this hypothesis as partly confirmed by the reaction to his own activities. Du Bois participated in an international movement for peace which gathered signatures protesting the atom bomb and circulated news about activities in favor of peace. He served as chairman of the Peace Information Center in 1950. His activities drew the attention of the Justice Department, which, even lacking any significant evidence (as the court case eventually found) prosecuted Du Bois

for failing to register as a foreign agent. He concluded "The Department of Justice . . . assumed that
our real crime was peace and not foreign agency."[84]

Du Bois' rejection of war did not entail support
for social nonviolence. Although he usually supported
nonviolence, he believed that at times such support
was futile. In 1957 he wrote a column in The National
Guardian about Martin Luther King's nonviolent tactics
in the South, entitled, "Will the Great Gandhi Live
Again."[85] King's activities did not solve the race
problem in Alabama, Du Bois argued. The reason given
for this was that non-violence as a tactic only works
against normal people. But in the South where the
doctrines of race hate and race superiority flourished,
people could not have been expected to respond in
normal ways: ". . . we have today in the South millions of persons who are pathological cases. They
cannot be reasoned with in matters of race. They are
not normal and cannot be treated as normal. They are
ignorant and their schools are poor because they cannot
afford a double school system and would rather themselves remain ignorant than let Negroes learn."[86] The
remedy Du Bois identified was an integrated education
for all children--just the sort of thing he found to
be blocked by racial prejudice. He offered no hope
for a solution but ended by saying: "If we cannot
civilize the South, or will not even try, we continue
in contradiction and riddle."[87]

VI

A further reason for pursuing peace, or perhaps
it is better to call it an assumption underlying the
four reasons given above, was that the world is inevitably marching towards socialism and welfarism. War
was judged to be a temporary block to these almost
natural movements. Thus, a movement against the main
block to socialism would, in fact, provide an aid to
the eventual dominance of socialism. In 1950 he claimed
that socialistic power would come to the masses regardless of any attempt to block it: "A new era of power,
held and exercised by the working class the world over,
is dawning and while its eventual form is not yet
clear, its progress cannot be held back by any power
of man."[88] In 1957 he confidently predicted that "the
United States will become a socialist state. . . . We
can't go on becoming a state which is ruled by business
for businessmen and for private profit. We have already

186

taken many steps toward socialism. We will take more.
Eventually we shall come to be a Communist state. But
how long that is going to take, I don't pretend to
say."[89]

Du Bois' belief in progress toward socialism and
eventually toward its extreme form in Communism was
based on what he saw to be a growing world-wide movement. He viewed the Soviet Union, a major part of the
movement, as a success. His 1959 visit to Russia
resulted in an image of the country as one in which
people were secure and happy, with a genuine voice
in their country's policies, confident in the future
and with a belief that they actually owned the
nation.[90] China was considered in even more glowing
terms. Looking back on its history, he contended that
the Chinese people faced 2,000 years of real misery,
worse than that faced at the lowest points of slavery
in America.[91] But even with such a debilitating past
China proved successful: ". . . I have never seen a
nation where human nature was so abreast of scientific
knowledge; where daily life of everyday people was so
outstripping mechanical power and love of life so
triumphing over human greed and envy and selfishness
as I see in China today."[92] China's progress was
characterized as miraculous. Added to the evidence
of the establishment of socialistic states in these
two large nations was the less spectacular evidence of
a gradual movement in socialism in nearly all nations.
He observed:

> Despite every effort in the
> United States to conceal and deny
> the facts, all civilized nations
> have been progressing toward
> socialism, especially since 1900.
> They own and run the railways, the
> telephones and telegraph, street
> cars, buses and subways; they
> largely conduct housing, sanitation,
> insurance and relief; they guarantee
> employment; they engage in industry,
> in manufacturing, foreign trade,
> mining, forestry and river control,
> in power conversion and control and
> wide ownership of land. Some nations
> like Britain go further than this;
> others like the Scandinavian lands
> plan less in theory but do ever more

in practice; while Communist lands
attempt complete social and industrial planning and ownership of
all capital.[93]

He claimed in 1950, that Roosevelt's "New Deal" which
he by and large supported, was pure socialism.[94]

Although Du Bois often seemed to have sided with
an extreme form of determinism in calling socialism
inevitable, he also expressed a more temperate version,
more in keeping with the doctrine's empirical foundation. "Time and again in the history of mankind
[progress] has faltered, and we have only to remember
that the progress of men, which is not to be doubted
in the long run, is never a straight march but is
always a lurching forward and a falling back, and we
only keep up hope as we see that progress has continued and will continue."[95] Du Bois was here more in
the spirit of pragmatism, which recognizes the limits
to determinism and the reality of chance. Du Bois did
express the view that social events were forged on a
mixture of chance and law: "Social problems change
more often and in more ways than physical problems
because of the unpredictable variations in human
feelings and choices. Probably most of these emotions
and conclusions are subject more or less indirectly to
the same physical laws as those which dominate sticks
and stones. But there is enough volition to make it
necessary for persons who are studying a human problem
or trying to conduct their action in accordance with
its present manifestations, to keep a wary eye on
changes and current facts."[96] With this sort of statement he could maintain a belief in a socialist future
and nevertheless admit the possibility, even if remote,
of a different future. In all, he insisted on keeping
an eye on developments and refused to dictate how or
when socialism would come about because he recognized
that this would be established by local and varying
conditions: "The question of the method by which the
socialist state can be achieved must be worked out by
experiment and reason and not by dogma."[97]

Even with his belief in the rising tide of
socialism and his agnosticism on the proper methods
for achieving socialism, Du Bois viewed the United
States as being in a "setback" period, and he sought,
through public activity (he ran for New York's United
States Senate seat in 1950 as the candidate of the

Progressive Party) and through his writings, to guide
the country, and especially black Americans, away from
capitalism toward socialism. With the death of
Roosevelt, he claimed that capitalists made an effort
to set socialism back at home and in the world.[98] While
failing in most of the world, Du Bois apparently believed that the attempt to block socialism in the United
States met with success.

His writings in the 1950's contain a critique of
America, centering on the power of wealth and the
impotence of the average person. Big Business in effect
was charged with controlling the American people,
including what is taught in school.[99] With the control
of industry in the hands of profit seekers he believed
that the welfare of the people was hampered. The distribution of wealth remained inequitable--in 1958 his
statistics showed 40 percent of the people receiving
less than $2,000 a year. The overall tone of his
critique of the United States was virtually the same
as that against the western nations in the 1940's,
including the use of the doctrine of racial inferiority
to keep workers in line. But he added the notion of
"psychological" poverty. Even those with enough income
become so desirous of material luxuries that they skimp
on necessities, causing a kind of poverty.[100]

Du Bois believed that Socialism was especially
necessary for black Americans whom he saw as permanently
subject to second class treatment under capitalism. For
the first time he explicitly rejected his former proposal of a group economy supporting a consumers' and
producers' cooperative. Instead he claimed that the
state must organize the cooperative movement and without state organization the cooperative movement could
not succeed. ". . . co-operation calls for Socialism,
and Socialism today is using co-operation in production
and consumption."[101] The earlier movement was inten-
tionally a non-state movement so as to counteract
racism in the government. In this way he seems to be
describing why his early plan failed. In effect, it
lacked the power it needed; that power could only come
from the state.

In this period his advice on establishing socialism
in the United States was usually limited to the suggestion that people use every opportunity to vote for
socialistic reforms and for peace. But in 1956 he
called for the establishment of a national third party

189

supporting increased government responsibility over
the welfare of the people:[102]

> Insist on a chance to vote for
> peace, for the total abolition of
> the color line; for no family income
> above $25,000 or below $5,000; for
> free education from kindergarten
> through college; for housing on a
> nationwide scale; for training of
> all for the work they can do in so
> far as such work is needed for the
> best interests of all. Insist on
> discipline for this work. Allow
> no laborer to be paid less than his
> product is worth; and let no employ-
> er take what he does not make. Curb
> corporations by putting them under
> government ownership.
>
>   Heal the sick as a privilege,
> not as a charity. Make private
> ownership of natural resources a
> crime. Stop interference with
> private and personal belief by
> religious hypocrites. Preserve
> the utmost freedom for dream of
> beauty, creative art and joy of
> living. Call this socialism,
> communism, reformed capitalism,
> or holy rolling. Call it any-
> thing--but get it done![103]

Du Bois recognized that Socialism was not without
costs. Its greatest cost, in his opinion, was the
discipline required--people must do certain things for
the common good that they do not want to do. But, on
the other hand, he observed that in America under
capitalism freedom was also restrained by law, cultural
patterns and by the planning done by capitalists,
since no modern society could exist without planning.
So in the final analysis the question of discipline
was the question of the end or goal of discipline,
rather than about its existence.[104]

In 1961, shortly before leaving the United States,
Du Bois ended his indecision over how to achieve
socialism in the United States. Instead of offering
ad hoc advice on voting in support of socialistic

measures, he decided that the best policy was to join
the American Communist Party. Previously he seemed to
believe that the United States would turn itself
around, albeit gradually, through reform of existing
institutions. In 1952 he viewed America as continuing
under a reform oriented capitalism, moving toward
socialism, albeit at too slow a pace.[105] This appeared
to be his usual position all during the 1950's. When
he joined the Communist Party he apparently rejected
this position, claiming that capitalism "cannot reform
itself" and is "doomed to self-destruction."[106] The
Communist Party will, he claimed, be a real alternative
for the voting public with its intent "to give all men
what they need, to ask of each the best they can contribute. . . ."[107] The platform he approved was
presented in his letter of membership to Gus Hall:

1. Public ownership of natural resources
    and of all capital.
2. Public control of transportation and
    communications.
3. Abolition of poverty and limitation of
    personal income.
4. No exploitation of labor.
5. Social medicine, with hospitalization
    and care of the old.
6. Free education for all.
7. Training for jobs and jobs for all.
8. Discipline for growth and reform.
9. Freedom under law.
10. No dogmatic religion.[108]

VII

Du Bois' conversion to the American Communist
Party, although it must be viewed as the climax of a
gradual development, left certain questions unanswered.
First of all, it represented a shift in his late thinking from the position that the United States was not
ready for communism, that this would take a considerable
length of time, and that the United States must be
subject to a gradualistic socialism. Du Bois' letter
of membership does not unequivocally reject gradualism;
but it does suggest such a rejection, and with the
statement that capitalism cannot reform itself, seemed
to shift him to a revolutionary approach. This change
is not especially difficult to understand: he had,
for a period of some 12 years, called communism the
eventual future for America. His support for gradu-

alism was simply tactical for the United States at a specific period. But he apparently despaired of the system's ability to change gradually--he often assayed the faults of capitalism; these may have eventually added up to the view that it was bad enough to vitiate reforms. Thus a thoroughgoing change was required. Note, however, that he never advocated revolutionary violence in America and gave his support to a political party to provide a choice for the American voter. This left tactical questions unanswered. How likely was an effective pro-communist vote? Why was not a vote for Communism simply a wasted vote as he had thought in the past? How would, say, a majority communist congress act vis-a-vis a Democratic president? Would a time come for violent revolution or would the process stick to constitutional methods? What would need to be done if a pro-communist vote remained low? Should blacks maintain a special role in the communist movement? Without specifics, Du Bois' position remained on the level of specifying goals and evils without recommending a programmatic solution. While Du Bois' membership in the Communist Party is consistent with his increasing attacks on the basic structures of capitalism, many questions remain unanswered.

Another sort of problem is even more troublesome. In the 1930's Du Bois clearly rejected communism both in its practical party manifestations and in its theory. The objections to theory and practice involved racial considerations: Blacks formed a special group without a significant class opposition, essentially a proletariat group. Yet blacks were separated from the proletariat movement by racism; the proletariat as an economic class was split on racial lines, an eventuality Du Bois viewed Marxism as incapable of explaining. Du Bois' letter in 1961 ignored special reference to blacks, except in historical recollection. The change, then, seemed dramatic on two counts. There was no longer an account of the split in the proletariat caused by white racism, and there was no longer mention of the homogeneous class structure of Afro-Americans.

Answering the latter point first goes a long way toward explaining Du Bois' willingness to ignore his former objections to communism. He no longer believed that blacks internally formed a monolithic proletariat. We previously saw that he recognized a _tendency_ toward the formation of economic classes in the black community. But after his indictment by the Justice department, he spotted an actual and meaningful class division in the black community: "The reaction of Negroes to this case revealed a distinct cleavage not hitherto clear in American Negro opinion."[109] Many of the better educated and the wealthier blacks did not, by Du Bois' account, speak out in his defense: he appeared to believe that their distaste for socialism and communism and their belief in American propaganda caused them to remain silent and thus showed their class interests. He added, "This dichotomy in the Negro group, this development of class structure, was to be expected, and will be more manifest in the future, as discrimination against Negroes as such decreases. There will gradually arise among American Negroes a separation according to their attitudes to ward labor, wealth and work. It is still my hope that the Negro's experience in the past will, in the end, lead the majority of his intelligentsia into the ranks of those advocating social control of wealth, abolition of exploitation of labor, and equality of opportunity for all."[110]

In 1953, Du Bois claimed that many American blacks tended to view their own problem as a civil rights fight without linking it to world problems. This was the base because American patterns of distribution and overseas injustices were not questioned. Consequently, he exhorted blacks to see themselves as in union with the world proletariat.[111] In 1955 this break was underscored by his claim that in the cold war tensions, fear divided black Americans from Africa. This signifies a break in the concept of race designed to find the psychological link between all people of African descent. With a partial breakdown in the race concept, the notion of class unity gains in significance.

In the late 1950's Du Bois' view on the development of classes in the Afro-American community solidified. He claimed that blacks were "flying apart" into economic classes. His hope that color caste would create social unity was explicitly seen as mistaken. "(T)he American Negro is today developing a distinct bourgeoisie bound to and aping American acquisitive society and developing an employing and a laboring class. This division is only in embryo, but it can be sensed."[112] He again called on black labor to join the world labor movement and thus signalled a belief

in a racially united proletariat movement: "As . . .
the Negro laborer joins the white unions, he is drawn
into a great labor movement and begins to recognize
black business exploitation."[113] Du Bois did, as in
earlier days, recognize that through gains from exploitation in foreign lands, part of the American labor
movement was more or less an extension of the bourgeoisie. He claimed, ". . . the main mass of American
labor is at present in conservative unions under
reactionaries like Meany."[114] Blacks in these unions,
he said, tended to follow the union's policies. Race
ceased to be the central gap within economic classes
as formally presented; the central issue became economic status and the relation of labor to profits and
foreign exploitation.

Du Bois believed that his trial freed him from
racial provincialism and caused him to see that a
coalition of black and white labor, progressives,
socialists, and communists could effectively work
together;[115] this can be understood in terms of a
further shift toward a more Marxian way of thinking.
Class, in Du Bois' final years, dominated race: the
theoretical block to joining communism fell.

Du Bois did not lose interest in racial minorities.
Indeed, he continued to consider the darker people of
the world as the main group facing excessive exploitation at the hands of capitalist countries. The
center of his interest late in his life was Africa.
Africans seem to a great degree to take over some of
the traits attributed formerly to Afro-Americans.
Africans, although differing in language, customs and
skin color, share the common experience of colonialism
and imperialism, thus putting them in union with all
third world peoples. But ties that were formerly
racial, were placed on an even more pronounced economic level, so that even whites were included: "Your
[internal] bond is not mere color of skin but the
deeper experience of wage slavery and contempt. So,
too, your bond with the white world is closest to those
who support and defend China and help India and not
those who exploit the Middle East and South America."[116]
Du Bois not only applied to Africans a concept analogous
to the later concept of race but he also reviewed
(although only in brief reference) the notion of a
consumer's cooperative for Africans. Viewed as having
some power as consumers[117] Africans were advised to
unite in a cooperative movement.[118] With the back-

ground of African communalism, similar to the background supporting the ground of his appeal to black Americans, Africa could readily move toward socialism and welfarism.[119]

Du Bois advised Africans to avoid capital development based on United States or Western European credit and to strive for cultural and educational development.[120] His program for the Congo, which seemed to be meant for all Africa, entailed a simple life, restrictions on the extraction of raw materials, and centering on agricultural development. He even recommended a return to a barter system with industry satisfying local needs.[121] He supported a disciplined approach to economic security and self-reliance:

> Here, then, my Brothers, you face
> your great decision: Will you for
> temporary advantage--for automobiles,
> refrigerators and Paris gowns-spend
> your income in paying interest on
> borrowed funds; or will you sacrifice
> your present comfort and the chance
> to shine before your neighbors, in
> order to educate your children,
> develop such industry as best serves
> the great mass of people and make
> your country strong in ability,
> self-support and self-defense? Such
> union of effort for strength calls
> for sacrifice and self-denial, while
> the capital offered you at high price
> by the colonial powers like France,
> Britain, Holland, Belgium and the
> United States, will prolong fatal
> colonial imperialism, from which you
> have suffered slavery, serfdom, and
> colonialism.[122]

In 1961 he moved to Ghana to direct the compilation of an Encyclopedia Africana. This, his final role, once again, was directed toward a scholarly project and not at social leadership (a role in which he never felt entirely comfortable). Significantly, the project was not to be centered on race; the concept of race by then was too diluted. He firmly stated, "My idea is to prepare and publish an encyclopedia not on the vague subject of race, but on the peoples inhabiting the continent of Africa."[123]

195

Du Bois was unable to do much more than begin the project; his health was gradually declining. He died in his sleep in Africa on August 27, 1963.[124]

NOTES

1. W.E.B. Du Bois, The Autobiography of W.E.B. Du Bois: A Soliloquy on Viewing My Life From the Last Decade of its First Century (New York: International Publishers, 1968), p. 336.

2. The labor theory of value, borrowed by Marx from classical economists such as Adam Smith and Ricardo is the doctrine that prices tend over the long run to approximate the worth of labor put into goods directly, or indirectly through labor put into producing, for example, capital goods and raw materials. Because price tends to equal the worth of labor in a product, profits come only by making labor put in more hours than are equal to its labor's price. Roughly, labor is worth what it takes to keep the class of laborers in existence. Thus labor tends to sink to a subsistence existence while creating a surplus product (amounting to that part of their labor for which they are not paid) going to those who live off this exploitation of labor.

3. W.E.B. Du Bois, "Marxism and the Negro Problem," The Crisis, XL (May, 1933), pp. 103-104.

4. Ibid., p. 104.

5. W.E.B. Du Bois, The Crisis, XXXVIII (September, 1931), p. 315.

6. Du Bois, "Marxism and the Negro Problem," p. 104.

7. Ibid.   8.   Ibid.

9. V.I. Lenin, "Imperialism, The Highest Stage of Capitalism" (1916), in James E. Connor (ed.), Lenin on Politics and Revolution (Indianapolis, Ind.; The Bobbs-Merrill Co., 1968), p. 115.

10. Ibid., pp. 120-127.

11. Aptheker, Correspondence, III, pp. 377-378.

12. Du Bois, "Marxism and the Negro Problem," p. 118.

13. W.E.B. Du Bois, "Social Planning for the Negro, Past and Present," (1936), in Julius Lester (ed), The Seventh Son: The Thought and Writings of W.E.B. Du Bois (2 vols.) (New York: Random House, 1971), II, p. 435.

14. Ibid., p. 436.

15. W.E.B. Du Bois, The Crisis, XXXVIII (September, 1931), p. 318.

16. Ibid., p. 315.

17. Du Bois, Autobiography, p. 290.

18. There is an exception presented later in this chapter.

19. W.E.B. Du Bois, Color and Democracy: Colonies and Peace (New York: Harcourt, Brace and Company, 1945), p. 17.

20. W.E. Burghardt Du Bois, "The Realities in Africa: European Profit or Negro Development," Foreign Affairs, 21 (July, 1943), p. 721.

21. W.E.B. Du Bois, "Phylon: Science or Propaganda," Phylon, 5 (First Quarter, 1944), p. 8.

22. Du Bois, The World and Africa, p. 56.

23. Ibid., p. 58; Eric Williams, Capitalism and Slavery (1944) (New York: Capricorn Books, 1966), p. 52.

24. W.E.B. Du Bois, What the Negro Has Done for the United States and Texas (Washington, D.C.: Government Printing Office, 1936), pp. 2-3.

25. Du Bois, The World and Africa, p. 66.

26. Ibid., p. 43.   27. Ibid., p. 163.

28. W.E. Burghardt Du Bois, "Colonies and Moral Responsibility," The Journal of Negro Education

(Summer, 1946), p. 311.

29. Ibid., p. 312.   30.   Ibid.

31. Ibid., p. 313.

32. Karl Marx and Friedrich Engels, The Communist Manifesto (New York: Appleton-Century-Crofts, 1955), p. 9.

33. Du Bois, The World and Africa, p. 163.

34. Du Bois, "Realities in Africa," p. 722.

35. W.E.B. Du Bois, "Black Africa Tomorrow," Foreign Affairs, 17 (1938), p. 100.

36. Du Bois, Color and Democracy, pp. 46-47.

37. Du Bois, The World and Africa, p. 6.

38. Ibid., p. 13.

39. Du Bois, Color and Democracy, p. 109.

40. Ibid., p. 110.   41.   Ibid.

42. V.I. Lenin, "The First Stage of Revolution," in Connor, Lenin, p. 152.

43. W.E. Burghardt Du Bois, "Prospect of a World Without Race Conflict," American Journal of Sociology, 49 (March, 1944), p. 453.

44. Ibid., p. 455.   45.   Ibid., p. 456.

46. Du Bois, The World and Africa, pp. 17-18.

47. Ibid., p. 252.

48. Du Bois, Color and Democracy, p. v.

49. Ibid., p. 14.   50.   Ibid., p. 19.

51. See, for example, Du Bois, "Black Africa Tomorrow," p. 103, and Du Bois, Color and Democracy, p. 136.

52. Du Bois, Color and Democracy, p. 136.

53. Ibid., p. 134.

54. Du Bois, "Prospect of a World Without Race Conflict," p. 456.

55. Ibid.

56. Du Bois, Color and Democracy, p. 115.

57. Ibid., pp. 14-15.

58. Du Bois, "Social Planning for the Negro, Past and Present," p. 435.

59. Du Bois, Color and Democracy, p. 120.

60. Du Bois, The Crisis, XXXVIII (September, 1931), p. 313.

61. W.E.B. Du Bois, "From McKinley to Wallace: My Fifty Years as a Political Independent" (1948), in Lester, The Seventh Son, II, p. 596.

62. Du Bois, Correspondence, Vol. III, p. 297.

63. See Ibid., pp. 335, 344, 348-349, 381, 387.

64. See Ibid., p. 415.

65. W.E.B. Du Bois, In Battle for Peace: The Story of my 83rd Birthday (with comment by Shirley Graham) (New York: Masses and Mainstream, 1952), p. 22.

66. Ibid., p. 23.   67. Ibid., pp. 22-23.

68. Speech by Dr. William E.B. Du Bois, A.L.P. Candidate for U.S. Senator at A.L.P. Rally, Golden Gate Ballroom (October 5, 1950), in Lester, The Seventh Son, II, p. 605.

69. W.E.B. Du Bois, "The Life of History as it is Taught Today" (1960), in Lester, The Seventh Son, II, p. 669.

70. Speech (October 5, 1950, The Seventh Son, II, pp. 605-606.

71. W.E.B. Du Bois, "Right," The Negro Digest, 8

(March, 1950), p. 11.

72. W.E.B. Du Bois, Peace is Dangerous (New York: National Guardian, 1951), p. 6.

73. W.E.B. Du Bois, "The Negro and Socialism," in H.L. Alfred (ed.), Toward a Socialist America: A symposium of Essays (New York: Peace Publications, 1958), p. 179.

74. Du Bois, "Right," p. 12.

75. W.E.B. Du Bois, "Statement Issued by W.E.B. Du Bois Before He was Arraigned on Charges of Being an 'Agent of a Foreign Principle'" (1951), in Lester, The Seventh Son, II, p. 610.

76. W.E.B. Du Bois, "The Hard-Bit Man in the Loud Shirts" (1953), in Lester, The Seventh Son, II, p. 616.

77. Speech (October 6, 1950), p. 606.

78. Du Bois, Peace is Dangerous, p. 6.

79. W.E.B. Du Bois, "A Program of Reason, Right and Justice for Today" (1960), in Lester, The Seventh Son, II, p. 673.

80. Du Bois, Peace is Dangerous, p. 6.

81. Ibid., p. 11.

82. W.E.B. Du Bois, "The Future of Africa: Address to the All-African People's Conference, Accra" (1958), in Lester, The Seventh Son, II, p. 659 and "The American Negro and the Darker World" (1957), in Freedomways (Third Quarter, 1968), p. 247.

83. Du Bois, Peace is Dangerous, p. 13.

84. Du Bois, In Battle for Peace, p. 56.

85. W.E.B. Du Bois, "Will the Great Gandhi Live Again," in Lester, The Seventh Son, II, pp. 644-647.

86. Ibid., p. 646.   87. Ibid., p. 647.

88. Speech (October 5, 1960), p. 604.

89. W.E.B. Du Bois, "Interview with Dr. W.E.B. Du Bois" (1957) in Lester, The Seventh Son, II, p. 702.

90. Du Bois, Autobiography, pp. 29-43.

91. W.E.B. Du Bois, "The Vast Miracle of China Today" (1959), in Lester, The Seventh Son, II, p. 663.

92. Ibid., p. 662.

93. Du Bois, In Battle for Peace, p. 171.

94. Du Bois, "Right," p. 13.

95. W.E.B. Du Bois, "Natural Guardianship" (1956), in Lester, The Seventh Son, II, p. 639.

96. W.E.B. Du Bois, "On the Future of the American Negro," in Aptheker, "Some Unpublished Writings of W.E.B. Du Bois," Freedomways (Winter, 1965), p. 117.

97. Du Bois, "The Negro and Socialism," p. 191.

98. Du Bois, "The American Negro and the Darker World," Freedomways (Summer, 1968), p. 249.

99. W.E.B. Du Bois, "The Independent at the Dinner Table" (1958), in Lester, The Seventh Son, II, p. 655.

100. Du Bois, "The Negro and Socialism," p. 188.

101. W.E.B. Du Bois, "Negroes and Socialism," in Lester, The Seventh Son, II, p. 650.

102. W.E.B. Du Bois, "The Theory of a Third Party," in Lester, The Seventh Son, II, p. 633.

103. Du Bois, "A Program of Reason, Right and Justice for Today," in Lester, The Seventh Son, II, p. 676.

104. W.E.B. Du Bois, Socialism Today - On China and Russia (Chicago: Afro-American Heritage

Association, 1964), p. 4.

105. Du Bois, In Battle for Peace, p. 162.

106. W.E.B. Du Bois, "Letter of Application for Membership in the Communist Party of the United States," in Lester, The Seventh Son, II, p. 722.

107. Ibid.   108. Ibid.

109. Du Bois, In Battle for Peace, p. 75.

110. Ibid., p. 76.

111. Du Bois, "On the Future of the American Negro," pp. 118-119.

112. W.E.B. Du Bois, "How United are Negroes," in Lester, The Seventh Son, II, p. 630.

113. Ibid., p. 631.   114. Ibid.

115. Du Bois, In Battle for Peace, p. 155.

116. Du Bois, "The Future of Africa," p. 661.

117. Ibid., p. 659.

118. W.E.B. Du Bois, "A Future for Pan-Africa: Freedom, Peace, Socialism" (1957), in Lester, The Seventh Son, II, p. 649.

119. Ibid.   120. Ibid.

121. W.E.B. Du Bois, "A Logical Program for a Free Congo," in Lester, The Seventh Son, II, p. 700.

122. Du Bois, "The Future of Africa," pp. 659-660.

123. W.E.B. Du Bois, "On the Beginnings of the Project," in Lester, The Seventh Son, II, p. 724.

124. His wife, Shirley Graham Du Bois, describes his last hours on His Day is Marching On: A Memoir of W.E.B. Du Bois (New York: J.B. Lippincott Co,, 1971), pp. 366-367.

ABOUT THE AUTHOR

Joseph P. DeMarco is chairperson of the Department of Philosophy at Cleveland State University. He began his teaching career at Tuskegee Institute in Alabama, where he also served as Head of the Philosophy Department. He has written numerous articles on American philosophy, ethics, the theory of justice, as well as articles on W.E.B. Du Bois. He is currently working on the development of a theory of justice, which has been influenced by Du Bois' notion of equality.